Rancho del Llano Seco

Northern California's Last Rancho

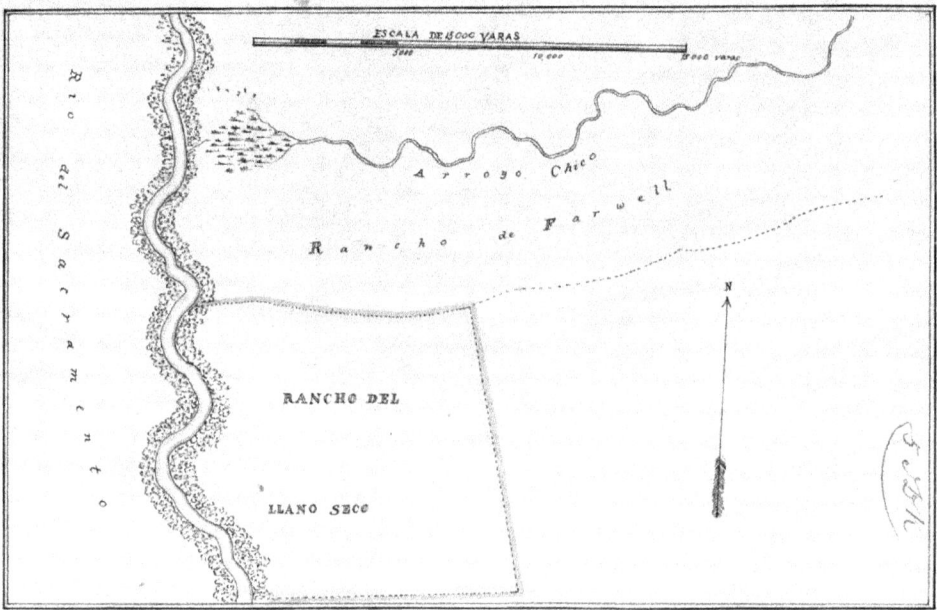

ESCALA DE 15000 VARAS

5000 10000 15000 varas

Rio del Sacramento

Arroyo Chico

Rancho de Farwell

RANCHO DEL

LLANO SECO

N

331

Rancho del Llano Seco

Northern California's Last Rancho

GREGORY G. WHITE, PH.D.

Sub Terra Consulting, Archaeology & Paleontology

B. ARLENE WARD

Mechoopda Tribe of Chico Rancheria, Chico, CA

ADRIAN FREDIANI

The Nature Conservancy

ANCHR

ASSOCIATION FOR NORTHERN CALIFORNIA HISTORICAL RESEARCH

FRONT/BACK COVER

"Residence and Ranch of John Parrot, Llano Seco Rancho, Butte County, California"

Pen and ink drawing in Smith & Elliott, 1877, *Butte County Illustrations, Descriptive of its Scenery, Residences, Public Buildings, Manufactories, Fine Blocks, Mines, and Mills.*

FRONTISPIECE

Diseño Rancho del Llano Seco by John Bidwell, 1852. Pen-and-ink and watercolor on tracing paper. United States Northern District Court, Land Case No. 398, Charles J. Brenham, et al., claimants.

"Llano Seco, Diseños 289, GLO No. 12, Butte County, and associated historical documents." (2018). Butte County. 7. https://digitalcommons.csumb.edu/hornbeck_usa_4_a_bc/7

ISBN 978-1-931994-15-6
Library of Congress Control Number: pending

Reviewed and edited by Matthew Meyer, Josie Reifschneider-Smith, Megan Bradshaw, Nancy Leek
Layout design by Josie Reifschneider-Smith
Printed by Heidelberg Graphics, Chico, California, 95926

Association for Northern California Historical Research (ANCHR)
PO Box 3024, Chico, California, 95927-3024
www.anchr.org • (530) 636-0778
facebook.com/anchrbooks/
anchr.books@gmail.com

Contents

LLANO SECO, CALIF.
SW/4 CHICO 15' QUADRANGLE
N3930—W12152.5/7.5

1948
PHOTOREVISED 1969
AMS 1663 III SW—SERIES V895
PHOTOINSPECTED 1976

CALIF

QUADRANGLE LOCATION

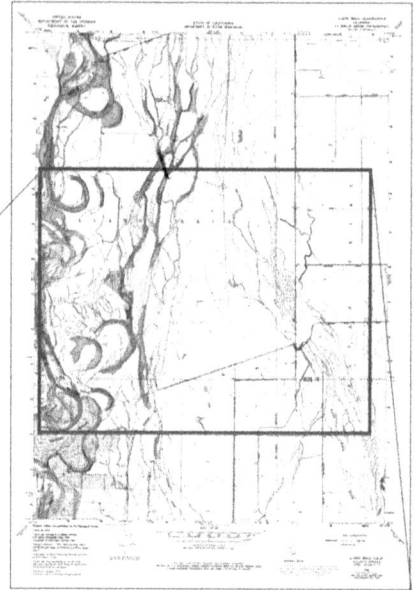

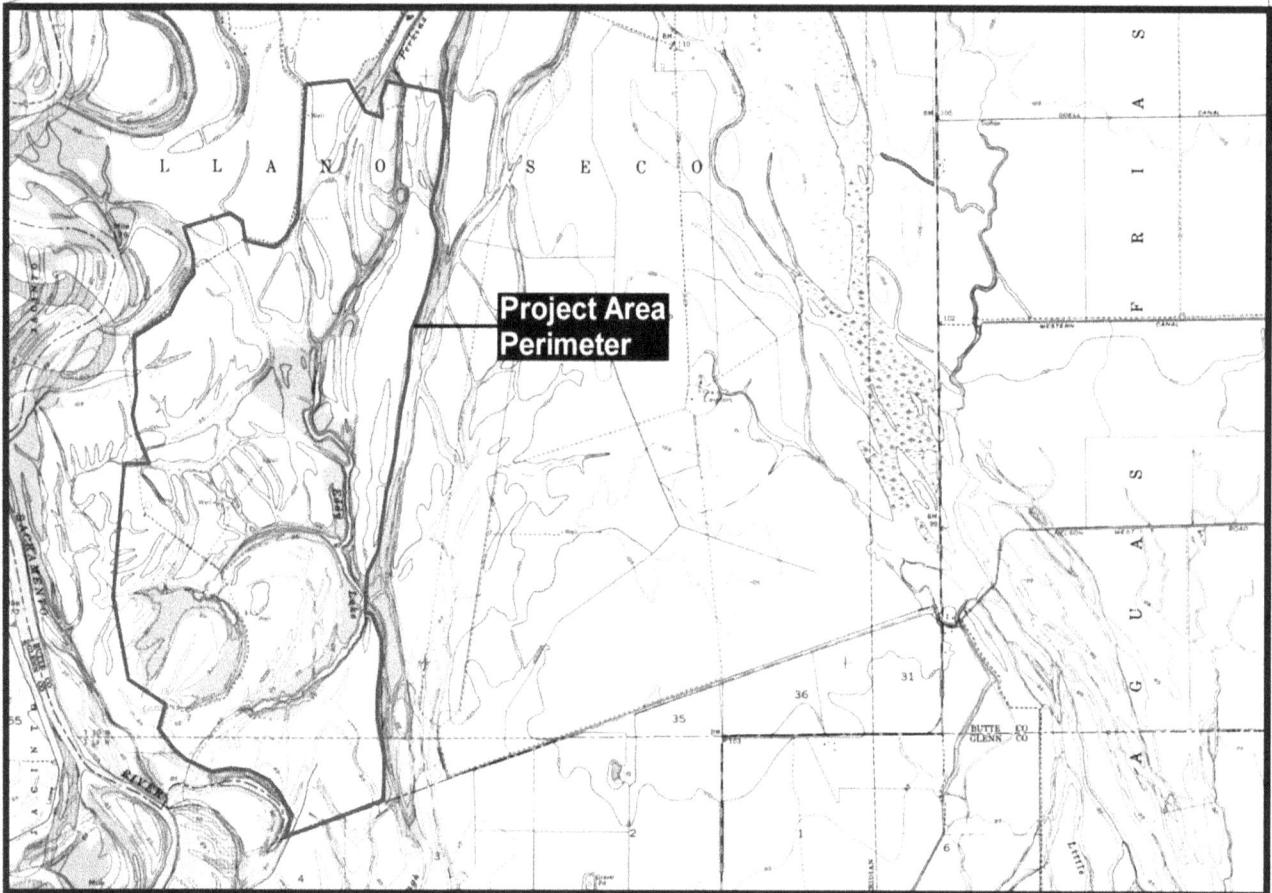

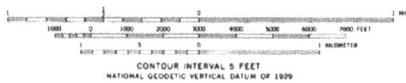

Project Area Perimeter

CONTOUR INTERVAL 5 FEET
NATIONAL GEODETIC VERTICAL DATUM OF 1929

Project Location, Llano Seco Ranch, Butte County, California.

Historical Research Methods & Sources

THIS BOOK IS AN ABRIDGED version of a much larger field report covering the archaeological investigations of a small portion of the Llano Seco Ranch, and it focuses solely on some of the ranch's general history, pre- and post-contact. Culturally sensitive information, archaeological findings, etc., are omitted. This decision was made to protect Native American interests and those of the current owners of the ranch, which is private property.

Beginning in 2019, The Nature Conservancy (TNC) began riparian and flood plain restoration efforts on approximately 2,000 acres of the 2,900-acre Project Area on the Llano Seco Ranch in Butte County, California. Phase 1 converted fields (approx. 750 acres) with the poorest soil quality to native grasslands; Phase 2 restored fields (approx. 670 acres) with higher-quality soil; and Phase 3 restored fields (approx. 670 acres) with the highest-quality soils—currently the irrigated fields. Riparian communities restored through Phases 2 and 3 included the planting of lower-, mid-, and upper-story native species.

Rancho Llano Seco (Rancho) is a historical 17,767-acre multi-purpose family ranch located in southwestern Butte County, California, ten miles southwest of Chico. The property is bounded by Ord Ferry Road to the north, 7 Mile Lane to the east, the Butte/Glenn County line to the south, and the Sacramento River to the west.

With respect to the history of Rancho Llano Seco, conventional sources for study of local history proved very disappointing. We conducted research in archives located at the Northeast California Special Collections facility, Meriam Library, CSU, Chico, and in local museums and libraries but with little success. Scant information about the Rancho had been published or archived. However, these studies expanded dramatically when Rancho Manager Joe Mendes informed our team of the existence of extensive primary historical documents on file in archives located at the Rancho Headquarters on Hugh Baber Drive. These included tons of documents stored in archive boxes, in original magazine files, on wood shelves and in steel bins, along with photographs, aerial photos, communications, and maps covering the Project Area. We re-geared our research efforts to focus on these materials which were then assembled, digitized, and studied closely. These investigations successfully compiled extensive field-by-field information on the location, context, composition, and function of structures, buildings, and other constructed features, some still extant, others dilapidated, and still others burned, razed, or plowed-under and indicated solely by scant archaeological traces. Documentation available in the archives spanned between 1874 and the modern era. For the twentieth-century time frame, the Rancho archives provided a detailed, field-by-field record including work orders, receipts and invoices, construction blueprints, and theodolite-produced land maps.

Archive Review

Prior to the field investigation, on April 30, 2018, the author conducted an archival document review at the Northeast Information Center of the California Historical Resources Inventory System. In order to achieve thorough coverage, supplementary county historical information sources were consulted including GLO Plats, historical topographic and aerial photo series, and county registers on file in regional repositories and on file at Sub Terra Consulting (STC). Document review resulted in a compilation and synthesis of information covering four topics and resulting in the products as follows:

1. To establish the nature and extent of ethnographically documented Native American traditional land use in the Project Area, primary documents related to the Konkow-Valley Maidu tribe were thoroughly studied.

Traditional activities and specific place names were recorded for the Project Area.

2. To determine the timing and events related to early non-Native exploration and colonization of the Project Area and consequences to Native American populations, the investigation was supplemented by research in the stacks on file at the Northeast California Special Collections facility of the Meriam Library, California State University, Chico, and the files of Butte County historical societies as identified below.

3. To establish expectations for the kinds of archaeological resources likely to occur in the Project Area, a document review was conducted of records housed at the Northeast Information Center of the California Historical Resources Information System, California State University, Chico. The review covered records of previous professional cultural resource studies contained within or immediately adjacent to lands of Rancho Llano Seco, an area measuring 6.3 x 5.3 miles (10.1 x 8.5 kilometers).

4. To identify the major research themes defined by scholarly research in the region, the document review was supplemented by a thorough search of reports, published articles, and books on file at the offices of STC. Key regional syntheses, especially Rosenthal et al. (2007) and White (2003A, 2003B) were consulted for this part of the investigation.

Documents

Prior to and concurrent with the field investigation, historical research was conducted in the stacks on file at the Northeast California Special Collections facility of the Meriam Library, California State University, Chico, and the files of Butte County historical societies.

These studies expanded when Rancho Manager Joe Mendes informed our team of the existence of extensive primary historical documents on file in archives located at the Rancho Llano Seco Headquarters on Hugh Baber Drive. These included several tons of documents stored in archive boxes and original magazine files, along with photographs, aerial photos, communications, and maps covering the Project Area. These sources were assembled, digitized, and studied closely. These investigations addressed two areas of research: 1) Rancho Llano Seco

history and 2) land use history between 1874 and the modern era. For the twentieth century time frame, the Rancho archives provided a detailed, field-by-field record including work orders, receipts and invoices, construction blueprints, and theodolite-produced land maps.

The Rancho archives were accessed, cleaned, and re-organized by this study, and the research team engaged in this effort was met with a regular supply of exciting finds which rewarded systematic and thorough investigations at every turn. For example, we found a raft of new historical maps and aerial photo montages making it possible to definitively track historical structures, clear-cut locations, roads and levee development, and crop and pasture changes through time. In addition, the Parrott Investment Company (PIC) Board Meeting minutes (privately published in 15 leather-bound volumes dating July 15, 1909 to September 25, 1969) were stored in the archives and consulted for this study. All references to the Rancho found in the minutes were identified and transcribed. These included reports from managers and accountants; discussion of impactful events such as fires, floods, pest infestations, and animal diseases; requests and mandates from neighboring operations and from federal and state agencies; discussion of the need for new construction or equipment upgrades; reports on the progress of land development, new construction, and purchase of materials and equipment; market conditions, harvest volumes and meat prices; discussion of record keeping; and management and labor practices.

Maps

For the purposes of historical research, nineteenth- and early twentieth-century maps are uncommon and typically of insufficient scale and detail to provide meaningful detail. However, our research produced eleven maps providing important historical context, and in some cases exceptional detail and accuracy. These maps became an important tool for identification and analysis of Rancho Llano Seco historical features.

Historical Maps

- **1847 Rancho Jacinto Map.** *Map of the Hyacinth Farm, the Property of W. H. McKee, M.D., Surveyed by W. B. Ide. Oct. 1847, C. S. Lymann, Del. Hyacinth Farm.* McKee's Hyacinth Farm consisted of eight leagues of land originally granted as Rancho Pleito y Toros by Governor Manuel Micheltoreña to Jacinto

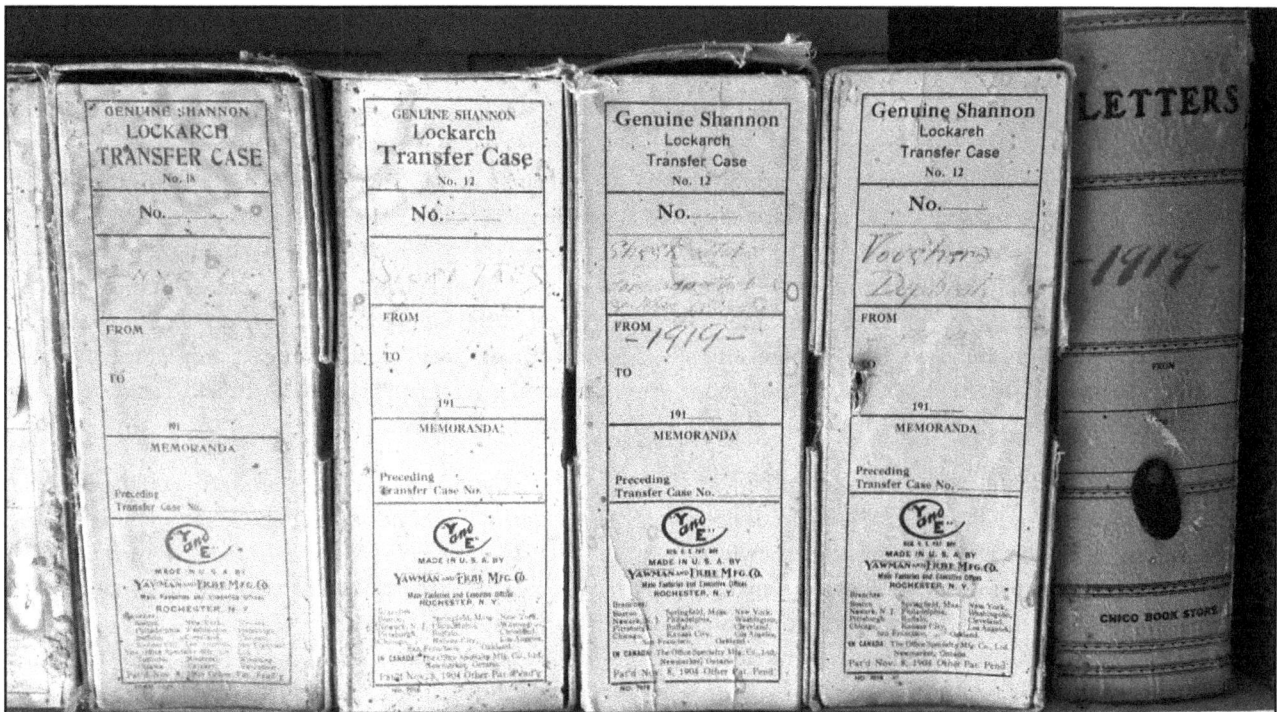

Invoices, sales tags, vouchers, and communications dating 1919 and stored in the Rancho archives.

Rodriguez, and purchased and renamed "Rancho Jacinto" by William H. McKee in 1847. Ide's map, as delineated (copied) by C. S. Lymann, depicts the west edge of Rancho Llano Seco on the east bank of the Sacramento River, in the USFWS Riparian Sanctuary Unit immediately west of the Llano Seco Project Area's Camp 2 Field. The map depicts several important built features directly relevant to the interpretation of Project Area cultural features. Location: Northeast Special Collections, Meriam Library, CSU Chico.

- **1851 Mapa del Valle del Sacramento.** Pen-and-ink illustration by John Bidwell, depicting the Rancho de Keyser and adjoining Mexican land grants. Location: Online Archive of California (cdlib.oac.org).

- **1874 John Parrott Map.** *Map Showing the Topography of the Llano Seco Rancho, the Property of John Parrott, Situated in Butte County, California, Surveyed and Drawn by Hoffmann & Craven, 1874, Containing 17,767 and 17/100 Acres.* Muybridge, Photo. Map on file, Rancho Llano Seco archives. This map, which covers the entire Rancho, is reproduced from a photographic plate by Eadweard Muybridge (1830-1904), renowned San Francisco

panoramic photographer and stop-motion cinema pioneer.

- **1900 (circa) Llano Seco Rancho Map.** This map, which covers the entire Rancho, was probably drawn on vellum from the 1874 John Parrott Map, but absent some detail and with no field names or acreage. The date is estimated based on the complete cutoff and revegetation of the original Parrott Landing loop, the elimination and revegetation of the Jacinto-Dayton Road, and the depiction of access via the River-Ranch Road at Parrott School. It appears to have been issued as the Rancho's first regular-use crop map. Location: Rancho Llano Seco archives.

- **1907 Abby M. Parrott Map.** *Map Showing the Topography of Llano Seco Rancho, the Property of Abby M. Parrott, Situated in Butte County, California. Exterior Boundaries Surveyed by A. W. Von Schmidt, Dep. U.S. Sur., July 1859, Containing 17,767 and 17/100 Acres.* This map, which covers the entire Rancho, is substantially similar to the 1874 John Parrott Map but contains additional inked detail and a record of modifications made at the turn of the century. Map on file, Rancho Llano Seco archives. This map is reproduced here from a high-density scan made of a linen-backed color-inked print. Location: Rancho Llano Seco archives.

- **1910 (circa) Parrott Investment Company Llano Seco Rancho Map.** This map, which covers the entire Rancho, is of unknown origin and produced by unknown engineers, and served as an early crop planning map. It depicts fields in active production, showing fencing ditch and drain, and levee details. Fields are unlabeled except for letter designations: **a** - agriculture; **ni** - non-irrigated; **p** - pasture; and **nc** - not cultivated. Location: Rancho Llano Seco archives.

- **1912 Soils Map.** *Soil Report, Proposed Cultural Program and Soil Map Prepared by G. W. Shaw on January 2, 1912.* This map is an interesting analysis of soil variation across the portion of the Rancho not overgrown with timber. The map accompanies a 25-page report by Shaw providing recommendations for land use that guided Rancho management for decades to come. Location: Rancho Llano Seco archives.

- **1913 Polk Map.** *Map of Llano Seco Rancho, Butte County, California, by M. C. Polk, County Surveyor.* This map, which covers the entire Rancho, depicts fields and field acreage, fencing, roads, levees, lakes, swales, and Rancho structures and buildings. It is mounted on a wooden roll-up dowel, and probably was hung in the Rancho Manager's office (Waugh and/or Shinn). Intended for use as a crop planning map, it has penciled-in notes naming crops and plotting sub-fields. Location: Rancho Llano Seco archives.

- **1924 PG&E Utility Map.** *Distribution Map, DeSabla Division, Vicinity of Parrott School, Approved by C. E. Y. and H. B.* This map, which covers the entire Rancho, depicts the final plan of Rancho electrical lines after installation of the electrical main from the Ord Ferry Road. Location: Rancho Llano Seco archives.

- **1938 Irrigation and Fencing Map.** *Llano Seco Rancho in Butte and Glenn Counties, California, by Hugh Stone, Licensed Surveyor #1865.* This map, which covers the western reach after comprehensive clear-cutting was complete, and was commissioned by Rancho Manager Hugh Baber to serve as the annual crop plan base map for the next two decades. Location: Rancho Llano Seco archives.

- **1939 Irrigation and Fencing Map.** *Llano Seco Rancho in Butte and Glenn Counties, California, by Hugh Stone, Licensed Surveyor #1865.* This map is identical to the 1938 Irrigation and Fencing Map except that it depicts 1939 development of the Camp 2 Field including construction of the Camp 2 Beef Cattle Operation and re-routing of the Rancho southwest access road through Camp 2 and dividing Camp 2 West and Camp 2 East Fields. Location: Rancho Llano Seco archives.

- **1971 Crop Map.** *Llano Seco Rancho in Butte & Glenn Counties, California, by G. F. N., Revised July 1973 by G. F. N., Revised February 1977 Revised April 1977.* This map, which covers the entire Rancho, depicts topography, section lines, field names, acreage, dedicated crops, fencing, access roads, and structures and buildings. It served as the annual crop plan base map through the next two decades. Location: Rancho Llano Seco archives.

USGS Topographic Quadrangles

- 1891 USGS 1:125,000 Topographic quadrangle Chico, CALIF. N3930–W12130/30.

- (USGS Topographic Map Explorer http:// historicalmaps.arcgis.com/usgs/), accessed February 2018.

- 1893 USGS 1:125,000 Topographic quadrangle Chico, CALIF. N3930–W12130/30 (USGS Topographic Map Explorer http://historicalmaps. arcgis.com/usgs/), accessed February 2018.

- 1912 USGS 1:31,680 Topographic quadrangle Newhard, CALIF. N3930–W12152.3/30 (USGS Topographic Map Explorer http://historicalmaps. arcgis.com/usgs/), accessed February 2018.

- 1948 USGS 1:24,000 Topographic quadrangle Chico, CALIF. N3930–W12145/15 (USGS Topographic Map Explorer http://historicalmaps. arcgis.com/usgs/), accessed February 2018.

- 1949 USGS 1:62,500 Topographic quadrangle Chico, CALIF. N3930–W12145/15 (USGS

Topographic Map Explorer http://historicalmaps.arcgis.com/usgs/), accessed February 2018.

- 1950 USGS 1:24,000 Topographic quadrangle Chico, CALIF. N3930–W12152.5/7.5 (USGS Topographic Map Explorer http://historicalmaps.arcgis.com/usgs/), accessed February 2018.

Historical Aerial Photographs

1922 Chambers Aerial Photo Montage

Among the remarkable and important research resources identified in the archives stored at the Rancho office building, a 1922 aerial photo mosaic is perhaps the most important to the greatest range of scholars, especially because it is 15 years older than the oldest previously available aerial photo set, it is substantially more crisp and detailed than photo sets far younger, and it depicts the status of the Rancho's western timber belt just prior to the Rancho management's sweeping clear-cuts. In my opinion, the photos are of sufficient quality to judge the density and canopy composition of the timber and the status and shrubaceous composition of native grasslands. It is also invaluable for pinpointing the location and composition of key historical features, including roads and trails, fence lines, irrigation, and structures and buildings.

The 1922 aerial mosaic has been preserved in three forms: 1) a wall-sized print measuring 12.5 x 7.0 feet hanging in a storage shed behind the office building; 2) a 4.0 x 2.5 foot framed print hanging in Ranch Manager Joe Mendes' office, and; 3) a set of 10 high-quality prints on matte photographic paper mounted on hardboard slabs, stored in a custom-made cedar cabinet located in the top floor attic of the office building. The latter is the most likely to yield good results for modern photographic prints and re-assembly in a Geographic Information System matrix.

In order to confirm the date of the aerial mosaic and provide some context for its unusual vintage, an effort was made to research its origin. These investigations found a passage in the PIC Minutes of April 28, 1921 (PIC Minutes 3:89) recording a presentation by a "Major Chambers of the Durant Aircraft Corporation" in regard to his company's offer to complete an aerial photographic map of the Rancho and various prints for the price of $2,860. Research in the archives also found a receipt for payment of the Durant bill in 1922.

According to the PIC Minutes, Chambers planned to begin work by setting central reference hubs and aerial targets with the assistance of Rancho civil engineers Polk and Robinson, who had recently completed the crop map template described above. Additional document review established that Major Reed Chambers was a World War I ace fighter pilot who in the post-war period partnered with Medal of Honor winner Eddie Rickenbacker in the Durant aerial survey operation. The Durant aerodrome and field, located in Oakland, California, was owned by Rickenbacker's father-in-law (Chant and Batchelor 2002, 72–74).

Durant had recently received favorable press for the high-quality aerial maps the company produced for Bay Area cities, a process described in the January 1922 issue of the journal *Buildings and Building Management*, which reported that this new type of map "is produced by a method adapted from the photographic observations of airplane scouts during the World War." A plane with a specially designed camera mounted in the belly was flown at a fixed altitude for a few minutes at 12:00 noon each day, and the machine was "flown directly between points established by transit working from triangulation points fixed by the United States Geological Survey." The plane carried a pilot and photographer, and one strip was photographed each day with the photographs ultimately joined together and "registered on one great plate from which the commercial maps are printed" (Zorn 1922, 17–18).

Despite enjoying commercial success, within a few years Chambers and Rickenbacker abandoned the aerial survey business for automobile performance design and aircraft manufacturing. Both also consulted with the U.S. military during World War II.

1937–1988 Aerial Photo Mosaics

The pre-field investigation also consulted 12 generations of aerial photos placed online by the Sacramento River Forum, including:

- 1937 USACE, 1:24,000 aerial flood imagery (Sacramento River – Geospatial Data Library https://www.sacramentoriver.org/forum/index.php?id=gismy&rec_id=133), accessed March, 2018.

- 1938 CADWR, 1:24,000 aerial imagery (Sacramento River – Geospatial Data Library https://www.sacramentoriver.org/forum/index.php?id=gismy&rec_id=39), accessed March, 2018.

- 1942 USBR/USACE, 1:24,000 aerial imagery (Sacramento River – Geospatial Data Library https://www.sacramentoriver.org/forum/index.php?id=gismy&rec_id=237), accessed March, 2018.

- 1947 USGS, 1:23,600 aerial imagery (Sacramento River – Geospatial Data Library https://www.sacramentoriver.org/forum/index.php?id=gismy&rec_id=37), accessed March, 2018.

- 1949 USBR, 1:20,000 aerial imagery (Sacramento River – Geospatial Data Library https://www.sacramentoriver.org/forum/index.php?id=gismy&rec_id=116), accessed March, 2018.

- 1958 CADWR, 1:20,000 aerial imagery (Sacramento River – Geospatial Data Library https://www.sacramentoriver.org/forum/index.php?id=gismy&rec_id=149), accessed March, 2018.

- 1964 USGS, 1:24,000 aerial imagery (Sacramento River – Geospatial Data Library https://www.sacramentoriver.org/forum/index.php?id=gismy&rec_id=35), accessed March, 2018.

- 1970 CADWR, 1:7,000 aerial imagery (Sacramento River – Geospatial Data Library https://www.sacramentoriver.org/forum/index.php?id=gismy&rec_id=239), accessed March, 2018.

- 1974 CADWR, 1:36,000 aerial flood imagery (Sacramento River – Geospatial Data Library https://www.sacramentoriver.org/forum/index.php?id=gismy&rec_id=38), accessed March, 2018.

- 1980 USGS, 1:20,000 aerial imagery (Sacramento River – Geospatial Data Library https://www.sacramentoriver.org/forum/index.php?id=gismy&rec_id=150), accessed March, 2018.

- 1982 CADWR, 1:24,000 aerial imagery (Sacramento River – Geospatial Data Library https://www.sacramentoriver.org/forum/index.php?id=gismy&rec_id=223), accessed March, 2018.

- 1988 USGS, 1:24,000 aerial imagery (Sacramento River – Geospatial Data Library https://www.sacramentoriver.org/forum/index.php?id=gismy&rec_id=52), accessed March, 2018.

SECTION 1

The Natural Environment

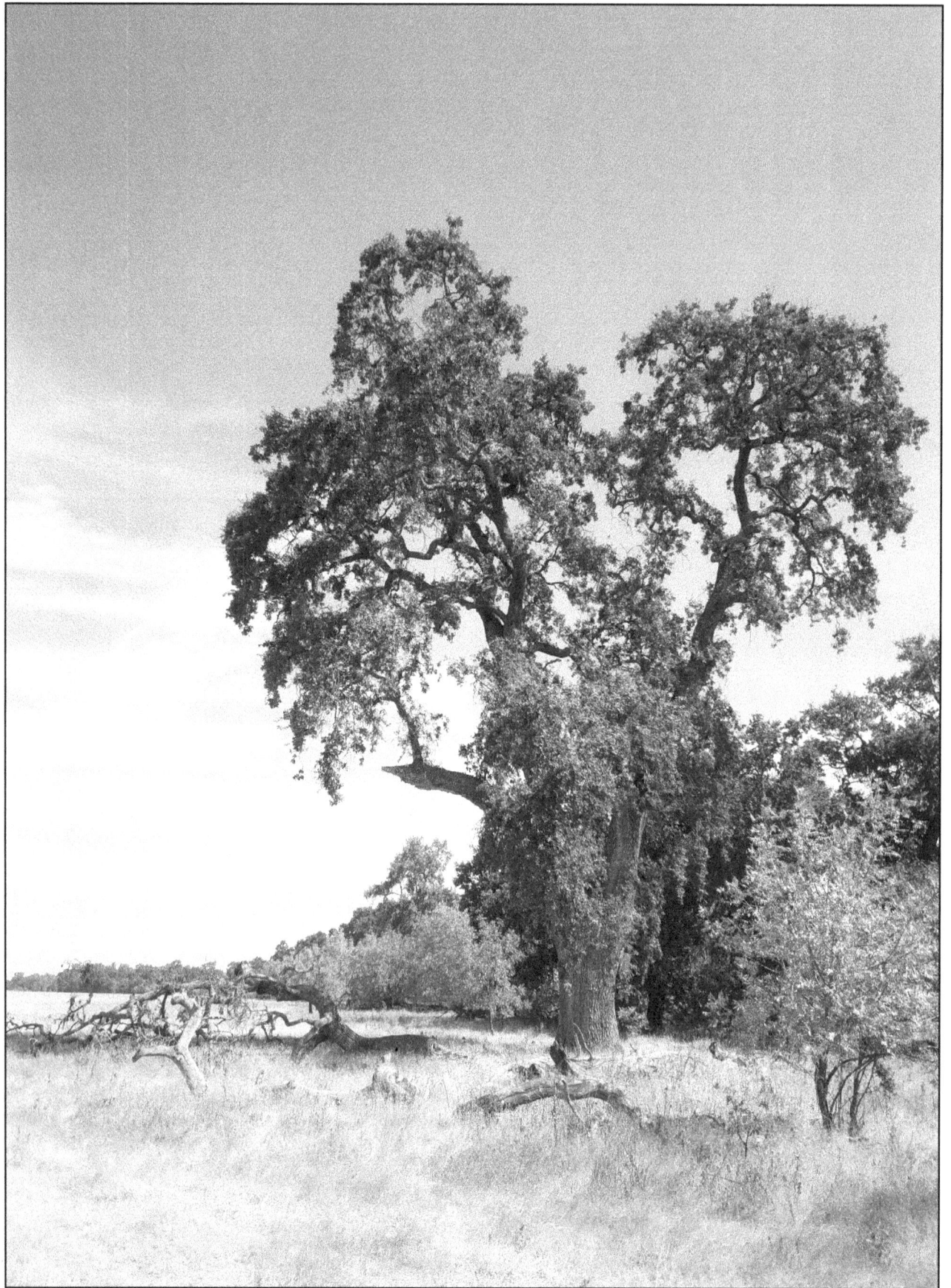

CHAPTER 1

Landscape & Soils

LANDSCAPE AND SOILS RECEIVE FIRST attention here because by examining the structure of landscape we can begin to define the factors that determined the pattern of prehistoric and historical human occupation of the Rancho Llano Seco Project Area. The record of human occupation is likely to span more than 13,000 years, and the human signature is embedded in the Llano Seco landscape, which also constantly evolved throughout this span. With respect to the prehistoric record, previous archaeological surveys in the Llano Seco Project vicinity have established the potential for buried archaeological deposits along the Sacramento River, with the identification of three previously recorded buried deposits (Ca-Gle-95, Ca-Col-245/H, Ca-Col-247) and several excavated sites with cultural deposits exceeding 3.5 meters (11.5 feet) deep (e.g., Ca-But-233, Ca-But-294, Ca-Col-247). The distribution pattern of archaeological sites has been further conditioned by erosion as demonstrated by several older recorded sites subsequently eradicated by river bank erosion (e.g., Ca-Gle-105). Thus, the first order of business here is to establish the extent to which the spatial and temporal distribution of archaeological sites in the study area has been conditioned by the river's propensity to create and remove habitable landforms and their associated habitation traces, and how these mechanisms changed over time. Can enough be learned about Quaternary landscape formation in the Llano Seco Project Area to relate the geochronology of the river corridor to the chronological structure of the archaeological record?

Landforms

Rancho Llano Seco has become an important laboratory for the investigation and analysis of the hydrological, geomorphological, and ecological evolution of the Sacramento River corridor. Two things make this an important place to conduct these lines of inquiry. First, only 4,500 acres—just 25 percent of Rancho Llano Seco acreage—has been leveled for flood-irrigated crops. The remainder, while generally under production for the last 80–120 years, has been used for low-intensity cattle pasture or dry row crop production relying on shallow tilling and meteoric moisture without levelling. As a result, the Rancho landscape stands apart from most of the Northern Sacramento Valley which has been levelled for flood irrigation, a practice that elsewhere has erased surface soil variation and topography, along with most if not all associated archaeological traces. The Rancho landscape preserves significant and well-defined ancient and modern relic landforms including abandoned channels, oxbows, lagoons, swales, natural levees and distal floodplain basins which have become an important focus of investigation. Another thing makes this place special: for most of the middle reach of the Sacramento River, east-west flowing streams draining either the North Coast Ranges or Sierra-Cascade introduce elevated alluvial fans composed of coarse-grained deposits that conflate with and modify fluvial floodplain formation. The Rancho is unique in its distance from these stream sources meaning that its landforms are conditioned solely by fluvial mechanisms.

A number of investigators have documented and interpreted the Rancho Llano Seco relic channel landforms and soils (e.g., Brice 1977; Helley and Harwood 1985; White 2003; Meyer and Rosenthal 2008; Dunne and Aalto 2013), but until recently these studies were based on map and aerial photo interpretation. This changed in the early 2000s when Michael B. Singer of the Earth Research Institute at University of California, Santa Barbara and Rolf Aalto of Exeter University sampled 18 cores in the Rancho's western and eastern relic river channel landforms with the intent of dating paleochannels. In the 2010s, Aalto's Exeter doctoral student Mathais Will followed up by digging an additional 45 cores and 15 trenches, the latter assisted by Rancho senior staffer Shannon Samuelson.

Will's primary research problems are also pertinent to the archaeology-geomorphology interface: 1) patterns and processes of Quaternary landscape evolution, and 2) links between these patterns and processes and events and conditions generated by paleoclimate and paleotectonics. In addition to completing standard profiles for each sample, Will characterized the lithology of gravel deposits to differentiate Sierra-Cascade from North Coast Range sources, characterized sedimentation rates and their change over time, and dated key stratigraphic units using a combination of absolute dating methods including radiocarbon (14C), OSL (Optically Stimulated Luminescence), and 210Pb decay methods.

General Structure

The subsurface deposits we are concerned with here, occupying the upper 6.0 meters (20.0 feet) of the Rancho landscape, are soils and sediments deposited in the last 33,000 years, during the late Quaternary period. The mechanisms of erosion and deposition responsible for late Quaternary landscape production in the Rancho were conditioned by fluvial transport and floodplain development associated with the ancient and modern Sacramento River. There is, however, evidence of an important structural shift at the Pleistocene/Holocene boundary. The Rancho Llano Seco surface slopes slightly down from north to south—100–110 feet AMSL on the north end of the Rancho and 95–100 feet on the south end (a drop of 1.0 foot for every 4,400 feet)—and slightly down from east to west—from 110 feet AMSL on the east border to 104 feet at the bank of the current Sacramento River channel forming the Rancho's western border (a drop of 1.0 foot for every 3,880 feet). This "strike-and-slip" appears to be a marker of the mechanism configuring the most salient local feature of the river's evolution—its steady eastward migration throughout the late Quaternary. The entire Rancho is composed of relatively shallow sediments and soils lying atop a marker late Pleistocene petrocalcic duripan dating approximately 13–17,000 years old capping a massive unit of dense, calcareous Pleistocene fluvial gravel and sand deposits dated 13–33,000 years old. In the eastern part of the Rancho the marker petrocalcic duripan occurs at relatively shallow depths of 1.7–2.6 meters (5.5–8.5 feet) below surface (elevation 95.5–92.5 feet AMSL), while to the west this marker also occurs but at depths of 3.3–3.5 meters (10.8–11.5 feet) below surface (elevation 90.0 feet AMSL), indicating approximately double the

east-west slope. Agreeing with previous researchers (e.g., Helley and Harwood 1985; Robertson 1987; Meyer and Rosenthal 2008; Dunne and Aalto 2013), Will (2015) argues that the east-to-west downslope of this contact was the product of gradual uplift of the Llano Seco Terrace beginning at the Pleistocene/Holocene transition, and this was the mechanism responsible for the river's gradual migration westward to its present position and the production of deeper floodplains in the western part of the Rancho. Figure 1 shows the principal landscape units of Rancho Llano Seco and the following describes research and findings to date, relying primarily on Will (2015).

Llano Seco Terrace

As defined by Will (2015) the Llano Seco Terrace occupies the eastern two-thirds of the Rancho (Figure 1) and is composed of relatively shallow clay and silty clay sediments and soils residing atop the marker petrocalcic duripan. The Llano Seco Terrace has channel and floodplain/basin facies:

- *Channel Facies.* The channel facies are composed of Llano Seco Series and Vermet Series soils consisting of old, well-developed clay loams to silty clay loams that have increased clay and carbonate content and blocky structure with depth (USDA 2018A, 2018B). Some older Parrott Series soils (USDA 2018C) situated on the Llano Seco Terrace and possessing linear north-south trending relic river channels are also included here. Will (2015) dated the linear channel deposits to the mid-Holocene, between 3219+/-138 and some time before 6206 ± 1583 cal BP. While he assumes that the Llano Seco-Vermet-Parrott soils date as early as the onset of the Holocene around 12000 cal BP, there is no specific demonstration in the dating record that this is the case. However, based on the complex and stacked "B-Horizons" comprising these soils it is likely that extreme instability at the onset of the mid-Holocene produced significant weathering and deflation of the Llano Seco Terrace deposits erasing some portion the early-Holocene record (see also Meyer and Rosenthal 2008). The channel facies has a "rolling" topography indicative of heavy weathering, and the terrace is dissected by linear north-south-trending relic river channels forming a classic woven anastomosed channel pattern typical of low-gradient

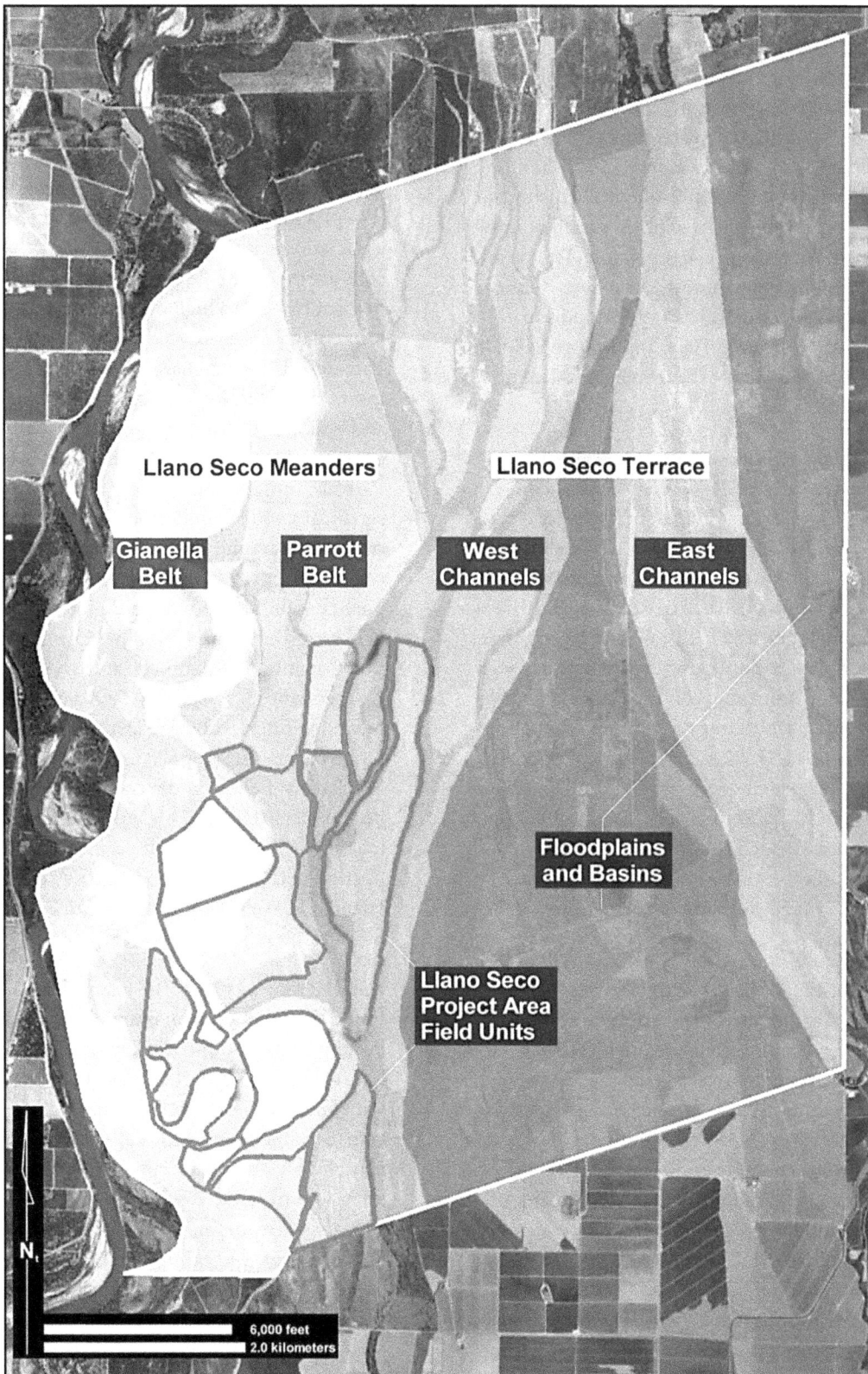

Figure 1. Rancho Llano Seco floodplains, basins, terraces, and meanders.

channels with durable, clay-dominated banks (per Dunne and Aalto 2013). There are also numerous runoff washes, calcareous alkali pans, and occasional elevated, mound-shaped remnant natural levee and bank features distributed throughout. There are two distinct channel alignments separated by a basin, and these alignments may be chronologically distinct and may have been produced by shifts in runoff or uplift at the Pleistocene/Holocene transition (Dunne and Aalto 2013). The westernmost Llano Seco Terrace channel facies occur in the current Llano Seco Project Area in Vermette, Hale, and Martin 1 Fields and in the west portions of Martin 2 and Martin 3 Fields (Figure 1).

- *Basin/Floodplain Facies.* The basin/floodplain facies are composed of Dodgeland-Whitecabin-Farwell Series soils consisting of massive deposits of 40.0–55.0 percent clay characterized by increased stickiness, alkalinity, and iron and manganese content with depth (USDA 2018D, 2018E, 2018F). Reflecting their position in distal flood basins, the basin/floodplain deposits are very shallow and less than one-half the thickness of the channel deposits; the transition to the petrocalcic duripan is just 135–183 centimeters (53–72 inches) below surface. The basin/floodplain facies occur outside and to the east of the current Llano Seco Project Area, in Bedrock, Burnham, and Crouch Fields (Figure 1).

Llano Seco Meanders

As defined by Dunne and Aalto (2013) and Will (2015), the Llano Seco meander belts occupy the western one-third of the Rancho (Figure 1) and are composed of relatively deeper silt and silty clay sediments deposited by late Holocene Sacramento River meander activity. As the river migrated west its vertical entrenchment was checked by the underlying duripan and calcareous gravels. This erosion-resistant basement complex forced the river's flood energy laterally, resulting in a meander migration pattern, and the uplift forced the trend west, resulting in meander age-progression to the west. Will's analysis of sediment composition in the Llano Seco meanders indicates that the river's progress west was slow because it came at the expense of coarse-grained distal fan toes originating from the Stony Creek Megafan, which still forms the west bank of the Sacramento River (Will 2015). The Llano Seco meanders are here separated into two

groups based on soil series associations: an older meander belt to the east composed of filled and inactive scars, and a younger meander belt to the west including active oxbows and other documented historical channels:

- *Parrott Belt.* Several ranks of older meanders exist in the eastern portion of the meander belt, grouped together here as the "Parrott Belt" based on association with Parrott Series soils. Parrott Series soils are moderately-fine silt loams with 18–27 percent clay and a high organic content. They are more oxidized, massive, and sticky with depth. Parrott soils include older alluvium deposited as inset terraces backfilled during the meander process and younger alluvium deposited in abandoned channels. Unlike the Gianella Meander Belt, the Parrott meanders lack clearly defined topographic signatures and are indicated at the surface only by subtle topographic and soil variation. The lack of profound topographic signatures is a product of post-channel abandonment floodplain deposition. Will found evidence for a rapid rate of deposition in the abandoned channel features (Will 2015, 97). Consequently, in a span of 2,000 years the older meander loops evolved from active channel to cut-off, to oxbow, to lagoon, and then to subtle swale. The Parrott Belt meander traces are non-contiguous because later Gianella meanders penetrated in several locations. The Parrott Belt occurs in the central portion of the Llano Seco Project Area, in Oil Well Island, Oil Well West, Little Grant, Fish Camp, and Stump Camp North Fields (Figure 1).

- *Gianella Meander Belt.* The Gianella meanders are found on the floodplain immediately east of the current Sacramento River channel, grouped together here as the "Gianella Belt" based on association with Gianella Series soils, composed of very friable, coarse-grained sand and silt loams with 5–14 percent clay and a high organic content. They are young, with an A/C profile, but deep because like the Parrott soils they are dominated by alluvium deposited as inset terraces backfilled during the meander process. Organic-rich alluvium that has accumulated in abandoned channels, oxbows, and lagoons is associated with the related Columbia Series soils. The Gianella Meander Belt is clearly defined by relic channels in the form of a series of overlapping oxbows, lagoons, crescent-shaped swales, and drainage features contained in the west portion of the Llano Seco Project Area.

- *Columbia Series Soils.* The Gianella Meander Belt is clearly defined by relic channels in the form of a series of overlapping oxbows, lagoons, crescent-shaped swales, and drainage features contained in the west portion of the Llano Seco Project Area, in Gangplank, Camp 2 West, Stump Camp South, DWR 1, DWR 2, and the west half of Martin 2 Fields (Figure 1).

- *Llano Seco Terrace Stratigraphic Structure.* Will's Llano Seco Terrace study established the shallow stratigraphic position and Pleistocene age of the underlying duripan and calcareous gravels at around 1.5–2.5 meters below surface, dating between 13800+1700 and 33500+6800 cal BP. He also established that the bulk of the overlying channels and floodplain clay and clay silt was produced when the Sacramento River occupied the Llano Seco Terrace during the early to middle Holocene, probably dating 3200–13000 cal BP. Will's dates for the Llano Seco Terrace lack profound vertical seriation, and it is likely that the early-to-middle-Holocene deposits are composed of a complex and interbedded set of channels, banks, and natural levees that have not yet been mapped or defined.

- *Parrott Belt Stratigraphic Structure.* Beginning sometime after 6200 cal BP, the river began a gradual migration west. In the new channels the underlying Pleistocene deposits forced flood energy laterally, leading to meander formation. Will's and Johnson's dates combined show that production of the Parrott Belt meanders began sometime before 4570 cal BP and continued through 900 cal BP. The five Parrott Belt dates form a well-seriated series with a strong date/depth correlation (r=0.79) and a curve suggesting the rate of deposition was slow between 1500–4500 cal BP and then accelerated after 1300 cal BP, probably when the primary channels drifted west, changing the Parrott Belt to an active floodplain and shifting the sediment balance from erosion-deposition to primarily deposition.

- *Gianella Belt Stratigraphic Structure.* The westernmost meanders began production sometime between 1900–1300 cal BP and were most active after 400 cal BP to the modern era. The Gianella Belt dates lack profound seriation, but this is consistent with Will's analysis of profiles and sediments suggesting that deposition was event-specific and varied significantly by floodplain versus abandoned channel feature association.

Endemism

SOIL ENDEMISM CONTROLLED THE PRINCIPAL features of Rancho Llano Seco's historical vegetation distribution patterns. For example, the earliest record of vegetation—the 1874 John Parrott Map—shows the eastern one-half of the Rancho as an "Open Plain" devoid of trees, and this is consistent with the ancient basin's predominant Dodgeland-Whitecabin-Farwell Series shallow clays, which because of poor drainage and high alkalinity resist timber colonization. This same map shows the Rancho's central belt, associated with the Llano Seco and Vermet Series clay loams, supporting only patchy stands and individual trees on the plains and dense timber confined to narrow strips bordering the immediate banks of the relic braided river channels where seasonal impoundments and flood-deposited loam prevailed. In sharp contrast, the map depicts dense timber in the western one-third of the Rancho associated with the deep, well-drained Parrott, Gianella, and Columbia Series loams.

Based on the patterns produced by perennial soil endemism, current vegetation trends in unmanaged tracts are likely to closely approximate habitats existing here before Rancho development began in the 1860s. In fact, by importing and geo-referencing historical maps and aerials this investigation found that many individual trees and stands depicted in old maps still exist today and are relics pre-dating the 1870s. The Rancho's natural vegetation follows three phases, each associated with the distinctive soil and landform types described above. A list of species and habitat associations observed during the cultural resource survey appears in Table 1, including notes on Native American uses as determined by ethnographic documentary research, previous archaeological finds made in nearby archaeological sites, and as specified during the course of the investigation by survey crew member and Mechoopda elder Chester Conway, who participated in Project Area field work.

Llano Seco Terrace Vegetation

The Llano Seco Terrace vegetation, found in the Llano Seco Project Area's Hale, Vermet, and Gangplank Fields, occupies the central axis of the Rancho, and is associated with an elevated relic floodplain containing old, weathered clay and silt clay loams capping a shallow duripan. Dense, non-native ryegrass, common wild oats, and thick patches of head-high bull thistle and chest-high yellow starthistle now cover most of the broad, flat to gently sloping plains of Hale, Vermet, and Gangplank Fields, but these species are products of lapsed permanent pasture cultivation in which rye and oats ultimately out-competed the original sown mix, and invasive thistles prevailed. In the prehistoric period native prairie grasses probably dominated on these landforms, including needle grasses, meadow barley, California oatgrass, hairgrass, and fescue, among others. Common native bulbs and forbs are still present but infrequent on the Llano Seco Terrace landform. Species observed during the field study included soaproot, brodiaea, buttercup, lupine, clover, and vetch. The floodplains are heavily weathered, crisscrossed by braided relic channels, swales, runoff washes, calcareous alkali pans, and occasional elevated, mound-shaped remnant natural levee features. The swales and alkali pans are seasonal wetland patches dominated by alkali-tolerant grasses and forbs including saltgrass, alkali sacaton, peppergrass, filaree, saltbush, tarweeds, hareleaf, and clover. Dispersed oaks and oak woodland patches occur on the remnant rises along the relic channels. In most instances the oaks are the sole arboreal species, sustained by deep tap roots capable of reaching the buried duripan contact where scant moisture might accumulate in dry months.

Table 1. Species list and habitat associations observed during the cultural resource survey.

* Native American uses as determined by ethnographic documentary research, previous archaeological finds, and comments by survey crew member and Mechoopda elder Chester Conway.

** Soaproot used as food, fish poison and soap.

Species and Habitats		Native American Uses* Food	Tools	Medicine
Floodplain Overstory				
California valley oak	Quercus lobata	X	X	
California box elder	Acer negundo	X		
California walnut	Juglans californica	X		
Oregon ash	Fraxinus latifola		X	
toyon	Photinia arbutifolia	X		X
California buckeye	Aesculus californica	X		
Floodplain Understory				
elderberry	Sambucus mexicana	X	X	
Douglas sagewort	Artemisia douglasiana			X
mulefat	Baccharis viminea			X
wild rose	Rosa californica	X	X	
coyote bush	Baccharis pilularis			
button-willow	Cephalanthus occidentalis			
Riparian Overstory				
western sycamore	Platanus racemosa		X	
Fremont cottonwood	Populus fremontii			
big leaf maple	Acer macrophyllum			
white alder	Alnus rhombifolia		X	
Riparian Understory				
Gooddings black willow	Salix gooddingii		X	X
red willow	Salix laevigata		X	X
black willow	Salix lasiandra		X	X
Riparian Vines				
wild grape	Vitis californica	X	X	
poison oak	Rhus diversiloba			X
pipestem	Clematis lasiantha		X	
blackberry	Rubus sp.	X	X	
Dutchman's pipe vine	Aristolochia californica			
greenbrier	Smilax californica			
California bedstraw	Galium californicum		X	
big mistletoe	Phoradendron tomentosum			X
Riparian Aquatic				
California bulrush	Schoenoplectus californicus	X	X	
cattail	Scirpus spp.	X	X	
pennywort	Hydrocotyle spp.			
duckweed	Lemna minor			

Species and Habitats		Native American Uses* Food	Tools	Medicine
Floodplain Grasses				
needle grass	Stipa spp.	X		
California oatgrass	Danthonia californica	X		
tufted hairgrass	Dechampsia caespitosa	X		
three-awn	Aristida sp.	X		
hairgrass	Deschampsia danthonoides	X		
fescue	Festuca spp.	X		
brome	Bromus sp.	X		
meadow barley	Hordeum brachyantherum	X		
wild oats	Avena sp.	X		
Pacific reedgrass	Calamagrostis nuthaensis	X		
wild rye	Leymus spp.	X		
junegrass	Koeleria cristata	X		
melicgrass	Melica spp.			
bluegrass	Poa Scabrella	X		
blue-eyed grass	Sisyrinchium bellum	X		
Floodplain Forbs				
soaproot	Chlorogalum spp.	X		X**
cluster lillies	Brodiaea sp.	X		
buttercup	Ranunculus spp.	X		
varicolored lupine	Lupinus variicolor	X		
clover	Trifolium sp.	X		
vetch	Vicia sp.	X		
Pans and Swales				
saltgrass	Distichlis stricta	X		
alkali sacaton	Sporobolus airoides	X		
peppergrass	Lepidium latipes	X		
filaree	Erodium sp.	X		
saltbush	Atriplex sp.	X		
hayfield tarweed	Hemizonia sp.	X		
tarweeds	Madia sp.	X		
hareleaf	Lagophylla sp.	X		
clover	Trifolium fucatum	X		

The three main relic channels coursing through the Project Area trend north-south and are framed by high bank walls (Figure 2, top). Historically, four of the channels contained impounded perennial water, identified on the 1874 John Parrott Map and the 1907 Abbey M. Parrott Map (from north to south) as Moorehead Lake, Perkins Lake, Eddy Lake, and Bundle Lake. The Rancho developed these lakes for irrigation by installing a series of dams, gates, pumps, and siphons to increase and manage the impoundments. The channel beds reside in the duripan and calcareous gravels, enhancing available water at the duripan contact in adjoining high floodplains. Consequently, even though the channel banks are high and steep and the floodplains rise 6–12 feet (1.8-3.6 meters) above the average lake water level, the channel banks support a dense vegetation belt. Valley oak is the predominant species and grows alongside California walnut and California sycamore which form a distinct second-tier overstory. An intermediate scrub overstory is composed of immature examples of the three, growing alongside Oregon ash, California box elder, elderberry, mulefat, wild rose, poison oak, button-willow, and California buckeye. Common vines and climbers included wild grape, poison oak, wild rose, blackberry, Dutchman's pipe vine, greenbrier, and wild clematis. The parasitic big mistletoe is found on overstory trees (c.f., Katibah 1984; Ornduff 1974; Roberts et al. 1980). Invasive water hyacinth and yellow flag iris have made inroads in portions of Eddy Lake.

Parrott Belt and Gianella Belt Vegetation

The 1874 John Parrott Map shows that the Gianella and Parrott Belts were originally characterized by dense, uninterrupted timber tracts, and the Llano Seco westernmost fields contained only 202 open acres, largely consisting of patches clear-cut in the 1860s by squatters clear-cutting for the Sacramento oak cordwood trade, and to develop small openings for wheat and pasture. This modest clear-cut pace continued through 1922; however, acting on a proposal advanced by William Parrott in June, 1921, in 1922 the Parrott Investment Company directed new Rancho Manager Hugh Baber to expand development of the western timber tract, and between 1923 and 1938 all but a few lake and oxbow borders in the Project Area's 12 westernmost fields were clear-cut to bare earth. Stumps were pulled and slash was burned in 1938, and by 1939 more than 1,900 acres of the Project

Area's 2,007 acres were open land in wheat, rye, and pasture production.

Since 1939 Parrott Belt vegetation has been primarily restricted to relic stands around the margins of the Llano Seco Project Area's Stump Camp South, Stump Camp North, Martin 1, Martin 2, Martin 3, DWR 1, and DWR 2 Fields. These stands are associated with Parrott Series deep, moderately fine silt loams produced by late-Holocene river migration and meander paths. The 1874 John Parrott Map suggests that the Parrott Belt's broad, flat floodplains, contiguous with the Llano Seco Terrace relic channel timber belts, were historically overgrown with mature oak woodland. Where they have not been levelled, the Parrott Belt's older meander scars are marked by subtle swales containing flood-deposited sandy loams. The deepest of these swales, for example the extinct oxbow curving through Stump Camp, is recorded in twentieth-century aerial photographs as a seasonal wetland containing dense wetland vegetation prior to the clear-cuts completed in 1938. Based on the pre-1923 maps and aerials, the Parrott Belt swales were characterized by mature riparian forest, with an overstory composed of occasional California valley oak, western sycamore, and Fremont cottonwood; intermediate arboreal species including California box elder, California walnut, Oregon ash, and California buckeye; and a shrubby understory composed of wild rose, coyote bush, mulefat, elderberry, button-willow, and Douglas sagewort.

Gianella Belt vegetation, contained primarily in unmanaged wetlands and oxbows located around the margins of Oil Well Island, Oil Well West, Little Grant, Fish Camp, and Camp West Fields, is associated with Gianella and Columbia Series loams produced by historical-to-modern river migration and meander paths. Gianella Belt floodplain vegetation is identical to and contiguous with the Parrott Belt oak-woodland. However, the historic oxbows and lagoons of the Gianella Belt contain active riverwash and frequently have sufficient depth to carry small lakes most of the year. These features are marked by an overstory of western sycamore and Fremont cottonwood and a second tier of big leaf maple, white alder, and willow, all overgrown with wild grape, blackberry, Dutchman's pipe vine, greenbrier, and California bedstraw (Figure 2, bottom). Lakes and ponds frequently generate dense stands of California bulrush, cattail, pennywort, and duckweed.

Figure 2. Llano Seco Terrace vegetation (top) – dense oak dominated riparian timber bordering the Eddy Lake relic channel; Gianella Belt vegetation (bottom) – dense vine-dominated riparian timber in an historic oxbow.

Animals

Only a few of the terrestrial animals that inhabited the Project Area historically can be considered exclusive to one or another habitat. Most carnivores/omnivores, including coyote (*Canis latrans*), gray fox (*Urocyon cinerargentus*), badger (*Taxidea taxus*), spotted skunk (Spilogale putorius), striped skunk (*Mephitis mephitis*), bobcat (*Felis rufus*), puma (*Felis concolor*), black bear (*Ursus americana*), and grizzly bear (*Ursus horribilis*) had widespread distributions and might prowl all three habitats in a single foray.

Of the three habitats, the California Prairie probably supported the highest proportion of large herbivores, including tule elk (*Cervus elophus nannodes*), pronghorn (*Antilocapra americana*), and black-tailed deer (*Odocoileus hemionus columbianus*). Tule elk was probably one of the most significant aboriginal game animals of the grasslands. While early historic extermination leaves open many questions about the behavior of this animal, we can infer the general properties of tule elk behavior in the region based on analogy to the behavior of modern herds in similar environments. Tule elk in the project area probably lived in small, fluid herds whose movements changed "in response to local conditions" (McCullough 1969, 47; see also Smith 1973 and Phillips 1976, 62). In response to desiccation, by September the elk probably accumulated in the vicinity of riparian woodlands within one mile of perennial water sources, presumably foraging succulents of the riparian zone and browsing oak leaves and green acorns. The rut probably took place near the end of September, characterized by bull-dominated cow groups of up to 30 to 50 individuals. Larger herds probably coalesced after the rut, feeding primarily on acorn mast until November, when they shifted to small, dispersed grazing groups occupying mixed prairie and oak woodland (McCullough 1969; Smith 1973; Phillips 1976).

Pronghorn were also common in the California prairie. Subsisting primarily on annual grasses and forbs and relying on open ground and speed for defense from predation, the pronghorn was most likely a permanent resident of the prairie. The rut took place in October, characterized by small, buck-dominated doe groups of 5 to 15 individuals. Larger herds might gather in the late fall through spring, dispersing into smaller herds in the summer.

Unlike the transhumant (seasonal movement) tule elk described above, black-tailed deer were probably fixed to specific territories, relying on cover provided by riparian woodland. According to Taber, for black-tailed deer in the chaparral (a comparable dense and woody habitat):

> an area of about 360 acres [1.46 km2] would represent the maximum home range size occupied by an individual deer... [further]... home ranges are not mutually exclusive, so that the same 360 acres might be occupied, in part at least, by as many as 80 or 90 deer. (Taber 1956, 113)

Exceptions to this pattern include yearling dispersal, buck travel during the rutting season, wandering by aged deer, disturbance from over-predation, desiccation, or burning. However, 90 percent of the time, an established animal can be found within a 450 m (500 yd) radius of the center of its home range. Black-tailed deer primarily subsist on green grass and browse in November through March, and oak and other browse between April through October (Taber 1956, 164-165).

Small game typical of the grasslands included the black-tailed jackrabbit (*Lepus californicus*), Beechey ground squirrel (*Spermophilis beecheyi*), kangaroo rat (*Dipodomys heermanni*), and pocket gophers (*Thomomys bottae*). Small game of the riparian woodland included gray squirrel (*Sciurus griseus*), ground squirrel (*Sciuridae sp.*), Audubon cottontail (*Sylvilagus audubonii*), brush rabbit (*Sylvilagus bachmani*), California quail (*Lophortyx californicus*), and ringtail (*Bassariscus astutus*), as well as many small perching birds, rodents, reptiles, amphibians, and bats.

Animals common to the river included beaver (*Caster canadensis*) Pacific pond turtle (*Clemmys marmorata*), molluscs (*Anodonta californiensis, Gonidea angulate, and Margaratifera falcata*), and predators such as raccoon (*Procyon lotor*), ringtail (*Bassariscus astutus*), weasel (*Mustela frenata*), mink (*Mustela vison*), and river otter (*Lutra canadensis*). Resident riparian avifauna included waterfowl such as ducks, teal, and shovelers (*Anas sp.*), wood duck (*Aix sponsa*), coot (*Fulica americana*), double-crested cormorant (*Phalacrocorax auritus*), western grebe (*Aechmophorus occidentalis*), and gulls (*Larus sp.*). Wading birds, some of which were migratory, included great blue heron (*Ardea herodias*), green heron (*Butorides virescens*), snowy egret (*Egretta thula*), great egret

(*Casmerodius albus*), and American bittern (*Botaurus lentiginosus*). The Project Area lies directly in the Central Valley path of the Pacific Flyway. Migratory waterfowl, including swans, geese, and ducks (Anseriformes) stopped over between approximately November and February. Ethnographic accounts describe the valley thick with waterfowl during the winter season. In general, they favored open ground or shallow water of the basin areas.

The extraordinary fisheries of the Sacramento River featured a number of resident and anadromous species. The largest resident fish was the white sturgeon (*Acipenser transmontanus*); however, the most common fishes belonged to the cyprinidae family, including hitch (*Lavinia exilicauda*), splittail (*Pogonichthys macrolepidotus*), hardhead (*Mylopharadon conocephalus*), and the western pike-minnow (*Ptychocheilus grandis*). Other common resident fish included the western sucker (*Catostomus occidentalis*), Sacramento perch (*Archoplites interruptus*), and tule perch (*Hysterocarpus traskii*). Each of these species was widely dispersed most of the year, but during the spring season could be found clustered in side streams, sloughs or shallow water habitats for nesting or spawning. Anadromous fishes primarily spawned in the late fall/winter but also had spring runs. These included the Pacific lamprey (*Lampetra lethophaga*) and several salmonids, including the king salmon (*Oncorhynchus tshawytscha*), Coho salmon (*Oncorhynchus kisutch*), and steelhead rainbow trout (*Salmo gairdneri gairdneri*).

SECTION 2

Native American Cultures

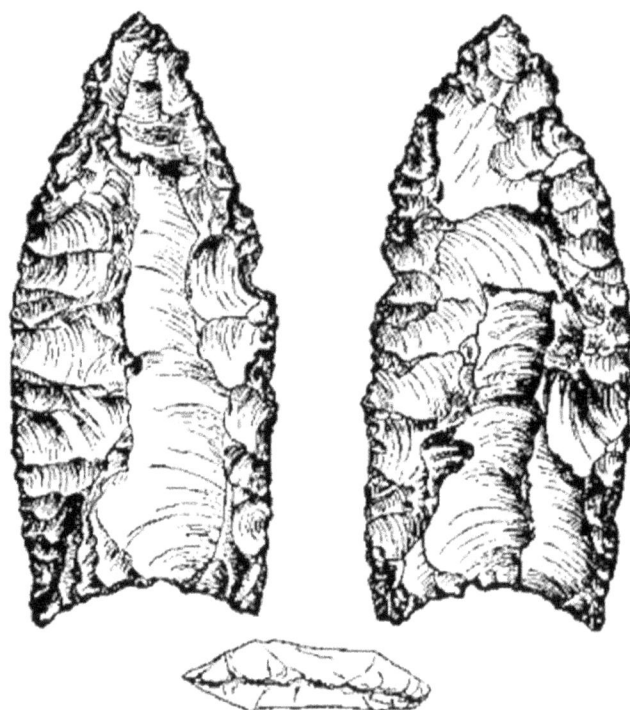

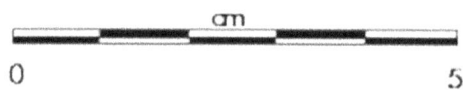

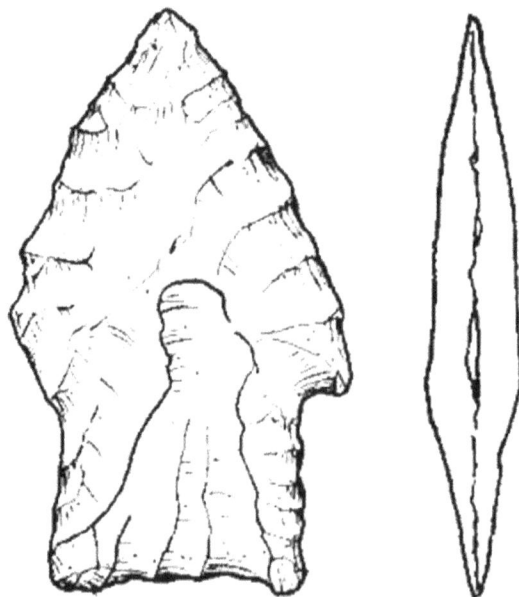

Figure 3. Clovis Fluted (top) and Borax Lake (bottom) wide-stemmed points from Northern California.

CHAPTER 3

Prehistoric Cultures

Paleoindian Cultures

RECENT SAMPLING AT BORAX LAKE near Clear Lake provides tentative obsidian hydration dating evidence indicating occasional obsidian quarrying activity as early as 16,000 years ago (White 2002, 448-449). However, the find remains unconfirmed and no other archaeological traces of this age have been identified in the Sacramento River watershed. Our most reliable evidence indicates that the region was first colonized at the end of the Pleistocene, around 13,500 years ago. Toolkits emphasizing heavily reworked multi-function equipment made from distant source materials indicate that these earliest peoples were culturally conservative, low-density hunters and foragers who moved between widespread resource patches and practiced technological traditions that were similar from region to region. Contemporaneity with Pleistocene megafauna is suspected but not demonstrated.

The most ancient confirmed cultural traces are associated with the Western Clovis Tradition and Borax Lake Pattern. The Western Clovis Tradition (Willig and Aikens 1988) dates between approximately 10,500 and 13,500 years before present (BP). Western Clovis is represented by one site and a few scattered artifacts in Northern California, marked by use of the distinctive Clovis fluted point (Figure 3, top). Diet remains a matter of speculation (Fredrickson 1984, 497; Fredrickson and White 1988; Rosenthal et al. 2007).

Lower Archaic Period Cultures

The Borax Lake Pattern is the Northern California manifestation of the Western Stemmed Tradition (Willig and Aikens 1988), dating between approximately 7,000 and 10,500 BP. The marker types are wide-stemmed projectile points (Figure 3, bottom) and handstones and millingstones. Deep, flutelike basal thinning, large

bladelet flakes and well worked unifacial tools are carry-overs from Paleoindian technology. A few sites have produced plant and animal remains indicating the Borax Lake Pattern diet featured large nuts and small and large game (White 2002). No artifacts or sites of this age have yet been identified in the Sacramento Valley proper; however, Borax Lake Pattern sites have been documented in the perimeter foothills of Butte, Colusa, Glenn, and Tehama counties.

Middle Archaic Period Cultures

The Middle Archaic corresponds to the Middle Holocene climatic period. Mid-Holocene instability is widely documented in North America and clearly established for Northern California (Adam and West 1983; Benson et al. 2002). Two consequences have been recognized in the regional archaeological record. First, climatic instability adversely affected the development of upland and lowland soils, diminishing the capacity of the landscape to store archaeological deposits. Consequently, Middle Archaic archaeology is uncommon and the available record problematic (Meyer 2002 in White 2002). Second, the density and distribution of economically significant resources also appears to have been impacted by climatic and landscape instability, leading to cultural responses such as local depopulation, interregional population movements, and dietary change (Rosenthal et al. 2007).

Concurrent with these ecological responses and related to them, there were a number of trends in prehistoric culture change that first emerged during the Middle Holocene, including the development of centralized settlement associated with ridgetops (Hildebrandt and Hayes 1993), river/marshes (Heizer 1949), and lake sides (Sampson 1985; White 2002), and dietary specializations on acorns, deer, and freshwater and anadromous fisheries. The Mesilla Complex, Mendocino Pattern, and Berkeley Pattern were also distinct regional cultural traditions that first emerged in Northern California during the Middle Archaic, and the archetypal Middle Archaic culture was the Windmiller Pattern, which appears to have been confined primarily to the Sacramento-San Joaquin Delta and Mt. Diablo regions. Windmiller material culture (Figure 4) featured artifacts made of varied stone materials such as quartz crystals, red ochre, chert, slate, obsidian, asbestos, biotite, and worked clay. Worked shell included ornaments and square beads or applique of red and black abalone and small Olivella beads. Twined basketry is known from impressions left in baked clay. Other baked clay objects include cooking balls, perforated disks, and grooved net sinkers (Heizer 1949, 25; Beardsley 1954, 69; Moratto 1984, 201). Based on the rarity of ground stone tools, abundant projectile points, and dietary bones from elk, pronghorn, deer, rabbit, coyote, beaver, lynx, bear, and waterfowl, it is assumed that hunting was the focus of Windmiller Pattern subsistence (Heizer 1949, 20, 27; Moratto 1984, 201).

Upper Archaic Period Cultures

Regional climates stabilized at around 2,800 BP, and by 2,500 BP the widespread, generalized technological traditions of the Middle Archaic were replaced by distinct regional specializations. Archaeologists have also found evidence of an increase over time in the scope and distance of intergroup trade patterns, a widespread change from less to more complex social forms, and from low to high population density (Rosenthal et al. 2007). The archetypal Upper Archaic culture is the Berkeley Pattern (Figure 5), constituting the basic Archaic adaptation of the rich alluvial basins of Central California. There was also considerable cultural diversity within the Berkeley Pattern, and distinct variants have been identified in the central Sacramento Valley, central North Coast Ranges, Napa Valley, Solano County, and Sacramento Delta regions (Bennyhoff 1994; Rosenthal 1996; White 2002). Certain traits are common to all Berkeley Pattern variants, including a highly developed bone tool industry, atlatl engaging hooks and dart-sized, non-stemmed points (Fredrickson 1974, 125a, 126; Lillard et al. 1939, 77; Beardsley 1954, 74). Inter-regional interaction intensified as evidenced by widespread shared stylistic traits and ceremonial practices, along with extensive trade from a few obsidian sources and common shell bead currency. Berkeley Pattern sites contain many features, especially fire-cracked rock heaps, shallow hearths, rock-lined ovens, house floors, cairns, and graves. Complete house floors

suggest that large, pole framed houses between 4-6 m in diameter were built, and clay daub with tule or bulrush impressions indicates that the houses were thatched and sod-packed. Berkeley Pattern economy varied regionally, generally focused on seasonally structured resources that could be harvested and processed in bulk, such as acorns, salmon, shellfish, and deer. The high frequency of mortars and pestles relative to chipped stone implies a heavy reliance on acorn processing (Fredrickson 1974, 125a; Moratto 1984, 209).

Continuing a pattern of increasing cultural diversity, in Central California Berkeley Pattern sites occur contemporaneous with Windmiller Pattern sites (Fredrickson 1974), and in the Sacramento Valley region, riverine Berkeley Pattern sites also occur contemporaneous with Mendocino Pattern and Martis Complex sites (White 2002). The Berkeley Pattern was endemic to alluvial basins while the Martis Complex and Mendocino Pattern were common to foothill and mountainous terrain, suggesting different ecological niches. The Martis Complex and Mendocino Pattern artifacts were also very different, including notched, concave-based, and thick leaf-shaped projectile points, shaped and cobble handstones and millingstones, cobble pestles and mortars, and basalt core tools. Trade goods were uncommon, and no formal domiciles have been identified. The Martis Complex and Mendocino Pattern components are generally non-midden deposits, ranging from attenuated materials typical of a brief stay to more substantial and diverse assemblages indicating seasonal base camps. Studies of plant and animal remains indicate a focus on small seeds and a mix of small and large game (Kowta 1988; White 2002).

Emergent Period Cultures

The relatively stable climatic regimes established at the outset of the Late Holocene continued through the modern period, although a "climatic anomaly" dating around 900 BP may have caused widespread disruption (comparable to the Mid-Holocene) (Jones et al. 1999). In Northern California, after 1,100 BP many Archaic technologies and cultural traditions disappeared, in each region replaced by the onset of cultural patterns and behaviors similar to those existing locally at the time of culture contact. The archetypal Emergent Period culture is the Augustine Pattern, a widespread tradition marked by the coalescence of long-distance, integrative trade

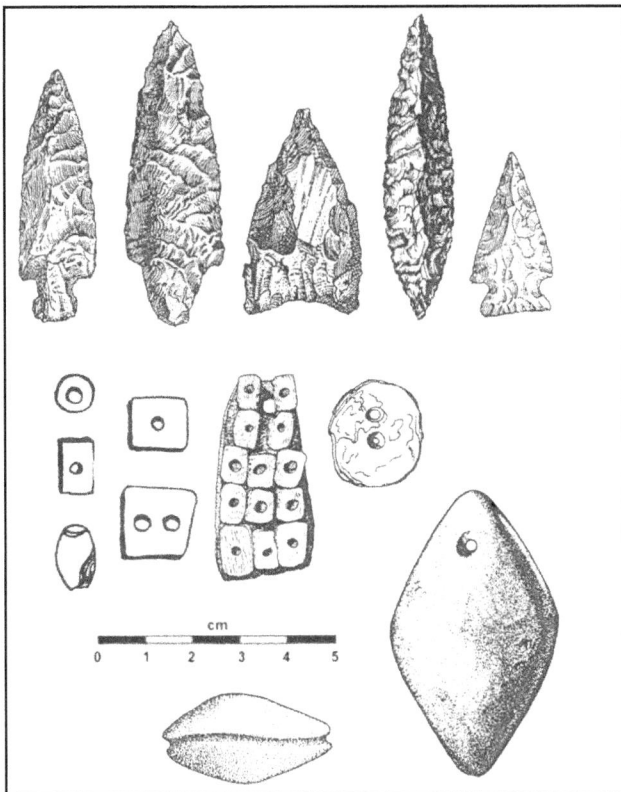

Figure 4. Artifacts typical of the Mid-Holocene Windmiller Pattern.

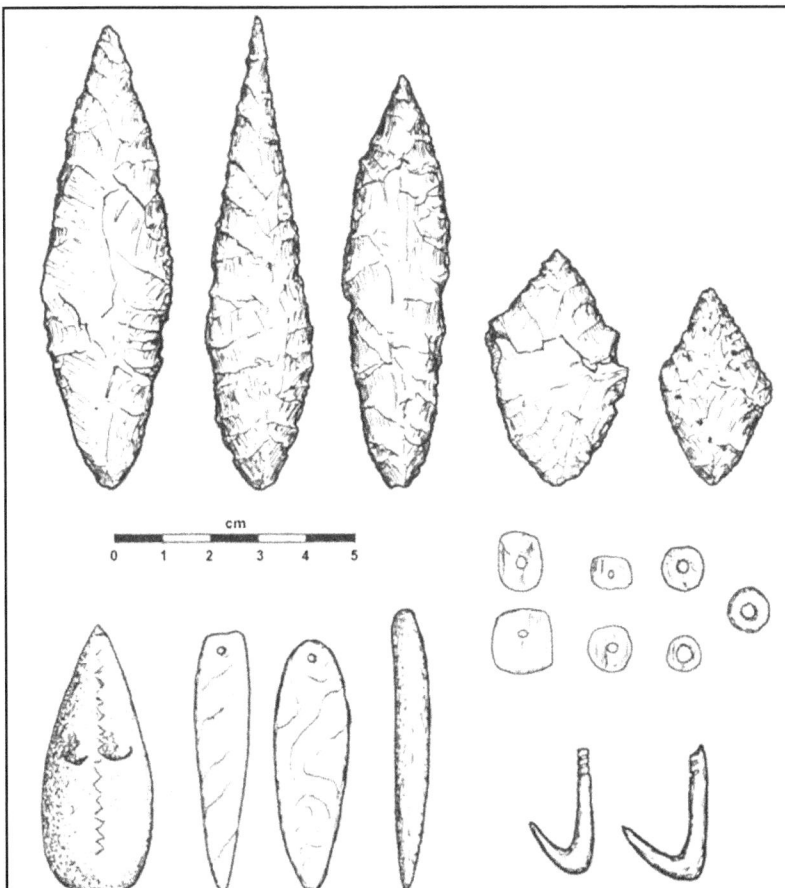

Figure 5. Artifacts typical of the Upper Archaic Berkeley Pattern.

spheres and the introduction of the bow and arrow, which replaced the atlatl as the favored hunting implement. The Augustine Pattern has been divided into two phases common to most or all localities. Phase 1 markers include Olivella whole and lipped beads. "Banjo" type Haliotis ornaments first appear with Phase 1 of the Augustine Pattern, as well as elaborately incised bird bone whistles and tubes, and "flanged" soapstone pipes. Phase 2 artifacts include small corner-notched and triangular points, clam disc beads (Figure 6) and bead drills, magnesite cylinders, bedrock mortars, and house pit sites often attributable to known ethnographic villages (Beardsley 1954, 77-79; Bennyhoff 1978, 44; Fredrickson 1984; Moratto 1984, 213). Other new traits which distinguished the Augustine Pattern include pre-interment grave pit burning with tightly flexed burials, and cremation, a form of burial apparently reserved for high status individuals during Phase 1 but widespread during Phase 2 (Fredrickson 1974, 127; Moratto 1984, 211). Grave offerings such as shell beads and ornaments regularly occurred with utilitarian items including mortars and pestles often "killed" before burial. In the Sacramento Valley area, fishing equipment is more common, elaborate, and diverse than in earlier phases and includes several types of harpoons, bone fish hooks, and gorge hooks (Beardsley 1954, 78, Moratto 1984, 211, Bennyhoff 1978, 44).

Basketry has been identified from charred remains found in graves, and a form of pottery is also known from sites in the Central Valley (Moratto 1984, 213; Beardsley 1954, 77). Baked clay balls, probably used for cooking, are a common constituent in Central Valley sites where stone is absent (Moratto 1984, 213; Beardsley 1954, 77). The Augustine Pattern economy was regionally variable, although fishing and acorn gathering appear to have increased in importance over time. Shaped mortars and pestles predominate, with charred acorns frequently found in middens. Culture contact between Native Californians and immigrant populations from throughout the world occurred at various times in Northern California, generally between 1750 to 1820 in the Central Valley to as late as 1850 in the gold-poor North Coast.

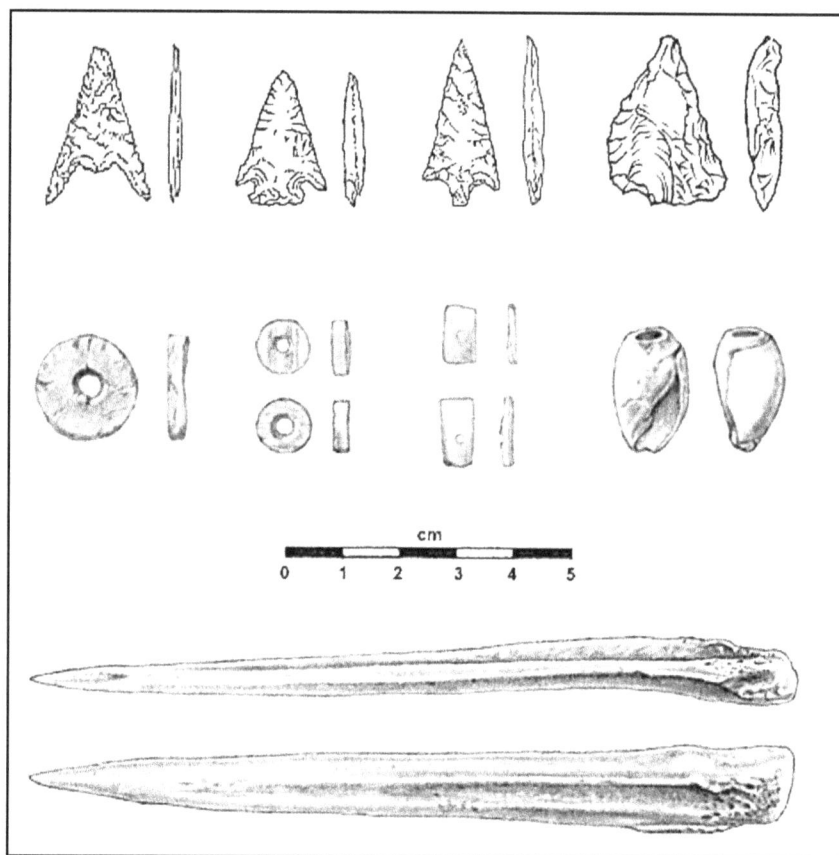

Figure 6. Artifacts typical of the late prehistoric Augustine Pattern.

CHAPTER 4

First Peoples: The Konkow

Geography & Population

Territory

Rancho Llano Seco is situated in the southwestern territories of the Konkow, also known as the Valley Maidu or Northern Maidu. The Konkow occupied a territory stretching from the foot slopes of the Southern Cascades to the west side of the Sacramento River. Along the Sacramento River, the Konkow shared their southern border with the River Patwin, their close economic, political, and social allies. The Konkow and River Patwin were so closely allied along the river that some inconsistencies appear in the ethnographic record regarding the exact boundary between the Konkow and Patwin in the Rancho Llano Seco area. For example, Kroeber (1925, Plate 34) placed a hard boundary at Princeton, while Dixon (1905, Plate XXXVIII) assigned the entire west bank of the Sacramento River to the Konkow from the mouth of Rock Creek on the north to the Butte sink on the south.

The most interesting and compelling evidence for the cultural composition of this portion of the Sacramento River comes from the journals of the region's earliest non-Indian explorers, Captain Luis Antonio Arguello, Commandant of the *Presidio de San Francisco*, and his chaplain, the Reverend Father Blas de Ordaz. Between October 17 and November 17, 1821, Arguello led an exploratory military expedition into northern California, pursuing rumors of white settlement in the valley. The expedition visited Konkow and Patwin settlements along the west side of the Sacramento River adjacent to the area which would become Rancho Llano Seco just 30 years later. Aguello's and Ordaz's expedition diaries (Fischer 1992; Heizer and Hester 1970) contain important details on native settlement names and population estimates, especially significant because they predate pandemics which decimated the tribes in the 1830s (Cook 1955).

Based on a translation of settlement names recorded by Arguello and Ordaz, Heizer and Hester ruled out Nomlaki occupation and list 17 Patwin settlements north of the town of Coru (now the City of Colusa, California, Colusa County), extending Patwin occupation just north of Ord Bend, California (Glenn County) approximately 18 miles (28.9 km) farther north than Kroeber's boundary (Heizer and Hester 1970, 81-85). This disagreement between investigators runs through much of the local ethnographic record. For example, according to the Heizer and Hester list, *Chan-no* was the northernmost River Patwin town, but the site was also identified by Kroeber as the Konkow settlement of *Ts'e'no* (Kroeber 1932, 266), visited by Arguello and Ordaz on October 30, 1821 and immortalized in the drawings of Henry B. Brown in 1851-1852 (Blackburn 2006) (see Figure 7). Another settlement in the area is identified by Heizer and Hester (1970) as the Konkow town of *Baht-che*, but is also identified by Kroeber as the Patwin *Batsi'* (Kroeber 1932, 267). Notably, Merriam, who conducted his field work in the area in 1902-1906, identified both *Chan-no* and *Baht-che* as "Wintoon Noemuk [Nomlaki] but shared with the Mitchopdo" (Merriam 1977, 316). White (2003, 56–61) re-examined the primary record and concluded that this difference may have been less a disagreement between sources and more a signal of a cosmopolitan area where settlements had a combination of Konkow, Patwin, and Wintun occupants and were known by similar names in the different languages.

Population

At the time of initial contact with non-Indian explorers, the Konkow primarily lived in large-scale settlements— essentially, small cities. In fact, in their survey of the pre-contact populations of North America, Driver and Massey (1957, 184-185) ranked the central Sacramento Valley along the Sacramento River among the highest population densities found in native North America,

Figure 7. The Konkow settlement of *Chan-no* illustrated by H.B. Brown, 1851-1852 (after Blackburn 2006).

Top – Dome-shaped, earth-covered pit houses spread along bank of the Sacramento River.

Bottom – Interior of a pit house showing central hearth and bunk beds with stored gear beneath. Note seated man in foreground with otter skin quiver and sinew-backed bow on the ground and flanked by a rack of duck decoys.

second only to agricultural societies of the Southwest and Mesoamerica. For example, the Arguello-Ordaz diaries recorded eight large River Patwin and Konkow settlements lying between Ord Bend and Knights Landing, with occupants numbering between 500 and 1,600 persons each (Fischer 1992; Heizer and Hester 1970). Cook (1964) estimates the pre-contact Konkow population at 12,000 persons. Notably, the person in the best position to produce an accurate estimate of pre-Gold Rush populations, John Bidwell, in a letter to John Sutter dated December 1847 included a census that placed the Indian population of the Sacramento Valley north of the Sutter Buttes at 19,000 persons, consistent with Cook's estimate (McKinstry 1872).

Structures & Facilities

Domiciles

The Konkow selected elevated river banks and rises for settlement locations. According to Kroeber (1925, 831), each settlement consisted of several extended family groups—often occupying house clusters—and a single settlement might have had between 15 and 50 houses or more. The houses were dome-shaped, covered with thatching, tule mats, and earth, and reached 10-15 feet across. Dixon recorded this description of Konkow houses:

> An excavation was made to a depth of not over one meter and over a circular area from six to twelve meters in diameter. The ground was loosened by the aid of digging-sticks, and then gathered into baskets, in which it was carried off and dumped to be used later in making the earth covering. Spring was the season usually selected for building a house, as at that time the earth was soft whereas later in the summer the ground becomes hard and baked. (Dixon 1905, 168-169)

According to Dixon, the interior post pattern and construction were similar to the larger dancehouse, with two main posts placed near the center fire and a circle of eight shorter posts of oak placed between the main posts and the walls (Dixon 1905, 168).

> The sides of the excavation were left vertical and lined or walled with logs either whole or split, set on end, or with large slabs of bark, forming

thus a solid wooden wall around the interior of the house. From the edge of the excavation, then, the long beams to support the roof were leaned toward the center, resting on the post already set, and tied to them securely with grapevines or osiers [willow rods]. . .. On these beams as a basis, cross-poles were laid; and on these, again, large pieces of bark, branches, leaves, and pine-needles; and lastly, a heavy covering of earth, generally from twenty to fifty centimeters [approximately eight to twenty inches] thick. In the center of the roof, at the top, an opening was left for a smoke-hole. This was covered, when necessary, by a skin, a basket, or a slab of bark. Directly in line with the two main posts, a door was made, less than a meter wide and from one meter to a meter and a half high; and a passage was built out about two meters in length, slanting up from the floor of the house to the level of the ground outside. In the Sacramento Valley area it would seem that these doors opened, as a rule, to the south or southwest. It also appears probable that originally in this region the doors were much smaller, having to be entered on hands and knees, and being really little more than draught-holes, and the real entrance and exit being by way of the smoke-hole. Since the coming of Europeans, however, the door has been enlarged, and the old entrance by the smoke-hole given up. When the latter was in use, however, a ladder composed of two poles, with cross-pieces tied with grapevine, afforded the means of ascent and descent, and ran almost vertically from the base of the main post to the smoke-hole. In some cases, it is said, a notched log was used instead of a ladder. It was through the draught-hole, however, that wood was generally carried into the house. (Dixon 1905, 170-171)

Dixon states that several families might occupy the larger earth lodges, and that each family had their own space within the structure. Every nook and cranny in the house contained stored food and gear (Figure 7, bottom; Figure 8). Food and property of various sorts were stored in baskets near the walls or under platforms. The earth lodge was tough and watertight:

> The roofs of their houses are strong enough to bear the weight of several persons, and the

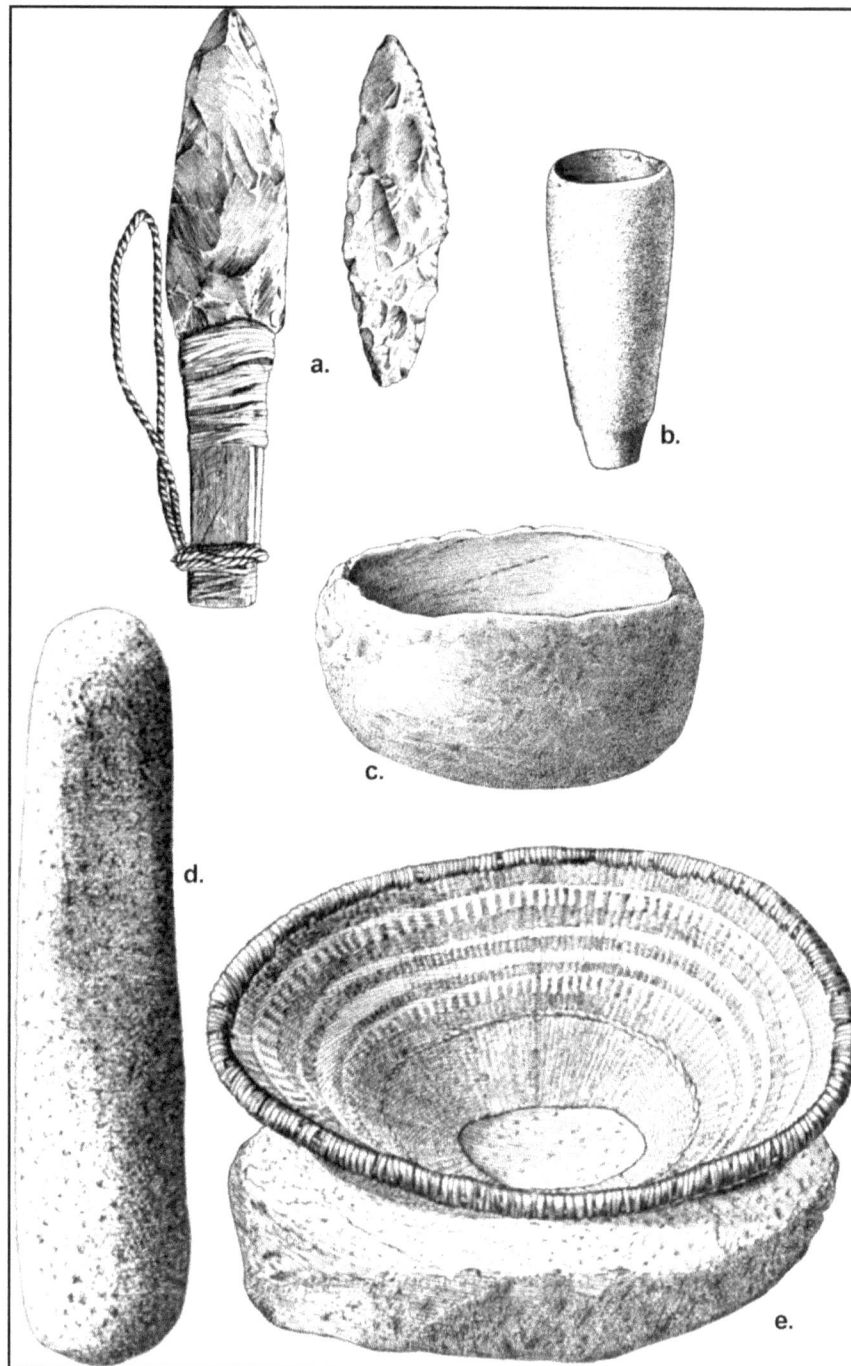

Figure 8. Konkow gear.

a. stone knives (Dixon 1905, Figures 1 a-b)
b. soapstone pipe (Dixon 1905, Figure 9a)
c. soapstone vessel (Dixon 1905, Figure 10)
d. pestle (Dixon 1905, Figure 8)
e. mortar and hopper basket (Dixon 1905, Figure 44)

Indians are usually seen sitting on the top of them. . . . Near the huts, large branches of trees had been stuck up for shade. (Wilkes [1845] 1958, 76)

Wilkes's description of rooftop congress is depicted in one of Brown's illustrations of Chan-no (Figure 7, top), which also shows a ramada like those described by Wilkes.

According to Dixon (1905, 169), the Konkow dancehouse was similar in construction to the earth lodge, although double in size. Located in the nuclear settlement, the dancehouse was a subterranean structure 3 to 4 feet in depth, constructed with large beams and two or four main posts then covered with brush, earth, or tule mats. The door faced east with a plank drum opposite and a smokehole at the top (Beals 1933). The two center posts of the dancehouse were set during a ceremony with the largest post or "spirit post" behind the fire pit. Only the dancers were allowed to walk near the spirit post.

Like the Patwin, the Konkow built acorn granaries used to store unprocessed acorns throughout the winter and early spring:

> one or more acorn-granaries of wicker-work stand around each lodge, much like hogsheads in shape and size, either on the ground or mounted on posts as high as one's head, full of acorns, and capped with thatch. (Powers [1874] 1975, 284)

Constructed using a pole and thatch design similar to the retaining walls described above, examples appearing in historical illustrations stand more than 6 feet high and 5 feet in diameter, built as a tall cylinder with an external frame of vertical and horizontal retaining rods and a barrel formed by woven thatch. These large storage structures were constructed to cache a large supply of unhulled acorns through the winter. Brown's illustration of Chan-no shows several granaries dispersed between houses (Figure 7, top).

Subsistence

The River Konkow, like their downstream River Patwin neighbors, relied heavily on salmon and acorns, intensively harvesting and processing both in the fall season for winter staples. William B. Ide's 1847 map of the Hyacinth Ranch depicts two fish dams spanning the river adjacent to the Project Area in the Llano Seco Riparian

Sanctuary unit. Commander Charles Wilkes of the U. S. Navy, who led an exploring and mapping expedition up the Sacramento River in 1841, encountered a similar structure blocking the river north of the current site of the City of Colusa (Figure 9):

> On the 31st, they again proceeded, and passed several Indian villages. Before noon, they arrived at a substantially-built fish-weir, of which the Indians began to take a part down, but Lieutenant-Commandant Ringgold deeming that this was the termination of his exploration, motioned to them to desist. This fish-weir was constructed with a great deal of art: stakes, pointing down the stream had been driven into its bed, having three openings, which led into square pens above; over each of the entrances into the pens was a platform, on which the natives stand to take the fish; on these also there were heaps of ashes, indicating that the natives make use of fire to attract the fish. (Wilkes [1845] 1958, 77-78)

John Bidwell also describes a fish weir he encountered in 1845, large enough for a mounted party to cross like a bridge:

> For the purpose of fishing they formed a fish-weir at a point some miles above Colusa, by using willow poles, the ends of which were rounded and sharpened, and then in some manner made to penetrate the sandy bottom to a depth sufficient to resist the force of the current. By the use of cross-sticks lashed with grape vine, the structure formed a bridge not less than eight or ten feet wide, for men to pass and repass upon. At this point the river was very wide and the bottom very sandy, and the water perhaps not more than four or five feet deep (J. Bidwell 1904, 286).

Later, passing downriver, the Wilkes party observed smaller features built much like the weir but representing individual fishing platforms (Wilkes 1845, reprinted 1958, 80). Wilkes ([1845] 1958, 76) also noted that "[a]round the huts were scattered vast quantities of the mussels' shells and acorns, which would therefore seem to be the principal articles of food. Annie Bidwell observed traditional acorn preparation still practiced by the Konkow well into the late nineteenth century:

31

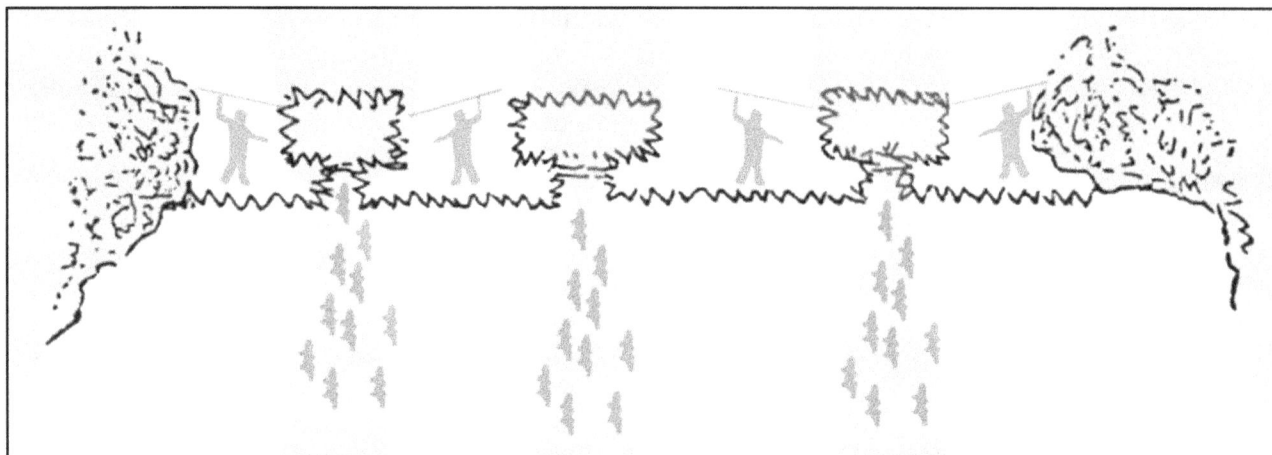

Figure 9. Adapted from Wilkes's salmon weir illustration (Wilkes [1845] 1958, 78).

Here and there lazily curled the smoke from fagot fires on which smooth stones were heating wherewith to cook acorn soup and bread, and other luxuries. Shallow circular depressions, some two feet in diameter, were made in the sand for washing the acorn meal, to remove the bitter, astringent properties. The acorns after being dried were pulverized in stone mortars of rude construction with stone pestles, and put into these shallow cavities. Water was then repeatedly poured on till the bitterness was gone. Then with the finger the dough was marked into squares, lifted by one hand, and the adhering sand removed by a dexterous application of water with the other. It was then transferred to the heated stones on which fresh grass or leaves were hastily laid to receive it. Then another handful of grass on top of the dough, and hot stones upon that, until it was baked. My husband says they also made the dough into balls and put it into holes in the ground, previously heated, and added stones on top. The meal not made into bread was diluted with water and boiled into soup in large water-proof baskets of beautiful shape and ornamentation, made of grass roots, wild similax, and certain shrubs. The stones were lifted from the fire with two long pointed sticks, dipped into a basket of water to remove the ashes, then dropped into the soup and on cooling returned to the fire. This was repeated until the soup was thoroughly boiled, bubbling like a mud geyser. The very aged still adhere to some of the old customs. (A. Bidwell [1896] 2002, 205–206)

Powers also noted two interesting snares used by the Konkow, which he claimed he had not seen in use elsewhere. Both snares were made of nets and rods and used for the capture of ducks (Powers [1874] 1975, 285).

Social Structure

The Konkow practiced a "tribelet" form of political organization—identified by Kroeber (1954) as the basic political and proprietary unit of the region—composed of a large nuclear village and surrounding camps and activity areas. Each tribelet community was considered autonomous (Riddell 1978, 373), and each controlled a local territory recognized by adjoining communities. Tribelet territories were generally "well-defined, comprising in most cases a natural drainage area" (Kroeber 1925, 831). The main village was the nucleus of this system. It was the population center, the site of the largest assembly lodge, men's sweat lodges, the residences of leaders and specialists, and held caches of ceremonial regalia, food, and trade goods. The central settlement was the chief's home. Chiefs generally inherited the position, but a chief could be chosen by acclamation, the current chief could name his successor, or a shaman might use his powers to aid the selection. Each extended family also had its own leader who would assist the chief. The Konkow chief's primary task was that of advisor, but leaders were expected to be wealthy and generous (Riddell 1978, 379). The chief's duties included leading his tribe into battle, keeping his people from trespassing, directing special festivals, arbitrating disputes, and acting as official host at ceremonial gatherings. He would also redistribute food when required (Dixon 1905). The chief could declare war or negotiate peace. Other than this right, he received no other privileges from the community (Riddell 1978, 379). If the chief had the support of the villages and the shamans his word was enforced. The chief lived in the men's lodge, which was burned on his death.

Ceremony

The Konkow followed a *Kuksu* ceremonial pattern closely similar to their River Patwin neighbors. In the Kuksu ritual cycle, detailed in A.L. Kroeber's *Handbook of the Indians of California* (1925, 364-390; see also Kroeber 1932, 312-329), young male initiates engaged in steps of passage by impersonating spirits, *Moki* being the highest level of achievement. The society functioned as a system for economic and social gain. In return for payment (usually in shell beads) to a director or older member, initiates received training in medicine, dance, and ritual. Membership resulted in higher social status. Rituals centered on the (symbolic) raising of the dead (new initiates), and the celebration of a good harvest or bountiful fish catch. Dancers wore masks, headdresses made of magpie feathers, and feather capes, their dancing accompanied by singers and a foot drum (Kroeber 1925, 384-388). The chief answered to a council of elder members of the Kuksu society, and it was generally understood that Kuksu members and not the chief held the real political power, controlling trade, craft groups, and resources.

The Konkow and Patwin also practiced the *Hesi* cult, which focused on elaborate ceremonial dancing (Kroeber 1925, 388-390; 1932, 329-340), and the Ghost Dance, or *Wai-Saltu* initiation, which focused on symbolic death and resurrection ritual (Bean and Vane 1978; Kroeber 1932, 308-311). A large dancehouse at the central settlement hosted all of the ceremonies, which were often scheduled during the winter season. According to Kroeber,

> Much of the systemization of Kuksu dances and their bewildering ramifications so unique in California and so reminiscent of Hopi and Kwakiutl . . . may be attributed to the fact that the Patwin [and Konkow] lived in good sized, permanent, water proof houses. Much of their religious activities were indoors. (1922, 366)

During Kuksu ceremonies, both dancehouse doorways came into use. The main or public doorway (opening

to the east) was used by the audience as well as some performers making entrances and exits. The doorway to the west, placed directly opposite, functioned like a back door to a stage. The performers, when not in costume, used this doorway to join the audience or to exit for the next performance (McKern 1923). The ceremonial foot drum was located adjacent this doorway. The audience was seated by family association along the northern half of the dancehouse, while the chief and his associates sat opposite along the southern wall. To the left of the chief sat dancers, drummers, ceremonial directors, guests, and initiates. New members were on the left near the foot drum. To the right sat singers, or the clown speaker, whose purpose was to entertain the audience (McKern 1923).

The *Wai-Saltu* was considered the most powerful and dangerous ceremony, though Patwin and Konkow may have viewed the performers as only impersonators of ghosts or devils, while to the Pomo and Yuki the performers were considered actual ghosts. The performers sought an altered state that resulted in the performer leaving the dancehouse to jump into the river or a marsh, a dangerous feat in this state of mind. Families then rescued performers and brought them back to sanity (resurrection).

The Konkow also practiced several additional ceremonial dances: a mourning ceremony in the fall, a *Kamin* Dance to initiate the spring, the *Weda* or flower dance in late April, and the *Lole* Dance for first fruits, the *Dape* or Coyote Dance, the *Omwulu* or Rabbit Dance, the Shaman's Dance, the *Nemusla* or Big Time Dance, and the *Husla* (Gifford 1927, 233-238).

Conflict

Feuds were common between communities, but it was uncommon for Konkow towns to unite for battle and this kept most conflicts localized. Warfare consisted of raiding and ambushing. Warnings of the coming attacks were common and given by smoke signal, with the attacks usually occurring at dawn. Prisoners, if taken, were tortured then killed (Dixon 1905).

SECTION 3

Rancho del Llano Seco

CHAPTER 5

Contact Era

Luis Antonio Arguello, 1821

ORDERED NORTH BY THE SPANISH Governor to pursue rumors of white settlement in the valley, Arguello and Ordaz led a troop of 70 men, their mounts, pack horses, and a horse-drawn cannon. The expedition was transported by launch to the Suisun area and from there followed a course up the valley, visiting Native American settlements along the west side of the Sacramento River and tracking the rumors north. In late October, 1821, Arguello's troop encountered Native American settlements in the vicinity of the Project Area.

Arguello was a military man under orders to secure territory and he approached each village with this intent, firing the cannon and engaging in skirmishes with settlements near present-day Grimes and Princeton. Nevertheless, many of the leaders he encountered sought peace, and this was often achieved with gifts of food and goods. Arguello wrote in 1821 that just south of present-day Glenn, CA (Glenn County) they approached a settlement where the inhabitants "showed themselves of sufficient peace and quiet and received the troops with much pleasure and celebration" (Fischer 1992, 27). Added Ordaz,

> We were received with great contentment by the inhabitants, who set out with several banners to meet us. All of the children up to the age of 14 years were arranged in the vicinity of the houses, forming an oval in each one of them. (Heizer and Hester 1970, 101)

By October 28, Arguello's party passed out of the vicinity of the Project Area, ultimately reaching a point four to seven miles north of Hamilton City where his interpreter could no longer communicate with villagers. Satisfied that the reports of white settlement actually referred to Indian stories about visits to known Russian settlements on the Pacific coast, Arguello's troop struck out to the west and probably followed Stony Creek to the foothills and then south through the eastern coast range on their return trip to the Presidio.

British Trappers

The Fur Brigades, 1827–1845

Final settlement of the Mexican War of Independence in 1821 and subsequent secularization of the Mission system eliminated the expansionist imperative that had driven the Mexican exploration of Alta California. Inroads by British and American-backed fur trappers quickly filled the void.

Beginning in the late 1820s a number of overland fur trapping and trading expeditions visited the Central Valley. In 1827, trapper Jedediah Smith of the Rocky Mountain Fur Company twice led parties of trappers through California, on both occasions being detained by Mexican authorities. On the second trip, following his detention at Mission San Jose, Smith's party was compelled to leave and ordered (by then-Governor Arguello) to follow a route northward through the Sacramento Valley. In early 1828, the party traveled along the Sacramento River to the Feather and then up the Feather to the forks and back overland to the Sacramento, apparently working their way through the Project Area and back again (Sullivan 1934; Weber 1990). In summer 1828, an American trapping party led by Ewing Young conducted a poorly recorded covert expedition into the Sacramento Valley, probably trapping in the Project Area. Acting on Smith's and Young's glowing reports of Sacramento Valley trapping prospects, beginning in 1829, the Hudson's Bay Company sent a number of trapping expeditions south from its headquarters at Fort Vancouver into the Sacramento Valley. In 1829, Alexander McLeod trapped the rivers south to Stockton, returning north in 1830 (Nunis 1968). In 1830, Peter Skene Ogden trapped down the north coast to San Francisco Bay, then moved inland and trapped the Sacramento Valley north to the Pit River.

The presence of the trapping parties had significant impacts on the region's Native American populations. The trappers' journals describe armed conflict and acts of murder and retribution similar to those described at a smaller scale by the Arguello expedition. The trappers also sought and relied on local Native American women to perform camp chores and to process hides. The trapping parties significantly depleted local game stocks, especially near their winter camps (Maloney 1945, ii-vi). The most destructive impact, however, came in the form of introduced disease.

In 1832 through 1833, John Work led an expedition that trapped along the Sacramento and Feather rivers in and around the Project Area (Maloney 1945). For a time, Work's party trapped alongside parties led by Ewing Young, who was again in California, and Michel Laframboise, who had come down from Oregon, a three-party nexus with disastrous consequences. In his fascinating *The Epidemic of 1830-1833 in California and Oregon*, S.F. Cook tracks the spread of malaria from the trapping centers of central California by the Hudson's Bay Company, resulting in the death in one year of at least 20,000 Indians in the Central Valley (Cook 1955).

In the Project Area, the results of the epidemic were especially stark and significant, and the onset and consequences were recorded in Work's 1832-1833 expedition log. During his initial trip down the valley, on December 2, 1832, Work observed the first signs of an illness, which he correctly identifies as malaria, emerging among the Valley Maidu he encountered near Chico, noting "[t]here appears to be some sickness resembling an ague prevailing among them (Maloney 1945, 19). Leaving the Chico area, in a day's march down the west bank of the Feather River Work's party encountered a remarkably high density of Native American settlements:

> The Indians are exceedingly numerous along the river. Our days journey was but short yet we passed 6 villages & are encamped near another, the inhabitants of each must amount to some hundreds. The country must be rich in resources when such numbers of people find subsistence. (Maloney 1945, 24)

After spending spring and summer on the western slope of the Central Sierra Nevada, on their return trip north Work first noted illness among his own group: "[S]everal of our people have been for some days unwell and some symptoms of the fever breaking out among them" (Maloney 1945, 69). On August 1, 1833, the party reached the southern edge of present-day Butte County where Work observed "[A] great many of the Indians are sick some of them with the fever" (Maloney 1945, 69). On August 6, Work's party first encountered a grim tableau:

> The villages which were so populous and swarming with inhabitants when we passed that way in Jnay or Febry last seem now almost deserted & have a desolate appearance. The few wretched Indians who remain seem wretched they are lying apparently scarcely able to move. It is not starvation as they have considerable quantities of their winter stock of acorns still remaining. We are unable to learn the malady or its cause. I have given the people orders to avoid approaching their villages lest it be infectious. (Maloney 1945, 70)

Work's progress up the valley was marked by increasing illness among members of his brigade. The brigade once again visited Valley Maidu settlements near the Project Area on Chico and Deer creeks that, in winter 1832, were raucous and thriving and now, in fall, 1833 were silenced and strewn with the dead and dying:

> Proceeded on our journey & made another very long days [*sic*] march, indeed we could not find water to make it shorter except along side of an Indian village & the villages we by all means avoid on account of the sickness prevailing among them. The natives here seem even more wretched than those on the feather river, the villages seen almost wholly depopulated.—The unhappy wretches are found in ones or twos in little thickets of bushes, and the men found two one of whom was dead & the other nearly so. The bodies of others were found partly devoured by the wolves . . . Here there is the materials for a fishing wear [weir] collected & prepared but probably the poor wretches were unable to construct it. (Maloney 1945, 71)

Cook considered the demographic implications of Work's observations and the consequences of the sweeping pandemic on the Konkow of Butte County:

> These Indians were very badly hit by the epidemic, which very possibly first began to be felt in 1832 and which reached its full intensity in the summer of 1833. Village life was utterly disrupted and the mortality was very great. (1955, 316-320)

Already frustrated with low take resulting from years of overharvest, the fur trapping parties also suffered heavily from the epidemic; Work reported that as many as 72 of his 100-member brigade contracted the fever (Work 1832-1833 in Maloney 1945). As noted by Haines (1971, xxiii), "[o]n one occasion Work reported that there was not a single person in the camp able to get to his feet," and Work himself spent the winter of 1833-1834 as an invalid at Fort Vancouver. According to Maloney (1945, foreword), the Hudson Bay and American fur brigades immediately curtailed, and by 1845, abandoned their valley expeditions, giving way in the Project Area to a slow trickle of American military expeditions, explorers, and settlers with the perfunctory Mexican citizenship required to seek and hold land grants. They found a land still reeling from the devastating epidemics of the 1830s.

One of the best journals of exploration dating to this decade was written by Commander Charles Wilkes, U.S. Navy, who was dispatched to reconnoiter the northwest frontier from 1839 to 1842. Wilkes visited central California in 1841, generating descriptions, maps, and coordinates for natural features, transportation routes, and population centers. Wilkes's party navigated up the Sacramento River to Sutter's New Helvetia settlement on August 20, and from there proceeded to the Sacramento River immediately south of the Project Area. In 1845, Wilkes commented on the area's depleted game:

> Game is represented to have decreased in this vicinity, from the numbers destroyed by the parties of the Hudson Bay Company, who annually frequent these grounds. (Sullivan 1934, 73)

Visiting a location at or near the former village site of Yo'doi near the confluence of the Feather and Sacramento rivers, on August 25, 1841, Wilkes's party encountered a disturbing scene:

> [T]he ground was strewed with the skulls and bones of an Indian tribe, all of whom are said to have died, within a few years, of the tertian fever, and to have nearly become extinct in consequence. (Sullivan 1934, 73)

Many similar accounts dating to the early 1840s cite abandoned former settlements along the Sacramento and Feather rivers. Based on comparison to these and similar midcentury census figures, Cook concluded that the Butte County Konkow population must have been reduced by 75 percent between 1833 and 1846, or a loss of more than 2,500 individuals (Cook 1955, 320).

Ranchos and Patronage, 1839-1850

Throughout the 1840s, the surviving river tribes were increasingly hemmed in by and dependent upon encroaching non-Indian colonizers. Living in reduced circumstances, with depleted game and restricted access to traditional lands and resources, and on the fringes of an unfamiliar economy, many Konkow survivors were physically compelled or forced by circumstances to work on ranchos newly established on the Mexican frontier, often living in traditional settlements (*rancherias*) now contained in rancho grounds.

This development was double-edged. Some economic gains must have been possible, based on journals and other accounts dating to the 1840s which demonstrate a partial demographic rebound in the Project Area, with locations dead or abandoned a decade prior now repopulated by Native American rancho workers and their families. On the other hand, these gains came at a high cost because typically the rancho bosses were autocrats accustomed to making extreme labor demands and requiring daily efforts and specific yields in return for meager goods or sustenance alone.

Many observers in this period cited peonage or slavery, and it is clear that issues of racial injustice and emancipation, soon to dominate the American political scene, were already much on the minds of many. In 1846, Clyman stated that:

> Capt. [Sutter] keeps 600 or 800 Indians in a complete state of Slavery and I had the mortification of seeing them dine I may give a short description of 10 or 15 Troughs 3 or 4 feet long ware brought out of the cook room and

seated in the Broiling sun all the labourers grate and small ran to the troughs like so many pigs and feed themselves with their hands as long as the troughs contain even a moisture. (Heizer and Almquist 1971, 19)

The frontier rancho owner's treatment of the Konkow Indians in this period is best understood in the context of their tutelage under traditional *Californios* rancho bosses (Gillis and Magliari 2003; Smith 2013). In fact, John Bidwell, owner of a massive rancho just north of the Rancho Llano Seco Project Area, sought to curb the worst abuses while at the same time frame statewide legislation around the basic injustices of the peonage system. In March, 1850, as a member of the newly formed California legislature, he introduced Senate Bill No. 54, "An Act Relative to the Protection, Punishment and Government of Indians" which proposed a parallel judicial system to hear and decide suits "wherein an Indian is a party," and provide for continuity of the rancho patronage system under U.S. rule. The bill proposed a statewide system of Justices of the Peace to be elected by the male Indians of that district, providing for Indian carriers to notify affected tribes of upcoming elections, and interpreters to be present at the polling place. The bill also contained provisions to ensure that proprietors of lands where Indians reside would continue to permit Indians and their descendants to reside on these traditional lands peaceably and to pursue traditional means of subsistence. The bill made it illegal to provide Indians liquor, set punishments for Indians convicted of stealing livestock, horses or dogs, and made it unlawful for any Indian to set fire to the woods or prairie, or for any Indian to not "exert full force of effort to extinguish said fires at pain of $50.00 fine or corporal punishment not to exceed 100 lashes."

Sections 7-12 of the Act defined the conditions of servitude on rancho lands. The bill stipulated that Indians residing and working on lands held by an individual by virtue of a Spanish or Mexican land grant, if they so desired, should remain in the employment of that rancho and "not be molested by any other person," thus ensuring continuity of the existing rancho patronage system. The Act determined that any rancho proprietor who treated his wards cruelly or inhumanely may be fined or lose rights of indenture to another to be determined by the justices. The bill made it unlawful to take minor Indians by force and also set fines of $50.00 to $500.00 for any

person convicted of forcibly compelling Indians to work in the mines. Section 38 provided that

> [w]hen minor Indians attain their majority, and desire to leave the persons who have had the care of them, such persons shall pay to such Indians in useful property the value of fifty dollars if female and one hundred dollars if a male, and two good suits of clothes.

Senate Bill No. 54 never reached the floor, but a replacement bill, Senate Bill No. 129, which was quickly passed and signed into law on April 22, retained many of its provisions. "An Act for the Government and Protection of Indians" prevented any person from forcibly compelling an Indian to work against his will, yet made it lawful to "apprentice" any number of Indians while providing food, clothing, and humane treatment. The bill also provided for the arrest and detention of "loitering, profligate, and vagrant Indians" who could then be hired out as apprentices for a term not exceeding four months. Bidwell coauthored the final draft of the bill with General Mariano G. Vallejo and David F. Douglas, the former, like Bidwell, a rancho master whose operations depended on low-wage labor and the latter an expatriate antebellum southerner clearly at home with these stipulations (Rawls 1984, 87-90). In some parts of California, the Act was interpreted to enable pernicious acts of slavery, including the kidnapping of children, both on- and off-reservation, by white slave dealers who provided "apprentice" labor to ranchers and miners under the color of law. The Act was repealed in 1863 (Heizer and Almquist 1971, 39-58).

American Settlement

The Mexican ranchos were frequently broken up and sold off to pay debts, in some cases almost as soon as they were acquired by absentee owners. Land speculation increased with the end of Mexican rule and California statehood in 1850, with landholders seeking to cash in on the influx of new American settlers. It is clear from the many contemporary reports published by Heizer (1979), Heizer and Almquist (1971), Rawls (1984), Trafzer and Hyer (1999) and others, that the new settlers were frequently responsible for new deprivations of the increasingly harried Konkow survivors. Some Konkow rebelled. In a letter penned on July 23, 1851, at his Sacramento River Rancho near present-day Jacinto, William B. Ide described the tensions and conflicts prevailing in the vicinity of Rancho Llano Seco:

At my nearest neighbor's at the east, across the Sacramento, about one mile distant, a man named James McKenney was shot while lying asleep in his bed, on the 17th inst., at 10 o'clock at night, and died on the 19th. The arrow entered the lower part of the abdomen, a little forward of the left hip joint, and ranged so as to lodge the point of the arrow against the inside of the pelvis. The only remedy decided upon by the attending physician, was to cut open the body, take out the entrails, wash them, sew them up and put them back, after having removed every foreign substance; —then sew up the body, and cover the wounded part with some light, adhesive plaster to exclude the air and water—then battle constantly with cold water, and apply glysters, as they did for two days; and if these operations could not save the man, there was no remedy. A surgeon was also called, who said it "was too nice a job for him": but I was in hopes he would recover, as he was free from pain. This is the fifth man who has fallen by the Indian's arrow, this summer, within a short distance of my house— four of them died and one recovered. Three Indian thieves have been shot by white men, within the same distance and time. (Ide 1880, 226-227)

Ide went on to describe a large gathering of Native Americans on the east side of the Sacramento River north of Rancho Llano Seco, which he took to indicate an imminent threat of open war:

The Indians are gathering together from all quarters at a place east of the River, about six miles north of my house, as we are told by a man who came down last evening—in numbers aggregating some 7 to 10 hundred men, women and children. Another man reports having seen 150 or 200, on their way thither from the south of this. All these are understood to be valley Indians, who have for three or four years been friendly to the settlers; but the conduct of the foreign miners has been such toward them, in common with that of the Mountain Indians (their enemies), that little or no dependence can be placed on their friendship. If they become enemies, they will be far more dangerous than the Mountain Indians, as they know all about our

business, occupation, &c., and where they can most successfully lie in wait for us. (Simeon Ide 1880, 227-228)

Wozencraft Rancho Chico Treaty of 1851

In 1847, the military governor of the newly secured territory of California identified regional Indian agents to conduct surveys and identify measures to maintain peace. In Northern California these agents were the same rancho bosses who controlled the labor of thousands of Indians in the last decades of Mexican rule, initially including John Sutter, subagent for the lower Sacramento/upper San Joaquin area, and Mariano G. Vallejo, subagent for the region north of San Francisco Bay (Ellison 1922, 41–42). In 1847, *Rancho del Arroyo Chico* owner John Bidwell was commissioned to survey the population, geography, and condition of Northern California Indians. These new commissioners defended the rancho system of forced labor and recommended legal measures to institutionalize and adapt it to the American form of governance. Many of these measures were enacted after statehood. In 1848–1852, a relentless and destructive wave of Gold Rush-era depredations of Butte County Konkow individuals and communities occurred. I will not enumerate events here but cite the sobering volumes that detail the institutional and pervasive discrimination which resulted in genocide, murder, rape, slavery, and starvation of Northern California Indians during this era (Cook 1955, 1976; Heizer 1979, 1993; Heizer and Almquist 1971; Hill 1978; Magliari 2012; Phillips 1981; Rawls 1984; Smith 2013; Trafzer and Hyer 1999). Gillis and Magliari (2003) and Shover (1998, 1999, 2000) provide detailed accounts of Butte County events.

Aware of these depredations statewide, in 1850, the U.S. Congress made appropriations and the President directed the Secretary of War to identify special agents and commissioners to undertake on-the-ground investigations in the Far West, resulting in reports that at once identified the harsh realities of the treatment of Indians on the California frontier yet also spoke to the issue from a deeply bigoted and martial perspective. The U.S. government enacted laws denying suffrage and rights of ownership of land to the Indians and at the same time approved Acts to appoint new agents to secure treaties for reservation lands and identify depots for the distribution of assistance to Indians on the California frontier (Ellison 1922, 47–49).

The three commissioners arrived in California and began work in mid-January, 1851. They found the newly minted state's legislature and governor busy authorizing funds for troops to defend the frontier against Indian uprisings, lending urgency to their mission (Ellison 1922). The commissioners' first efforts were jointly focused on the San Joaquin Valley, and then in May they separated. Commissioner O. M. Wozencraft reached Rancho Chico on or about July 30, 1851, with wagons and a mounted 53-man military escort including a major, two lieutenants, and 50 infantry. Wozencraft was in communication with Bidwell in the months before this visit, and Bidwell responded by directing his superintendent, Alex Barber, to map out a planned reservation area in the foothills to the east, and to visit Indian settlements in the valley and mountain districts around Chico and invite community leaders to attend the treaty summit and feast (Shover 2000). In response to Barber's invitation, some groups arrived at Rancho Chico three weeks early. On the day Wozencraft arrived, 300 or more Indians, including a mix of Konkow from rancherias located on major ranchos in the valley and Indians living in independent settlements in the mountains were waiting for him at Rancho Chico (Shover 2000; U.S. Court of Claims 1861, John Bidwell Deposition). Notably, among the recorded participants and treaty signatories were the leaders of three tribelets situated on or near the Rancho Llano Seco Project Area, including *Baht-che*, *Chan-no*, and *Soo'-noos*.

Before Wozencraft's arrival, Bidwell directed his workers to build a podium to draw attention to the speaker, and Bidwell supplied two interpreters, one his longtime houseboy and interpreter and the other the daughter of the Mechoopda headman. Wozencraft offered the assembled Indians a reservation spanning approximately 227 square miles immediately east and south of Rancho Chico. Big Chico Creek and Upper Butte Creek at Nimshew formed the north boundary and the Feather River from Thermalito to Concow formed the south boundary. Wozencraft promised that the tribes, if they signed, would reap a bounty of individual and community goods and benefits, and in accepting these terms, the signatories would provide the U.S. government right-of-way

> over any portion of said territory, and the right to establish and maintain any military post or posts, public buildings schoolhouses, houses for agents, teachers, and such others as they may

deem necessary for their use or the protection of the Indians.

The treaty also stipulated that

> [t]he said tribes or bands, and each of them, hereby engage that they will never claim any other lands within the boundaries of the United States, nor ever disturb the people of the United States in the free use and enjoyment thereof. (U.S. Court of Claims 1861; Exhibit C)

In 1858, Bidwell was deposed in a federal claim dispute concerning cattle supplied to this and other Wozencraft treaty meetings around the state (U.S. Court of Claims 1861, John Bidwell Deposition). Bidwell's testimony sheds light on his misgivings about Wozencraft's conduct and expressed his lack of confidence in the value of the effort itself:

> The Indians asked him when they were going to get all these things, and my impression was that they understood these things to be present in the baggage wagons which belonged to the escort … from what occurred immediately after I was convinced the Indians did not understand, for they commenced a great clamor for the blanket, shirts, pantaloons, &tc, which he had promised them; when they found that they were not there they left the ground without much ceremony and started off. (U.S. Court of Claims 1861, John Bidwell Deposition)

Bidwell's concerns were echoed by Heizer (1972), who argued that Wozencraft and his fellow commissioners lacked practical knowledge of California Indians and did not comprehend the nature of their small-scale social and political organization:

> [M]ost of the so-called tribes were nothing more than villages. We can also assume that men listed as "chiefs" were just as likely not to be chiefs, or at least tribelet heads who are called chiefs by anthropologists. Further, since land was owned in common, even chiefs had no authority to cede tribelet or village lands. (Heizer 1972, 4)

The presence of American claims and interests, objections about the dedication of too much land to tribes, and concerns about the peace and stability of nearby Anglo American communities led to strong opposition to the

California Treaties. The treaties reached Washington in February, 1852, and the California congressional delegation strongly opposed ratification. The California Treaties were rejected in committee, June 1852 (Heizer and Almquist 1971, 65–79).

Indian Removals

First Removal

After 1852, on the heels of the failed Wozencraft treaty conflicts between Anglo Americans and Native Americans escalated and intensified in Butte County. U.S. Government measures failed to produce a solution. In 1853, the U.S. Congress authorized funds to form the Nome Lackee Reservation, located across the valley in the coast range foothills 20 miles west of Corning. In 1854, a military post was established at the location. By August, 1855, in a series of military actions known as the "First Indian Removal," Konkow from rancherias located along the Feather and Sacramento Rivers were forcibly moved to the Reservation, and their rancheria homes burned to the ground. By 1857, the Reservation housed 2,500 individuals including many members of mountain tribes in constant conflict with Anglo American settlers. The reservation was temporarily successful but foundered on the U.S. government's failure to meet commitments resulting in increasing ill health and starvation experienced by reservation residents. By 1860, groups began to drift off. By 1863, few were left in the confines of the reservation. The government ultimately put the land up for auction. Many of the Native Americans displaced by the failure of Nome Lackee returned to Butte County where few found homes or work, and all found a growing Anglo American population increasingly hostile to their presence.

Second Removal

In the 1860s a number of factors conspired to physically marginalize local Maidu. Epidemics of cholera, typhoid, malaria, smallpox, pneumonia, influenza, and diphtheria swept through Maidu populations, leading to 3,500 deaths from disease by 1865. Most at this time also found themselves homeless and landless, a product of empty treaties, failed reservations, and the breakup of the old rancho system as owners of the large estates sold off lands and new owners drove out the Maidu from longtime settlements, some located on traditional village grounds occupied for hundreds if not thousands of years.

The displaced people faced constant, deep, and abiding racism. During this same period, Anglo American-on-Native American homicide accounted for another 500 deaths (Cook 1976, 255–277). Rare instances of Native American retribution were met with overwhelming, brutal, and indiscriminate Anglo American reprisals. Anti-Indian sentiment in Butte County ran rampant. Editorials in Chico, Red Bluff, and Marysville newspapers called for all-out war and scalp bounties. For example, one local newspaper ran an editorial demanding extermination:

> The man who takes a prisoner should himself be shot. It is a mercy to the red devils to exterminate them, and a saving of many white lives. Treaties are played out—there is only one kind of treaty that is effective—cold lead. (*Chico Weekly Courant* July 28 1866)

A series of conflicts in 1863 culminated on July 5th in the murder of two Anglo American children by Native American perpetrators in the mountains 12 miles east of Chico. This precipitated a watershed confrontation carried out by a local militia with Secessionist sentiments, which commenced to scour the region seeking to round up or murder every Native American in Butte County. On July 26th, Bidwell, in communication with Indian agents, agreed to harbor more than 100 Native Americans from Feather River Rancherias at his Bidwell Landing on the Sacramento River six miles west of Rancho Chico headquarters. As the militia's sweep continued, Bidwell was fearful for the fate of the Rancho Chico Native American families. Militia leaders then threatened to attack Rancho Chico and destroy his operations, forcing Bidwell to attend a meeting on July 27th where he promoted a distinction between the Rancho Chico Native Americans and all others, promising Rancho Chico people would stay productively engaged on his ranch. On July 31st Bidwell telegraphed the commander of the U.S. Army Department of the Pacific, who dispatched a captain and 40 mounted troops to Rancho Chico. This troop established what would be called "Camp Bidwell" at the Rancho Chico headquarters, eventually augmented to include 100 men. The Rancho Chico Indians remained under military protection while the militia's war of extermination raged all around. On August 28th the California Superintendent of Indian Affairs attended another militia meeting and agreed to a forced removal of Native Americans to Round Valley Reservation in the North Coast Ranges 74 miles west

43

of Chico. In this "Second Indian Removal," a U.S. Army force of 150 began to assemble Native Americans from the foothills and mountains, collecting them together with the group already established at Bidwell Landing, all with the express consent of Indian Affairs and the U.S. Army to leave the Rancho Chico Mechoopda community in place and under Bidwell's care. On September 4, 1863, the troops and 435 Native Americans began the long march to Round Valley.

Rancho Llano Seco and the *Soo-noos*

It is clear from William B. Ide's writings of July 23, 1851 that at least 700 Konkow Maidu lived on the east side of the Sacramento River in the vicinity of Rancho Llano Seco six years after Sebastian Keyser acquired the original grant. No documentation was found to confirm their places of residence, but it is likely that some if not many of these individuals resided on the vacant Rancho lands, in the territory identified as the tribelet of *Soo-noos* located "on the east side of the Sacramento River south of Parrott Landing and on Parrott Ranch," and identified by C. Hart Merriam who conducted his field work in the area in 1902-1906 (Merriam 1977, 116). John Bidwell, who attempted to negotiate representation by all major Butte County tribes for the July 30, 1851 Wozencraft treaty negotiations at Rancho del Arroyo Chico, successfully sought participation by tribal leader *Wa-Tel-Li* of the *Soo Noos*. *Wa-Tel-Li* endorsed the treaty (Heizer 1972, 48-49) but like the other signatories, saw no good come of the event.

The 1874 John Parrott Map is based on the original July 1859 traverse by A. W. Von Schmidt, Deputy U.S. Surveyor, done in conjunction with the State Land Commission's adjudication of the Rancho Llano Seco Land Grant. The 1874 print plots the locations of five separate Native American settlements within the boundaries of the Rancho, including three located in the current Llano Seco Project Area in Hale Field and one located in the nearby USFWS Llano Seco Riparian Sanctuary Unit. Because the traditional Spanish term *rancheria* (little rancho") was used it is likely that these settlements were plotted by or reported in relation to the land grant by Von Schmidt. The timing here makes it likely that the five Rancherias were composed of the tribelet center of *Soo-noos* and its satellite hamlets, probably occupied by refugee Konkow and others who escaped the 1853 First Removal in addition to those who fled the confines of the Nome Lackee

Reservation in 1858-1859. These individuals probably found refuge on Rancho Llano Seco due to its absentee owners and the prevailing legal limbo which prevented owner-occupation. The occupants of these Rancheria communities may have worked on squatter farms on the Rancho, but no records were found to indicate this was the case. Within four years, the new conflicts carried along by Civil War-related insurrectionist militancy resulted in the Second Removal of 1863, corresponding roughly to the timing of John Parrott's acquisition and initial development of the Rancho. It is likely that the Rancheria occupants were caught up in the second removal, and there is no clear evidence that Native Americans occupied the Rancho when John Parrott's full acquisition and tenure began.

Native American Labor on the Rancho

In order to address the mystery surrounding the fate of the *Soo-noos* and to assess the possibility that the Rancho served the same refugium role for the *Soo-noos* that the Mechoopda found on Bidwell's Rancho Chico, Ms. B. Arlene Ward, former Tribal Council Member and tribal historian for the Mechoopda Tribe of Chico Rancheria joined our research team in the month of September, 2018. Ms. Ward brought unique and invaluable experience to the study because she was able to use her command of tribal ancestry to search the Rancho archives for records of Native American laborers. The Rancho's extensive archives provided detailed payroll ledgers beginning in 1874. We established a study area in the attic loft of the historic Rancho office building and, joined by Project Historian Ms. Josie Reifschneider-Smith, Ms. Ward combed through tons of documentation seeking and flagging entries related to Native Americans, successfully identifying dozens of entries reflecting the participation of important Mechoopda Tribe ancestors, including grandfathers, great-grandfathers, and great-great-grandfathers of current tribal members. Other ledger entries were not specific enough to determine relationships to known ancestors of the Mechoopda Tribe, for example, "Johny Indian" listed in several 1877 entries in relation to sheep operations (Figure 10). Table 2 lists key ledger entries relating to verified Mechoopda Tribe Native American labor on the Rancho. The following provides biographies prepared by Ms. Ward for each of the Mechoopda Tribe Rancho laborers identified in the entries.

Table 2. Mechoopda labor on Ranch Llano Seco, 1874–1928.

* Caido Sparks and Pamaho compensation listed with expenses related to sheep, orchards, general labor.
** May be Edward Wilson, son of Santa Wilson
*** Santa Wilson charged $2.65 for "sundries," September 1920.

Year	Month	Name	Type	# Days	Wages	Amt	Amt Pd	Check
1876	July	Caddo (Caido Sparks)	Labor*	21 1/4	$ 2.00	$ 42.50	$ 42.50	
			(expenses)			$ 5.00	$ 5.00	
1876	July	Caddo (Caido Sparks)	Labor*	30 3/8	$ 2.00	$ 60.75	$ 60.75	
1876	July		(expenses)			$ 10.00	$ 10.00	
1876	July	Parmeho (Pamaho)	Labor*	18	$ 2.00	$ 36.00	$ 36.00	
1876	July	Parmeho (Pamaho)	Labor*	22	$ 2.00	$ 44.00	$ 44.00	
1876	July	Parmeho (Pamaho)	Labor*	10	$ 2.00	$ 10.00	$ 10.00	
1876	August	Caddo (Caido Sparks)	Labor*	19	$ 2.00	$ 38.00	$ 38.00	
1876	August	Caddo (Caido Sparks)	Labor*	16 1/2	$ 2.00	$ 33.00	$ 33.00	
			(expenses)			$ 10.00	$ 10.00	
1916	September	D. Conway	Orchard	4.5	$ 1.50	$ 6.75	$ 6.73	
1916	September	W. J. Conway	Orchard	5	$ 5.00	$ 10.00	$ 10.00	
1916	September	I. Conway	Orchard	5	$ 2.00	$ 10.00	$ 10.00	
1916	September	J. Conway	Orchard	5	$ 1.50	$ 7.50	$ 7.50	
1917	September	Roy Nuckolls	Orchard	4.5	$ 2.25	$ 10.15	$ 10.15	
1917	September	D. Conway	Orchard	1/2	$ 3.00	$ 1.50	$ 1.50	
1917	September	Earl Nuckolls	Orchard	1/2	$ 3.00	$ 1.50	$ 1.50	
1918	September	Mike Jefferson	Orchard	4	$ 0.40	$ 1.60	$ 1.60	
1918	September	E. Wilson**	Orchard	4	$ 0.40	$ 1.60	$ 1.60	
1918	September	S. Wilson	Orchard	3/4	$ 4.00	$ 3.00	$ 3.00	
1918	September	E. Nuckolls	Orchard	3/4	$ 4.00	$ 3.00	$ 3.00	
1918	September	J. Azbill	Sheep Dipper	4	$ 4.00	$ 16.00	$ 16.00	#6296
1918	September	J. Azbill	Sheep Shearer	796	$ 0.13	$ 99.50	$ 99.50	
1920	September	Santa Wilson	Prunes	450 boxes	$ 0.25	$ 112.50	$ 109.85	*** #6252
1920	September	J. Azbill	Sheep Shearer	908	$ 0.15	$ 136.20	$ 136.20	
1920	September	J. Azbill	Sheep Bucks	3	$ 0.40	$ 1.60	$ 137.15	#2483
1920	September	Santa Wilson	Sheep Shearer	770	$ 0.15	$ 115.50	$ 115.50	
1920	September	Santa Wilson	Sheep Bucks	3	$ 0.40	$ 1.20	$ 116.70	
1922	November	Joseph Mitchell	Sheep Herder	20 (11/12-31)	$ 2.00	$ 40.00	$ 40.00	
1922	December	Joseph Mitchell	Sheep Herder	3 (12/1-3)	$ 2.00	$ 6.00	$ 6.00	
1923	May	Joseph Mitchell	Herder	6 (5/26-31)	$ 2.00	$ 12.00	$ 12.00	
1924	January	John Azbill	Herder	15 (1/6-20)	$ 2.00	$ 30.00	$ 30.00	
1924	February	John Azbill	Herder	3 (2/2-4)	$ 2.00	$ 6.00	$ 6.00	
1925	October	Carl Cook (Delgado)	Labor	1/2	$1.50	$ 1.50	$ 1.50	
1925	October	Carl Cook (Delgado)	Labor	2 1/4	$2.50	$ 2.45	$ 2.45	
1925	November	John Azbill	Sheep Herder	5 1/2	$ 2.00	$ 11.92	$ 11.92	
1925	December	John Azbill	Sheep Herder	21	$ 2.00	$ 65.00	$ 65.00	
1926	January	John Azbill	Sheep Herder	31	$ 2.00	$ 65.00	$ 65.00	
1926	February	John Azbill	Sheep Herder	25 1/2	$ 2.00	$ 53.25	$ 53.25	
1926	March	John Azbill	Sheep Herder	1	$ 2.00	$ 2.00	$ 2.00	
1926	October	John Azbill	Sheep Herder	2 1/2	$ 2.00	$ 5.42	$ 5.42	
1926	October	John Azbill	Sheep Herder	4 1/2	$ 2.00	$ 9.75	$ 9.75	
1926	November	John Azbill	Sheep Herder	26 1/2	$ 2.00	$ 57.42	$ 57.42	
1926	December	John Azbill	Sheep Herder	21	$ 2.00	$ 65.00	$ 65.00	
1927	January	John Azbill	Sheep Herder	31	$ 2.00	$ 65.00	$ 65.00	
1927	February	John Azbill	Sheep Herder	28	$ 2.00	$ 65.00	$ 65.00	
1927	March	John Azbill	Sheep Herder	4 1/2	$ 2.00	$ 9.75	$ 9.75	
1927	May	John Azbill	Sheep Herder	7	$ 2.00	$ 52.00	$ 52.00	
1927	November	John Azbill	Sheep Herder	6	$ 2.00	$ 13.00	$ 13.00	
1927	December	John Azbill	Sheep Herder	31	$ 2.00	$ 65.00	$ 65.00	
1928	January	John Azbill	Sheep Herder	21	$ 2.00	$ 65.00	$ 65.00	
1928	February	John Azbill	Sheep Herder	29	$ 2.00	$ 65.00	$ 65.00	
1928	March	John Azbill	Sheep Herder	13	$ 2.00	$ 28.17	$ 28.17	

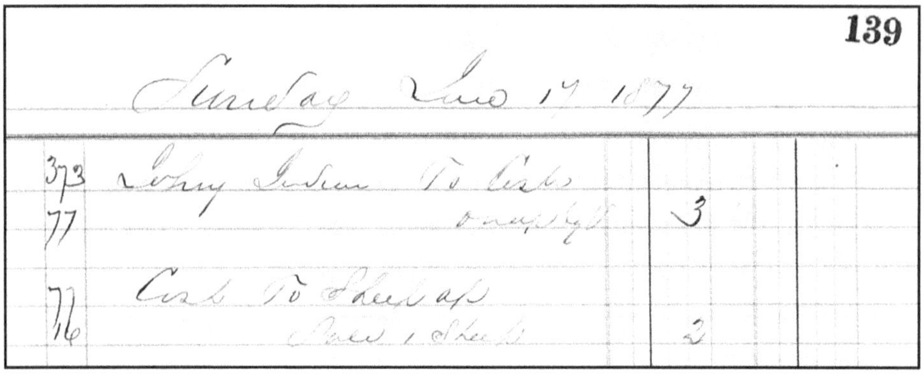

Figure 10. Rancho cash ledger entry for Sunday, July 17, 1877 listing "Johny Indian."

Parmeho (*Pamaho*) of Chico Rancheria, 1876

The 1874-1877 Rancho Ledger lists several entries for wages and expenses paid to *Parmeho*, who worked in sheep operations, orchards, and general labor in 1876 (Figure 11). This is likely to be Mechoopda Tribe ancestor *Parmeho*, who was truly a transitional figure who survived the 1851 Treaty, both removals, and lived on to enter the economic life of Butte County. *Parmeho*, who may have been between 50 and 60 years old when he worked on the Rancho, is listed as signatory of the 1851 Wozencraft Treaty, where he was identified as headperson of the *Sim-sa-wa* tribelet (Heizer 1972, 49). He is also mentioned in several places in Annie Bidwell's diaries archived at Bidwell Mansion State Historic Park, and in John Bidwell's Diary for February 22, 1876, in which he stated, "Pamaho and Hookmis (2 old Indians) called on me" (J. Bidwell [1876] 2002). *Parmeho* went on to reside at the Mechoopda Tribe settlement on Sacramento Avenue.

Some disagreement appears between sources regarding the identity of *Parmeho*'s family, wife, or wives. Bibby (2002) indicates that Mechoopda Tribe ancestor Ann (*Kayyopehne*) was first married to *Parmeho* and later married George Barber. McDonald (2004) claims that Mechoopda ancestor George Clements's mother was *Parmeho*'s wife. Ms. Ward is skeptical of the latter claim because George Clements's mother fell very ill and died June 8, 1875, while Mrs. George Barber is mentioned in Annie Bidwell's diaries after that date. On this basis Ms. Ward concludes that there were two different women. Ms. Ward continues to research this question, of special interest to her because George Clements was Ms. Ward's great-grandfather and therefore, his mother was her great-great grandmother.

Ms. Ward also calls attention to a Bureau of Indian Affairs family tree prepared for the Mechoopda Tribe which lists Mechoopda tribe ancestor Amanda Lafonso Wilson's parent as "*Parmeho*," based on documentation compiled by the late Donna Mae Rickert (Elmer LaFonso's daughter) who passed a couple of years ago at age 94. Ms. Ward will also continue to pursue this lead.

Caddo (*Caido* Sparks) of Chico Rancheria, 1876

The 1874-1877 Rancho Ledger lists several entries for wages and expenses paid to *Caddo*, who worked concurrently with *Parmeho* in sheep operations, orchards, and general labor (Figure 11). *Caido* is likely to be Mechoopda Tribe ancestor *Caido* Sparks. A tribal census letter dated September 13, 1914 from the U.S. Department of the Interior, Indian Services, in Redding, California, to H. G. Wilson, Supervisor, stated *Caido* Sparks was full blood, age 80, living with a band of Indians at Chico. This would make *Caido* 42 years of age when he worked on the Rancho in 1876. The census letter also listed Delbert (or Dalbert) Sparks, full blood, age 26, living in Chico, who had attended District School. An 1888 letter from George Clements to Annie Bidwell, who was at the time in Auburn, Placer County, reported that *Caido*'s wife was very sick. "She has fever every day. Dr. Oliver is waiting on her now but she don't seem to get any better" (California State Library, Box 62). Annie Bidwell's diary of December 27, 1905 contains an entry indicating she had visited *Caido*, arranged for new bed and bedding for him, delivered a sweater to Delbert, and got groceries and beef for *Caido*. In a January 1906 diary entry, Annie Bidwell noted a visit she made to *Caido*, who was suffering from a broken hip. By March, *Caido* was still confined to bed but his hip was better and he was able to sit up in bed. Annie Bidwell mentioned his son, Dalbert in

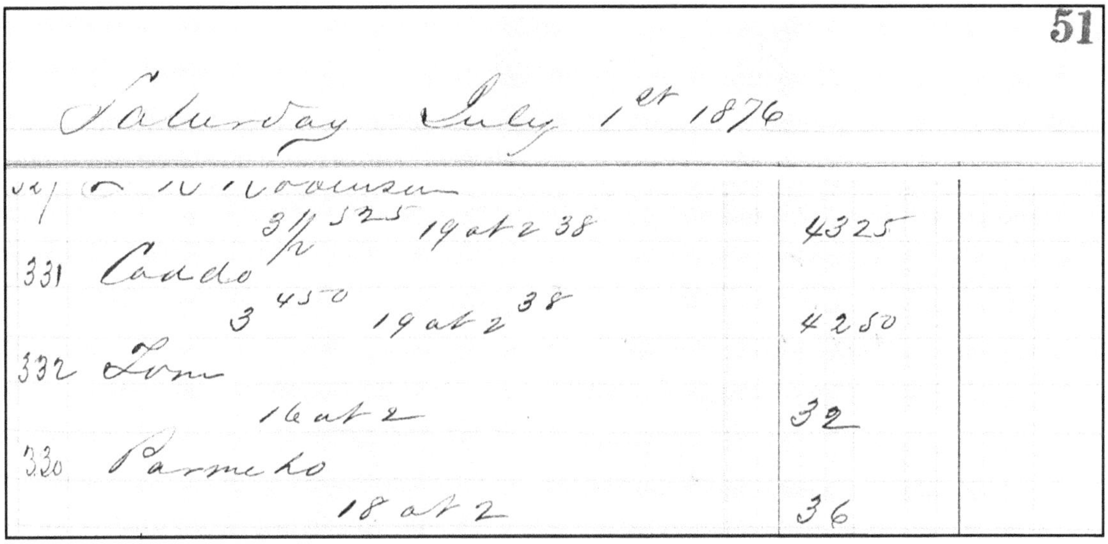

Figure 11. Rancho cash ledger entry for Saturday, July 1, 1876 listing Mechoopda ancestors Caido Sparks (Caddo) and Pamaho (Parmeho), the latter being the former headperson of the Sim-sa-wa Konkow.

her diaries between 1906 and 1908, when Dalbert played in the Indian Brass Band.

Santa Wilson

The 1918-1920 Rancho Ledgers list entries for wages and expenses paid to Santa Wilson, who worked in the orchards concurrently with John Azbill, who worked in the sheep operation. According to documentary and oral history evidence, Santa Wilson would have been about age 60 when he worked on the Rancho. Santa Wilson is a very important Mechoopda Tribe ancestor, a survivor of the forced march from Chico to the Round Valley Indian Reservation in Covelo, Mendocino County, California, in 1863.

The Azbill family's oral history reveals that Santa's mother was ill and near death, and with concern for her child, laid him under a bush for protection in hopes that someone would pick the child up and care for him (as told by Thelma Wilson, in a presentation to the Rotary organization in 1973 and reported in the *Chico Enterprise Record*, December 12, 1913). Thelma recalled hearing that Santa was taken on to Round Valley, eventually adopted by a white family, and later became a bookkeeper. Confirmation of Santa Wilson's role on the Reservation appears in Bauer (2009, 77) which notes that a Concow man, Santa Wilson, was employed as clerk in Round Valley by the Office of Indian Affairs around 1880.

Another family story is revealed by Craig Bates's personal research notes on file in the Mechoopda Tribe (Chico, CA) offices, which contain a transcript from an interview with a tribal elder who stated "Aunt Sally" was on the Round Valley trek and said that her sister was killed the night before as she was exhausted and a soldier had stuck her with a bayonet and killed her. The consultant claimed that the baby left on the road was Santa Wilson, and that "Old Lady Fuller Clark" saw the baby on the road and that Aunt Sally took the baby to Round Valley. The consultant reported that Aunt Sally identified the baby as Santa Wilson, father of Sherman Wilson. "Old Lady Fuller Clark" could be Sacramento Avenue Mechoopda Rancheria occupant Flora Clark, who was a very old, blind woman in the early twentieth century. Eva Pierce, daughter of Santa Wilson and Amanda Wilson, said in an interview reported by Dorothy Hill (1978) that Flora Clark, originally from Round Valley, lived with Sherman Wilson at the Sacramento Avenue Mechoopda Rancheria "toward the last" and died at Sacramento Avenue. Eva Pierce stated that Flora used to tell everyone, "I'm a Helltown Indian," and she was "known to hunt, could ride a horse and kill her deer, and I guess put deer up on the horse. Tough Indian." Eva said she called her "Aunt Flora." Grover Ramirez, great-grandson of Santa Wilson, in a conversation with Ms. Ward in early 2000s, stated that he recalled that as a very young boy he had been instructed, when in Aunt Flora's home, never to move any furniture or anything out of its location as Aunt Flora was blind, but Grover recalls he never would have known that because she moved around, swept and cleaned her place as if she could see.

The Indian Census of 1885 lists Santa Wilson as a husband, 27 years of age, with wife, Virginia, 19 years of age, and with Virginia's sister, Minnie Mackey, 12 years old. The 1887 Indian Census listed Santa with a new wife, Delia, aged 20. The 1916 Indian Census listed "Sandy" Wilson as now married to "Manda" (Amanda) Wilson, both in their 50s, and living in Butte County (associated with the Greenville Rancheria Agency). The April 13, 1914 census letter lists Santa Wilson as full blood, age 45, resident of Chico Rancheria with Mandy Wilson, half blood, age 50. In an interview with Dorothy Hill on December 12 1997, Eva Pearce reported that her father, Santa, was a minister of the Indian Church and ordained by Annie Bidwell. Mathes (1982, 159) mentions that Santa Wilson was a great asset to Annie Bidwell's Indian Church on Sacramento Avenue, verbally translating her sermons from English to Maidu. A 1914 letter report from H. G. Wilson, Supervisor, Indian Affairs to the Commissioner of Indian Affairs in Washington, D.C., stated that Annie and John Bidwell built houses occupied by the Indians, two of which cost over $3,000, and naming the house occupied by "Sandy" (Santa) Wilson, a minister, and Elmer "Lafonte" (Lafonso), a young educated Indian. By 1934 the only known surviving certificate of property titles issued by Annie Bidwell on June 4, 1901 to certain Mechoopda residents, was the one issued to Mr. and Mrs. Santa Wilson granting and conveying a tract of land described as Lot 25 of Me-choop-da Subdivision of the John Bidwell Rancho, map of April 30, 1909. This title document is still preserved by Mrs. Wilson's son, Elmer Lafonso.

Joseph Mitchell

The 1922 Rancho Ledger lists wages and expenses paid to Joseph Mitchell, who worked concurrently with John Azbill in sheep operations. Joseph Mitchell is a significant name in Mechoopda history because of his brief marriage to Maggie Lafonso in 1907 (December 21). Maggie Lafonso is the daughter of Amanda and Holi Lafonso, and the granddaughter of John Bidwell and Amanda's mother, *wi sum too* (as related by family oral history by Henry Azbill, and corroborated by Sherman Wilson, Amanda's son, and his daughters, Thelma Wilson and Harriet Ramirez). Maggie is often reported in Annie's and John's

personal diaries participating in personal family dinners. Maggie was a devout Christian and greatly influenced by Annie Bidwell, and undertook the church pastoral duties, assisted with Sunday school, and cared for the village community during Annie Bidwell's failing health.

On December 21, 1907, Annie Bidwell wrote in her diary that Maggie Lafonso married Joseph Charles Mitchell of Grand Island, Colusa County, age 27 years. They married in the Bidwell Mansion parlor with those witnesses including Santa and Amanda Wilson, Billy Preacher, Pablo, Hayce, and Martha (bridesmaid). A week later on December 29, 1907, Annie Bidwell baptized Joe Mitchell and provided him with a Bible for Christmas.

In a diary entry dated July 12, 1909, Annie wrote that Lafonso reported that Joseph Mitchell was taken to the County rest-house by Constable Barnes. Annie sent Elmer Lafonso to Oroville to learn about Mitchell's condition and sent letters for Joe and his doctor. Tragically, on November 7, 1909, Maggie died in childbirth and her baby died one day later. These deaths deeply impacted Annie Bidwell and the Sacramento Avenue Mechoopda Rancheria. Services for Maggie were held November 9, 1909, and memorial services were held on November 20 1909. In a diary entry of November 13, 1909, Annie Bidwell wrote that Elmer Lafonso reported to her that Joseph Mitchell "will remain on Rancho in response to Annie's pleading and overtures."

William Jennings Conway and Sons

The 1916-1917 Rancho Ledgers list entries for wages and expenses paid to father W. J. Conway, and sons D. Conway, I. Conway, and J. Conway, all of whom worked in orchard operations. Notably, William Jennings Conway is a direct ancestor of Project participant Tribal Elder Chester Conway. The earliest mention of William Jennings Conway found to date is John Bidwell's dairy entry for April 25, 1876, which identified William as a half-breed who had called on Bidwell to write a "letter to get things at Tehama." Later that summer, Bidwell's diary notes that Conway's mother died on July 5, 1876 and was buried the next day.

As reported in the 1880 Butte County Census, William Jennings Conway (single, laborer) age 18, was the son of Billy Walters (laborer) age 45 and Polly (keeping house) age 25. The April 13, 1914, Indian Service census letter listed William J. Conway as "age 53, educated in public schools of Butte County, claims to be an engineer and band leader." William Conway was a fluent speaker of the traditional Konkow Maidu language, and served as a consultant for anthropologists and linguists in the late nineteenth and early twentieth centuries. For example, William Conway served as a consultant to Gatschet (1877, 1879), who was in the Chico area in August of 1877, gathering linguistic material. Gatschet included in his manuscript many Indian names of his informants. Gatschet noted the orthographic spelling of Conway as *ka' nue*. Bates (n.d.) lists the Indian name of William Conway was *Saowaylexse*. Henry Azbill, born in the Mechoopda Tribe Rancheria on Sacramento Avenue, and known widely as a historian of Mechoopda culture and history, recalled that William Conway was inducted into Chico Society (traditional Kuksu dance society) when he was a young man and became a deer dancer, a very difficult dance. Henry also noted that William manufactured the Chico type headnet as "his business in American society," and made things for people on order (Hill 1978). Prior to "coming into American Society" men did not cut their hair and the traditional head nets with down feathers were tied over the top of the head, but after cutting their hair, the old style nets would not hold the down and the down began being woven into the net.

William Jennings Conway was a man of many accomplishments. He served as lay preacher in the Indian Church on Sacramento Avenue. For example, John Bidwell's diary of November 3, 1886, notes an "event," of which he writes that "Wm. Conway & wife went to church intending to unite next Sabbath" and the following Sabbath, William and his wife united with John and Annie Bidwell's church. Annie Bidwell's diary notes that in July 1891, during a missionary meeting "conducted solely by Indians," William Conway "expounded" on the Bible, reading "as well as any clergyman could have done it." There are many entries in Annie's diaries about the participation of William Conway in chapel services. Conway was an accomplished teamster for Annie Bidwell, and in 1883 and 1904 Annie noted in her diaries that William drove a four-horse team and a four-horse carryall. Conway was also a musician, and he was among the 12 who were recruited for the Mechoopda Tribe Indian Brass Band in 1904, assembled after Annie Bidwell offered to supply all the instruments if the Indian men formed a second band. William played the cornet, and his three boys, Isaiah, Dewey, and Jode were also members of the Brass Band. The Band was well known in the area and played for Annie at prohibition rallies and other local events.

William had gained a lifetime of knowledge of the healing properties of plants and herbs by direct experience and contact with the natural world, and with this intimate knowledge of medicinal uses of local trees, plants, grasses, and roots, he operated a lucrative nineteenth-century business, the Arrowhead Indian Herbs Company, "Manufacturers and Dispensors [*sic*] of Conway's Arrowhead Herbs, Remedies, Ointments and Liniments." His reputation as a healer attracted customers from all across the United States, even as far as New York City. His personal herbal recipes were known to cure and treat many ailments. However, Chico physician Dr. Newton Thomas Enloe accused William Conway of violating the State Medical Practice Act and sought a legal remedy. A hearing was held in January 1932 and William and his son, Dewey, were charged jointly and fined $200 in March of that year.

William and Nellie had five children: Eamyo, who died in 1908; Lucy, who died in 1893, and the three boys most remembered: Isaiah, Dewey, and Jode. Nellie died in May 1907 and was a great loss to William, who continued to raise his four boys. On April 4, 1932, William Conway suffered a fatal heart attack as reported in the *Chico Daily Enterprise*. His sons, Isaiah, Dewey, and Jode, and his granddaughter, Juanita, continued the business after his death. William's great grandchildren live in the Chico area and Nevada.

Carl Delgado

The 1925 Rancho Ledger lists two entries for wages paid to Carl Delgado, who worked concurrently with John Azbill. Carl Delgado was 13 years old when he worked at the Rancho. Carl's mother was Martha Silvers, his grandmother was Haycey, and his great grandmother was Lizzie Pulisse (1830-1907). Haycey was a child from a union prior to Lizzie's marriage to *Pullisse*. Lizzie (1840-1896), was the daughter of *jeponi* (yeh poh nee) or headman *Yolosa* (yo low sah) of the *ćeno* [Chan-no] people on the west bank of the Sacramento River near the northwest corner of Rancho Llano Seco. *Yolosa* was a signer of the 1852 Treaty (Beckham 2006, 20). Carl later took his adopted name of Delgado.

Lizzie married *Pullisse* (poo lees see), a leader of the kume (coo meh) men's society, of *mikćʔapdo* (meek cho'op doh). *Pullisse* was *yom nedi* (yome neh dee) (a doctor of dreams) and Lizzie was known as a woman dreamer (DuBois 1939, 75). After he came to Chico from Tehama County in his twenties, *Pullisse* worked for Rancho Chico as a laborer for many years. Lizzie and *Pullisse* had a son, *Oloso* (oh low so), also known as Rufus (1874-1950s), who had no children. As an older man, Rufus could often be heard singing the old *kume* songs in the Mechoopda Rancheria along Sacramento Avenue.

Carl Cook Delgado was raised in Chico, CA, and attended Chico State College. He was the first Mechoopda graduate of Chico State College, earning an A.B. Degree in Education in 1939. Carl was well known for his singing voice (tenor soloist with the a cappella choir) and was captain of the Chico State football team and President of Block C Athletic Club, earning All-American in two positions, center and fullback. The squad was known as the "team of the century" under Coach Art Acker. Carl Delgado was inducted posthumously into the California State University, Chico Hall of Fame in 1987. After graduation Carl entered the teaching profession, returning to Chico State College to earn five teaching credentials and spending 31 years as a teacher, principal, and coach at schools in Round Valley, Covelo, and Lower Clear Lake.

In the mid-1950s Carl was elected President of and by the Mechoopda Indians (Bidwell Indians) to represent them as they fought termination of federal supervision over their land (Currie 1957, 322). He retired in 1971 and in 1973 became an in-service specialist with Northern Indian California Education (NICE) Project, headquartered in Eureka, CA, a pilot project operating in six northwest counties, designed to help both Indians and non-Indians to understand and respect Indian culture and tradition. Carl Delgado had great pride and respect for his *mikč?apdo* heritage. He made many presentations and narrated a film, *Roots to Cherish*. He passed away as he was working on his doctoral degree at the University of California, Berkeley, in August 1974.

John Asbill/Azbill (1861-1932)

The 1918-1928 Rancho Ledger lists numerous spring, fall, and winter entries for wages paid to John Azbill, who worked as a sheep shearer and sheepherder concurrently with Santa Wilson, Joseph Mitchell, and Carl Delgado. Frank Azbill, father of John, was from Basque Country in the Pyrenees between France and Spain. He arrived in California about 1844 and settled on the Mendocino County coast. John (1861-1932) was born to Frank Azbill and a Wailiki woman, *Henockmeh Woto Kakini*. Henockmeh died when John was about 10 years old. Frank then married a white woman, Mary Frost, who wanted no part of Frank's half-Indian son. John then lived with Wailiki people and went on to graduate from Santa Clara University.

John attended the Mid-Winter Fair in San Francisco, July 1894, and met "Mary" *Mele ʻkainhua Keʻaʻaʻla*, who was an attendant for the Hawaiian booth. They were soon married and settled in as farm workers around Wheatland and Sheridan. Their oldest son, Pierce, was born in this area. John and Mary later came to live on the Chico Rancheria where in 1900 they had the first of four children, Henry. Of the four children only two boys, Henry (1900-1973) and Johnnie (1907-?), survived into adulthood. Their sister, Cora, died at a young age in 1905 (A. Bidwell [1905] 2002, entry June 10, 1905).

A USDI Indian Service, Redding, CA letter dated April 13, 1914, shows John Asbel, half blood, age 45, allotted at Covelo, was living at Chico Rancheria with Mary (40 years), Henry (15 years) and Johnie (later changed his name to John Brady). About 1906 the family name was changed from Asbel to Azbill (Bates n.d.). The 1916 Indian Census Rolls for the Greenville Agency shows John, Mary and two sons living in Greenville, perhaps while tending summer sheep range.

John Azbill's obituary, printed in the *Chico Daily Enterprise* of May 9, 1932, reported that John died in Susanville, where he had gone the month before. He was a sheep shearer for 35 years and a resident of Chico Rancheria for 40 years. Luther LaVerne Clements (1925-) recalled that John was recognized as the fastest sheep shearer around the country and "that was with hand operated shears." His wife, Mary, followed John in death in September 1932.

THE HISTORY OF THE FIRST three decades of ownership of Rancho Llano Seco is complex and confusing but illuminated by two documents found on file in the Rancho archives: a Parrott court filing associated with an 1872 lawsuit by Caleb T. Fay, and a 1960 treatise by Parrott Investment Company board member Marc de Tristan (1960). The de Tristan analysis was particularly thorough, based on a review of Mexican grant filings, pertinent Butte County Title Company volumes, probate documents, and 27 deed documents dating 1844-1918 and on file in the archives of the Parrott Investment Company. Copies of several of these resources along with supporting documents were found on file in the Rancho archives and accessed by the present study. The de Tristan analysis *Historical Notice and Resume of Transactions Involving the Llano Seco Ranch from 1844 to this Date* (March, 1960) is distilled here in Table 3, showing the 28 individuals who held at least partial title in the Rancho before John Parrott assumed complete control in 1869.

Sebastian Keyser, 1844

Keyser's name appears in various sources in at least three different spellings, settled by a self-published notice appearing in the *California Star* newspaper of September 4, 1847. Born in the Austrian Tyrol region, Keyser was one of a group of Germans who migrated west from Missouri to Oregon territory with John Sutter in 1838. Sutter then booked passage to California via Hawaii, where he stayed four months to wait for a California-bound ship. While in Hawaii, Sutter learned about the Sacramento Valley and convinced the Hawaiian monarchy to dedicate ten Hawaiian laborers to his plan to develop an inland farm and trading post. Sutter arrived in California (then known as Yerba Buena) in 1839, establishing a rough camp near the confluence of the American and Sacramento rivers. Sutter immediately sought Mexican citizenship and petitioned Governor

Juan Bautista Alvarado for two land grants totaling 48,827 acres (Dillon 1967). Keyser came south with a California-bound trapping party in 1843 and joined Sutter at his New Helvetia settlement, where Sutter assisted him in securing Mexican citizenship and acquisition of the 17,767-acre (71.90 km2) Rancho del Llano Seco land grant, issued to Keyser on July 26, 1844, by Governor Pio Pico. It is unclear if Keyser ever took formal possession by occupation and improvement of Rancho del Llano Seco, but it is unlikely that he did. According to de Tristan (1960), Keyser sold the grant even before it was finalized on November 10, 1844. A brief biographical sketch published in 1891 indicated that Keyser was a member of the Donner Party Fourth Relief in April 1847, and in 1849 purchased a land grant on the Bear River, Cosumnes County, where he built an adobe and ran a ferry. Keyser died in 1850 at age 39, drowning when the craft sank (*Memorial and Biographical History of Northern California* 1891).[1]

NOTICE.

My Wife, Elizabeth Keyser, having left my bed and board, the subscriber would inform the public that he will not be accountable for any debts of her contracting after this date.

SEBASTIAN KEYSER.
Bear Creek, August 20th, 1847.   35-3t.   .

---

1. A more thorough history about Sebastian Keyser and key people and events of the era can be found in the appendix

Table 3. Rancho ownership, 1844–1869.

* Farwell Estate administered by John Bidwell, 1845L-1849L
** J.H. Varbass Estate administered by T.A. Varbass, 1852L-1853E
*** Fay Estate administered by H. Maria Fay, c. 1868-1869

Year	1844E	1844L	1845E	1845L	1846	1847	1848	1849L	1849L	1849L	1850E	1850E	1850L	1851	1852E	1852L	1852L	1853E	1853L
Sebastian Keyser	100.00%																		
Edward Farwell (d. 1845)*		100.00%	50.00%	50.00%	50.00%	50.00%	50.00%												
John Bidwell			50.00%	50.00%	50.00%	50.00%	50.00%												
Thomas L. Chapman								50.00%	33.33%	33.33%	33.33%	33.33%	33.33%	33.33%	33.33%	33.33%	33.33%	33.33%	
Thomas A. Varbass								50.00%	33.33%	33.33%									
John H. Varbass (d. 1850)**											33.33%	33.33%	33.33%	33.33%	33.33%	33.33%	33.33%		
Bezer Simmons									8.33%										
Titus Hutchinson									8.33%										
John F. Pope									8.33%		16.67%								
William H. Stowell									8.33%										
Orin Farnham										16.67%									
William H. Stowell										16.67%	16.67%	16.67%							
Frederick Billings													5.56%	5.56%	5.56%	5.56%	5.56%	5.56%	5.56%
James R. Bolton													5.56%	5.56%	5.56%	5.56%	5.56%	5.56%	5.56%
Henry W. Halleck													5.56%	5.56%	5.56%	5.56%	5.56%	5.56%	5.56%
George G. Pope												4.30%	4.30%	4.30%	4.30%	4.30%	4.30%	4.30%	4.30%
Overton C. Pope												2.15%	2.15%	2.15%	2.15%	2.15%	2.15%	2.15%	2.15%
C. J. Brenham												2.69%	2.69%	2.69%	2.69%	2.69%	2.69%	2.69%	2.69%
John Hoskins												7.53%	7.53%	7.53%	7.53%	7.53%	7.53%	7.53%	7.53%
Joshua Norton																		33.33%	
Caleb T. Fay																			33.33%
Samuel C. Bruce																			33.33%
Archibald C. Peachy															U.S. Land Patent Aplication				
George F. Sharp																			
Thomas Hill																			
Sullivan Fay (d. c 1868)***																			
Andrew J. Pope																			
J. S. Doc																			
John Parrott																			
	100.00%	100.00%	100.00%	100.00%	100.00%	100.00%	100.00%	100.00%	100.00%	100.00%	100.00%	100.00%	100.00%	100.00%	100.00%	100.00%	100.00%	100.00%	100.00%

(Table 3 continued from page 52)

Year	1854E	1854L	1855E	1855L	1856E	1856L	1857E	1857L	1858E	1858L	1858L	1859E	1859L	1859L	1860E	1860L	1861E	1861L	1869
Sebastian Keyser																			
Edward Farwell (d. 1845)*																			
John Bidwell																			
Thomas L. Chapman		33.33%	33.33%	33.33%	33.33%	33.33%	33.33%	33.33%											
Thomas A. Varbass																			
John H. Varbass (d. 1850)**																			
Bezer Simmons																			
Titus Hutchinson																			
John F. Pope																			
William H. Stowell																			
Orin Farnham																			
William H. Stowell																			
Frederick Billings	5.56%	5.56%	5.56%	5.56%															
James R. Bolton	5.56%	5.56%	5.56%	5.56%															
Henry W. Halleck	5.56%	5.56%	5.56%	5.56%															
George G. Pope	4.30%	4.30%	4.30%	4.30%	4.30%	4.30%	4.30%	4.30%	4.30%										
Overton C. Pope	2.15%	2.15%	2.15%	2.15%	2.15%	2.15%	2.15%	2.15%	2.15%										
C. J. Brenham	2.69%	2.69%	2.69%	2.69%	2.69%	2.69%	2.69%	2.69%											
John Hoskins	7.53%	7.53%	7.53%	7.53%	7.53%	7.53%	7.53%	7.53%	7.53%										
Joshua Norton																			
Caleb T. Fay	33.33%	33.33%	33.33%	33.33%	33.33%	33.33%	33.33%	33.33%	83.34%	100.00%	66.67%	66.67%	41.67%	22.11%	22.11%	75.00%	63.00%		
Samuel C. Bruce	33.33%																		
Archibald C. Peachy					16.67%	16.67%	16.67%	16.67%											
George F. Sharp									2.69%										
Thomas Hill											33.33%	33.33%	33.33%	13.77%	13.77%				
Sullivan Fay (d. c 1868)***													25.00%	25.00%	25.00%	25.00%	25.00%	25.00%	
Andrew J. Pope														39.13%	39.13%				
J. S. Doc																	12.00%		
John Parrott																		75.00%	100.00%
	100.00%	100.00%	100.00%	100.00%	100.00%	100.00%	100.00%	100.00%	100.00%	100.00%	100.00%	100.00%	100.00%	100.00%	100.00%	100.00%	100.00%	100.00%	100.00%

U.S. Land Patent Granted

Edward August Farwell and John Bidwell
1844-1849

According to *The Memorial and Biographical History of Northern California* (1891), Edward August Farwell was a Boston printer and sailor who arrived in Northern California from Honolulu in 1842. In 1844, concurrent with Keyser's Rancho del Llano Seco grant, Farwell obtained the 22,193.93-acre Rancho de Farwell grant bordering Rancho Llano Seco to the north side (Figure 12). According to de Tristan (1960, 1), in 1844 Keyser sold the Rancho Llano Seco land grant to Farwell for 17 heifers at $5.00/head, giving Farwell control of 40,146.17 acres bordering Big Chico Creek and the Sacramento River. Wells indicates that Farwell settled in a small cabin south of Chico Creek that same year, thought to be the first non-Indian structure built in Butte County (Wells 1882, 129).

At the present time it is unclear what role John Bidwell may have had, if any, in Keyser's Rancho Llano Seco acquisition or in Keyser's immediate transfer of ownership to Farwell. Nevertheless, Bidwell was to some degree caught up in these affairs. Bidwell arrived at Sutter's New Helvetia trading station in 1841 and immediately went to work for Sutter as an accountant, manager, and engineer, producing the first formal *diseños*, or legal land grant maps, to be filed with the Mexican government for Sutter, and also providing similar services to other Alta California grant applicants (e.g., Figure 12). Bidwell was the author of the initial Rancho del Llano Seco land grant map submitted to Governor Manuel Micheltorena, and given his role in Sutter's operation it is likely that Bidwell was also involved in preparation and submittal of Spanish-language grant documents as required by the Governor's office, which de Tristan notes were submitted on April 1, May 1, and July 26, 1844.

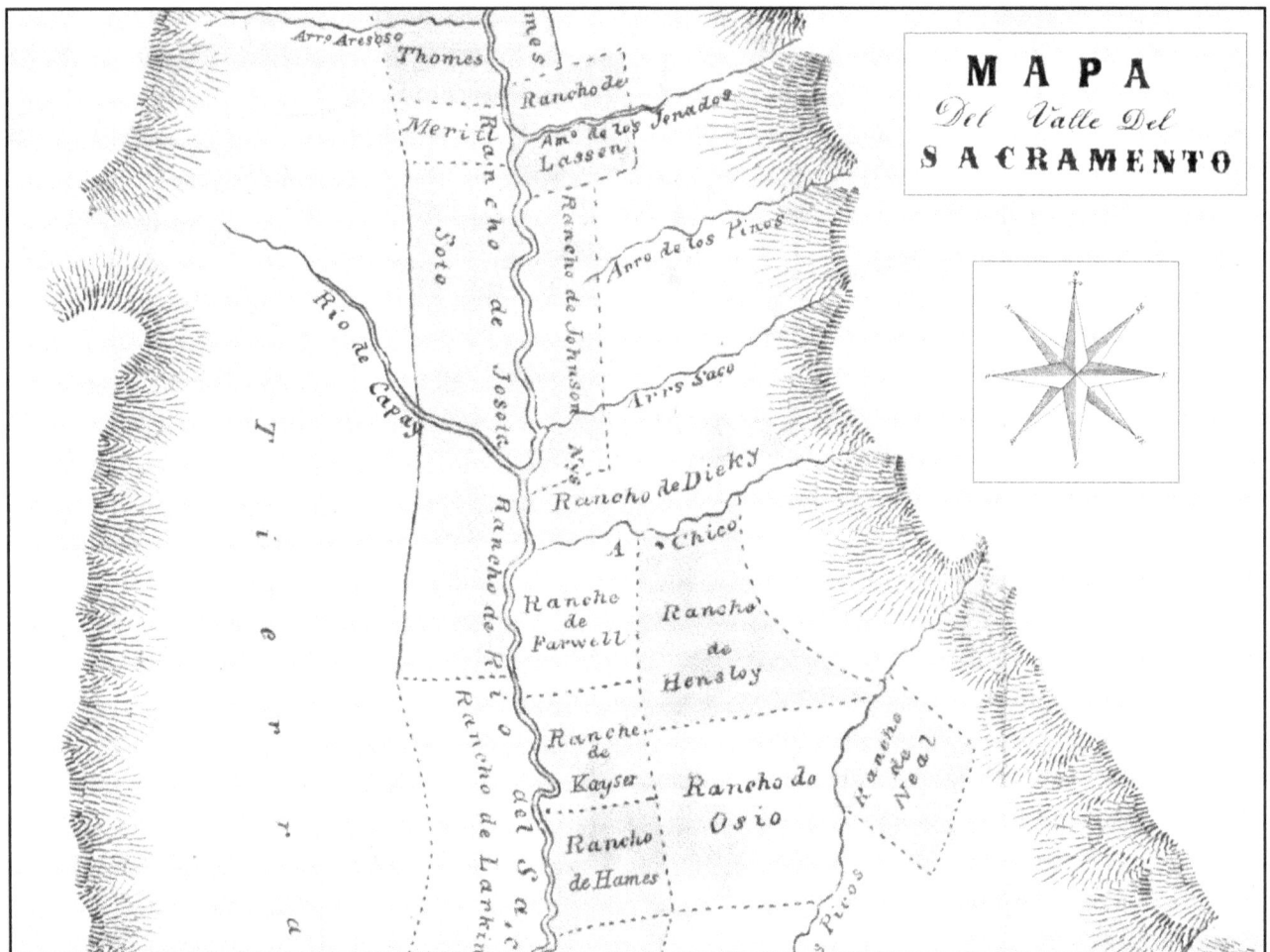

Figure 12. "Rancho de Keyser" and adjoining Mexican land grants detail depicted in the *Mapa del Valle del Sacramento* pen-and-ink illustration by John Bidwell, 1844 (detail; California State Library, California History Room).

Bidwell visited western Butte County on several occasions in 1843-1845, deciding at once to settle here as soon as an opportunity arose. In his *Reminiscences*, Bidwell recounts a summer 1844 visit to future Colusa and Glenn counties to map new grants sought by Thomas O. Larkin, American consul to the Mexican government in Monterey, during which he had a fortuitous meeting with Edward Farwell. The encounter took place after Bidwell left the Coast Range and travelled to the mouth of Stony Creek near present-day Hamilton City:

> The next day, July 5th, 1844, I reached the Sacramento River and met Ed. A. Farwell, with two canoes, coming up the river to begin occupation of a grant located on the east side of the river and south of Chico Creek. (Bidwell 1904, 379)

Whether Bidwell and Farwell discussed the Keyser-Farwell transfer on this occasion, on another occasion, or at all cannot be determined here, but it is clear that Bidwell visited Farwell again and also assisted Farwell's land grant application process. In April 1845, Farwell deeded Bidwell a half-interest in Rancho Llano Seco for "all the trouble and expenses of obtaining the proper and valid title for said land" (de Tristan 1960, 1). Most sources cite Bidwell's acquisition of the "south one-half" of Farwell's holdings, assuming that Bidwell acquired this portion of Rancho de Farwell, but given the timing Bidwell's half-interest may have been the aforementioned Rancho del Llano Seco deed. In 1847, Bidwell took his first major step toward establishing residency when he built a small cabin and drove cattle onto the property. Waterland describes the cabin as "made of oak and sycamore and chinked with mud," adding:

> It had a door as entrance, covered in deer skins. On the veranda were two bunks, a window over each covered with cloth. The fire for cooking was built on a dry floor outside the cabin, and was partly roofed sheltering it from the rain. The effort was made to always keep a fire, so there would be coals to replenish it. (Waterland 1934–1940, vol. I, 28)

Like many secondary sources, Wells (1882) and de Tristan (1960) claim that Farwell died in 1845, but *The Memorial and Biographical History* (1891, 113) indicates that in 1845 Farwell travelled overland to the East Coast "seeking relief for his weak eyes," and that he returned

in 1848 to assume command of Sutter's launch on the Sacramento River. According to this document, Farwell died in San Francisco in January, 1849.

In spring 1848, Bidwell left Sutter's employment in order to establish successful gold diggings along the Middle Fork of the Feather River near present day Oroville. By fall, 1849, he closed the diggings, having collected considerable wealth. Shifting his focus to agriculture and merchandise to provision the growing immigrant population of California, Bidwell acquired the Rancho del Arroyo Chico (Rancho Chico)—a 22,214-acre land grant issued in 1844 by Governor Micheltorena to William Dickey—in two purchases in 1849 and 1851.

Fractional Interests, 1849-1861

In October 1849, Bidwell sold his and the Farwell estate's Rancho Llano Seco interests to Thomas L. Chapman and Thomas A. Varbass, who in turn initiated a decade-long slate of fractional land sales and debt settlement to an increasingly long list of owners, none of whom appear to have occupied or made improvements to the Rancho. The de Tristan (1960) analysis admirably untangles the transactions (see Table 3). The first major event in this span occurred in July 1850, when the nine active Rancho title holders—Chapman, Varbass estate administrator John H. Varbass, F. Billings, J. R. Bolton, C. J. Brenham, T. L. Chapman, H. W. Halleck, J. Hoskins, G. G. Pope, and G. G. Pope acting as administrator for O. C. Pope, a juvenile—filed a petition with the State Lands Commission for recognition and confirmation of the Rancho Llano Seco Mexican land grant. It is likely that all of the purchasers acquired fractional title to the Rancho on speculation that the Mexican grant title would pass muster, three of the investors selling out when the Board of Land Commissioners rejected the petition for recognition, and others cashing out after the U.S. District Court of Appeals reversed the decree and decided in favor of the applicant in May 1857.

Between 1844 and 1860 the Rancho Llano Seco had absentee owners and there existed considerable and widely known uncertainty regarding the validity of the land grant title, especially after the State Land Commission's initial rejection of the 1852 application. In the interim, ad hoc county roads were established through the Rancho, a commercial operation was opened ferrying travelers across the Sacramento River to and from the Rancho lands, and as the Newhart example suggests, portions of the Rancho were occupied by squatters who viewed it as unclaimed land. It is likely that all three of the named clearings depicted in the 1874 John Parrott Map—Miller, Johnson, and Newhart—identify pre-1860 squatters and their clear-cuts.

In the 1850s, a series of transactions took place that led, circuitously, to John Parrott's ultimate acquisition and consolidation of the Rancho. In 1853, Caleb T. Fay, a San Francisco investor, speculator, and future United States Internal Revenue Assessor and candidate for Governor (*Daily Alta California* April 1885), purchased the Varbass holdings and, in 1858, he bought the Thomas L. Chapman interests, giving him 66.66 percent of the Rancho. By the end of 1858 Fay also purchased minor titles held by six other individuals, and for a brief time held 100 percent of the Rancho. In late 1859, Fay lost more than 77 percent of the Rancho to a tax-lien sale and to creditors for debt settlement. Enabled by a series of poorly secured loans and encouraged by the final land patent decree of June 18, 1860, in late 1860 Fay reacquired a 63 percent title, being ultimately unable to purchase 12 percent held by creditor J. S. Doc and 25 percent held by cousin Sullivan Fay. It is unclear from the record what Caleb T. Fay's ultimate objective might have been in buying up the Rancho titles, but there was nothing in his career that might lead us to conclude he aimed to be a rancher. Nevertheless, his near success in consolidating the Rancho titles did pave the way for John Parrott, who was interested in the Rancho as a meaningful and productive enterprise.

In March 1861 the Parrott & Co. banking concern loaned C. T. Fay & Company a sum of money to be made payable in 30 days at an interest rate of 2% per month. By June 4th, neither principal nor interest had been paid and Parrott initiated a court action of attachment filed as a lien upon the Rancho. The court action exposed additional liens against Fay's Rancho titles held by Thomas Hill and John S. Doc. In July 1861 Parrott purchased these debts and also took possession of the Hill and Doc titles; that same month Parrott secured title from Caleb T. Fay, bringing Parrott's total holding to 75 percent. Sullivan Fay retained his fractional title for another three years, but in December 1864,

> Sullivan Fay gave John Parrott a general power of attorney to handle his interests in the Llano Seco. Sometime later Sullivan Fay died, and in his will he named his wife, H. Maria Fay, his sole heir

and executrix. By deed dated February 13, 1869, H. Maria Fay sold to John Parrott the undivided ¼ interest in the Llano Seco for $10,000. (de Tristan 1960, 8)

This sale was confirmed by the court on May 20, 1870, giving Parrott complete title to all of the lands deeded by the original 17,952.24-acre Rancho del Llano Seco land grant. According to de Tristan, Parrott's total purchase price for the Rancho Llano Seco was $69,650.00.

John Parrott, 1861-1884

John Parrott was born in 1811 in Virginia (San Mateo County 1870 Census) to a family of sufficient means to provide a solid education and commercial opportunities to John and his older brother, William. Later that same year, the family moved to the area of Carthage, Tennessee.

In 1829, at age 18, John left home and joined William in Mexico City where he went to work in William's mercantile and trade company as a bookkeeper. In 1834, William was appointed U.S. consul in Mexico City by President Andrew Jackson, exposing John to political circles, which assisted his own advancement. In 1837 John was appointed U.S. consul to Mexico on the Pacific Coast at the Port of Mazatlán. By 1840 he also founded the trading firm of Parrott, Scarborough & Co., later absorbing a new partner in the firm of Parrott, Talbot & Co. (*Daily Alta California* March 2, 1880). In his consular duties and in his business affairs John was focused on American commerce in the Pacific, maintaining careful records of shipping arrivals, departures, incoming and outgoing cargos, and their value. As part of his duties, John Parrott maintained communication with U.S. Secretary of State Daniel Webster (Jostes 1972, 2-5).

With the collapse of Mexican rule in California and growing tension between the U.S. and Mexico over U.S. western expansionism and territorial border disputes under the Polk administration, John Parrott's role as consul took on new dimensions. At the time Great Britain, which still held the Oregon Territory, hoped to quietly initiate a military action to annex Alta California in the event of an outbreak of U.S.-Mexico hostilities in Texas, and in 1845, the British had amassed a naval fleet on the Pacific coast of Mexico poised to act at the first report of the outbreak of war. Parrott was instructed to maintain constant communication with Thomas O. Larkin, U.S. Consul in Monterey, Alta California, in order to coordinate the U.S. military response and thus forestall British action (Jostes 1972, 5-25). Parrott described his role in the ensuing events:

> There had been rumors of the likelihood of a war breaking out between Mexico and the United States. Both England and the United States were prepared to take a decisive step to seize on the territory of Upper or Alta California, on the first official announcement that war had been declared between the two Republics. Both had fleets at San Blas and Mazatlán, ready to sail on the receipt of the first news of the inauguration of hostilities.
>
> In April, 1846, [I] left Mazatlán on board the United States ship *Warren*, Captain Hull, for San Blas, accompanied by Dr. Wood, Fleet Surgeon of the United States Navy. We landed at San Blas, and took horse for Tepic, about 18 leagues from the port of San Blas. After resting a few days at Tepic, we took fresh animals, and left for the city of Guadalajara, distant from Tepic about 180 miles. While at Guadalajara, an express was received from San Luis Potosi, giving an account of the first engagement between the Mexican and American troops on the Rio Grande, in which it was stated the Americans had been defeated under Captain Thornton.
>
> This news created excitement. Bells were rung and bonfires lighted on the public square at that city. Knowing this news to be of the greatest importance, I requested a friend to get an express in readiness to start at once for Tepic. I sent my letter for Mr. J. R. Bolton, at Mazatlán, acting United States Consul, under cover to Barron, Forbes & Co., of Tepic, requesting them to send on at once another express to Mazatlán with the despatches [*sic*] for Mr. J. R. Bolton which contained information of the commencement of hostilities between Mexico and the United States. Mr. Bolton gave at once the desired information to Commodore Sloat, who despatched [*sic*] some war vessels to California, and sailed himself the next night on board the flagship Savannah. Everything was excitement, and we momentarily expected the news of the declaration of war. The English squadron, under command of Admiral Seymoure, were waiting

> news of actual declaration of war when a race was to be run by the English and American ships for the port of Monterey, the then Capital of Upper California. Communication was difficult at that time with the Atlantic or Pacific seaboard from the interior—no mails or coaches, but everything by mule or horse.
>
> On the 24th of June, 1846, George Bancroft, then Secretary of the Navy, wrote to Commodore Sloat, commanding the American squadron in the North Pacific, to wit: "If you should ascertain with certainty that Mexico has declared war against the United States, you will at once possess yourself of the port of San Francisco, and blockade or occupy such other ports as your force may permit."
>
> Commodore Sloat, on receiving the news through James R. Bolton, now a resident of this city [San Francisco], sailed out of the harbor, bound south, apparently for Acapulco or Panama. When night fell he stood to the north, bound for Monterey. The English fleet did not receive the news until three days later, the American squadron having three days' start. It was a race for the possession of Alta California. If the English had arrived first, and planted the English flag at Monterey, the British Government would have held possession of Upper, or, as it was called, "Alta California," and might have plunged the United States in a war with England. (*Daily Alta California* February 25, 1880)

With the cessation of hostilities in 1848, Parrott resumed his consular duties and business interests, but having amassed considerable wealth in international trade in Mazatlán, Parrott grew restless as he witnessed the burgeoning business opportunities in Alta California resulting from U.S. acquisition and the new gold discoveries. Frustrated with his inability to receive satisfactory compensation from the Mexican government for the wartime seizure of 469 mules and horses purchased and imported by Parrott for fulfillment of U.S. Cavalry contracts and 4,196 bales of American tobacco imported by Parrott for the Pacific trade, on April 9, 1850 Parrott resigned his consular post and move to the new center of commerce on the Pacific coast, San Francisco, where Parrott had developed business interests prior to his arrival.

Parrott (Figure 13) immediately set about purchasing and developing properties in downtown San Francisco, and by 1852 his assets included three lots with existing buildings, two lots with fire-proof multi-story buildings newly constructed by Parrott, one empty lot, the New Almaden Quicksilver Mine, and a long list of credits, debits, and trade goods totaling $627,659.32. In 1855, Parrott acquired the assets of a financial company via debt settlement and re-opened the concern under the business name "Parrott & Co., Bankers," with partner Walter Comstock, the new firm providing banking, exchange, investment, and lending services. This new firm was the conduit for Parrott's acquisition of Rancho Llano Seco.

Soon after completion of the Rancho Llano Seco acquisition, Parrott began a long correspondence with John Bidwell on issues relating to their common ranching and mining interests. Parrott visited the Rancho and initiated construction of the central headquarters complex, expanding cattle, horse, and wheat production as well as irrigation projects that enabled new rice production in the eastern fields. Parrott also installed a new steamship landing, "Parrott Landing," on the Sacramento River due east of the headquarters complex, focused on shipping Rancho products to Sacramento and Bay Area ports and transportation hubs. John Parrott's first wife died when their two children, Tiburcio and Maria Magdalena, were in the eastern U.S. for school.

Abby Parrott, 1884-1907

Abigail "Abby" Ann Eastman Meagher (Figure 13) was born in Maine on June 7, 1829, to a prosperous lumber mill operator and ship builder. As with Parrott and his brother, Meagher's family wealth enabled them to send her to a private finishing school, and it was in St. Joseph's Academy in Maryland, where Abby met and formed a fast friendship with Maria Magdalena Parrott. Two years after both girls' graduation in 1848, Abby was invited west to San Francisco where she met John Parrott, 18 years her senior. They married in 1853 and had eight children. John Parrott died on March 29, 1884 at age 74 of respiratory failure.

John Parrott's will assigned one-half of his separate and common property to Abby Parrott, including a half interest in Rancho Llano Seco, the other half interest in trust to be divided among the children at Abby's discretion (de Tristan 1960, 10). Abby Parrott, widowed at age 54, took an increasingly active and vital role in the

family's business interests, and in a transaction in 1884 secured a deed for all rights to John Parrott's property from Tiburcio Parrott, John's son by his first wife.

During Abby Parrott's tenure two parcels were added to the Rancho inventory and one was subtracted, all three changes related to meander loop cut-offs shifting lands to different access points. Two of these were parcels of 74.79 and 95.76 acres purchased from the estate of Hugh Glenn, adding meanders formerly accessed from Glenn's Jacinto Rancho to the western Rancho boundary. Similarly, a 118.93-acre parcel of land formerly connected to the southwest corner of Rancho Llano Seco was transferred to a neighboring landholder who benefitted from the new cutoff. These transactions, recorded by deed in Glenn and Butte counties, brought the Rancho's total area to 18,003.86 acres.

Parrott Investment Company (PIC) 1907-Present

Records contained in the archives suggest that, in the mid-1880s and early 1890s, John Parrott II took a principal on-site role in management of Rancho Llano Seco, and he may have been the first family member to take up significant residence at the Rancho during this time. This role scaled back in the late 1890s and ended completely in 1907 when he relinquished all claim to Rancho Llano Seco and "as the result of financial transactions with his mother" conveyed all of his interests and rights to the Rancho to his mother, Abby M. Parrott (de Tristan 1960, 10-11). This move appears to have been precipitated by and occurred in coordination with events in July 1907, when the remaining family shareholders initiated a much different management scheme, transferring by deed all individual interests in Parrott holdings to the Parrott Investment Company (PIC), a corporation held in shares by the beneficiaries of the trust specified in John Parrott's will. Abby M. Parrott died on October 6, 1917, at which time all her remaining private interests also transferred to PIC. The PIC manages the Rancho to the present-day.

Figure 13. John Parrott (c. 1877) and Abby M. Parrott (c. 1915).

Roads and River Landings

THE HISTORY OF RANCHO LLANO SECO roads and transportation mirrors the region at large, and for a time some of the region's most important transportation routes were linked to the Rancho. Within a few years after the Llano Seco land grant was first issued, the Mexican War concluded with the annexation of California and the U.S. acquired Oregon Territory from the British, prompting a number of American settlers to colonize the Far West. With word of sizeable Northern California gold deposits, the move west became a continuous flood of people, prompting an acute need for transportation; roads and river travel along the axially-oriented Sacramento River soon served a key role.

The Shasta Road, Jacinto-Dayton Road, Butte City-Dayton Road, and Newhart Landing Road

The Sacramento Valley's two main axial roads were first established in the mid-1840s. The principal west-side road, the "Shasta Road" was a crude dirt track following the west bank of the Sacramento River in the approximate alignment of present-day Hwy 45. Shasta Road connected the head of navigation on the Sacramento River at Colusa to newly formed settlements along the west side of the Sacramento River to Red Bluff. The 1847 *Map of the Hyacinth Farm, the Property of W. H. McKee, M.D., Surveyed by W. B. Ide. Oct. 1847, C. S. Lymann, Del.*, clearly depicts the road and an adjunct "Waggon Ford" crossing the river toward Rancho Llano Seco (Figure 14). This "Waggon Ford" was probably the precursor to the Jacinto-Dayton Road.

In 1848-1849, Gold Rush traffic changed this from a simple track to a heavily travelled main road used to transport goods and people north by pack train (Hardwick and Holtgrieve 1996, 120; Johnson 2001, 15). An ever-increasing volume of people and supplies needed

to be moved north, and in 1849-1850, mule train and freight wagon companies were quickly organized. These were soon supplemented by stage lines, the first of which was established on the Shasta Road in spring 1851 (Dyke 1932, 35-38).

The meager road system and rough river fords were unable to meet the growing transport needs, especially related to goods and commodities moving to and from westside communities (Willows, Glenn, and Jacinto) to eastside communities (Grainland, Dayton, Chico, and Oroville). In 1862, local farmers and business interests presented a petition to the Colusa County Board of Supervisors for new county roads, one to connect

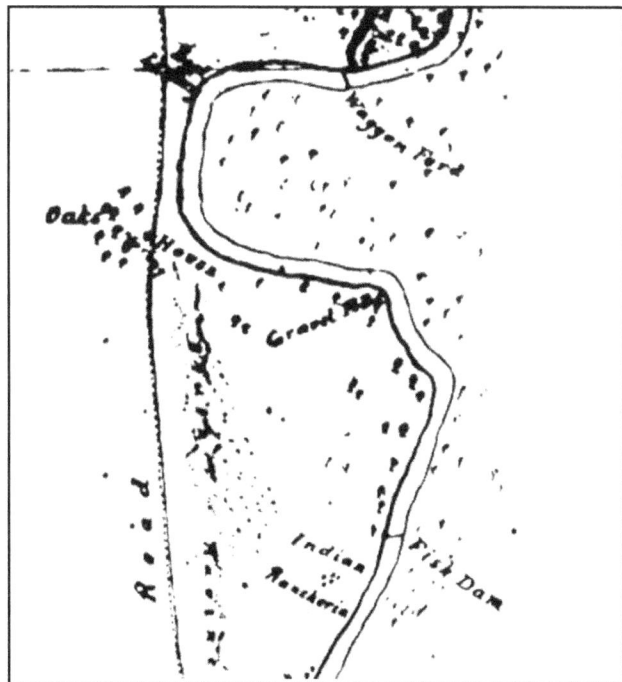

Figure 14. Detail of the northeast corner of the 1847 Map of the Hyacinth Farm, the Property of W. H. McKee, M.D., Surveyed by W. B. Ide. Oct. 1847, C. S. Lymann, Del., showing the old Shasta Road and a wagon ford crossing into Rancho Llano Seco.

the Shasta Road at Jacinto to Dayton and Chico, and the other to connect the newly founded community of Butte City to Dayton (Figure 15). In response, the Board directed County Supervisor and Colusa pioneer Will S. Green to survey and oversee engineering of the improved roads and the Board voted to commit county funds to expand the pioneer tracks and maintain the new roads which passed through Rancho Llano Seco (*Weekly Colusa Sun* September 27, 1862). The Board also granted a license for a ferry at Jacinto Crossing, replacing the informal pioneer ford (Weekly Colusa Sun September 8, 1862). Emphasizing the local importance of these early roads, an 1884 Postal Route Map for Colusa and Butte counties depicted the Jacinto-Dayton road as the principal east-west route in the vicinity of Chico (Preston 1983, 34-35). Newspaper reports from this era cite Chico business interests describing the Jacinto-Dayton road as one of Chico's most important to local commerce. Meeting with early success, Jacinto Ferry operators E. A. Barnes and M. V. Loy built a hotel on the Jacinto side of the new crossing (Figure 16). The hotel and associated residences and outbuildings are depicted on the 1874 John Parrott Map (Figure 15). Notably, the hotel site is still evident today, marked by a parallel row of date palms and other ornamental trees adjacent to the junction of Hwy 45 and Bayliss-Blue Gum Road.

John Parrott inherited these ad hoc roads, and it is evident—after he completed consolidation of Rancho Llano Seco in 1869—that he increasingly regretted the lack of formal easement agreements and the uncertain liabilities and unregulated public access that came as a result. A rash of Rancho grass fires ignited in the vicinity of the roads in the 1870s may have also played an important role in Parrott's decision, in 1878, to file an order with the County of Colusa to "abandon the road from a spot opposite Jacinto and the 'Milk Ranch' for and in consideration of easements for a road along the north edge of the grant to the river" (Figure 17). The Board of Supervisors adopted the resolution and committed funds to construct the road and four bridges required to cross the prominent ravines along the north border of the grant. A similar proposition was delivered to Butte County to replace the ad hoc Butte City-Dayton Road through the grant with a deeded route on the east boundary of the grant. This measure, adopted by Butte County, resulted in construction of 7-Mile Lane. The Jacinto Ferry and the Jacinto-Dayton Road through Llano Seco were formally abandoned in summer 1880, and the

county purchased a new right-of-way from the estate of Dr. Hugh Glenn and commissioned a new north-south county road linking Jacinto to a new ferry at Ord Bend. The 1907 Abby M. Parrott Map depicts these changes and how they impacted Rancho access. The Jacinto-Dayton and Butte City-Dayton roads through the Rancho were generally abandoned with some portions adapted to Rancho use. On the east boundary of the Rancho, the "County Road to Butte City"—7-Mile Lane—is clearly labelled. The newly constructed Ord Ferry Road and its four bridges along the north boundary of the Rancho are also clearly depicted on the 1907 map, as is a schoolhouse (Figure 18). Records contained in the Rancho archives suggest that land for the school was set aside by John Parrott concurrent with the road deed, and the school was in part funded by Parrott and attended by the children of Rancho staff. The old schoolhouse is still visible in the present day on the north side of Ord Ferry Road, in a stand of trees 200 feet east of the junction with River Road. Finally, it is notable that the 1907 map also shows Rancho access strictly limited to a single, gated entrance off Ord Ferry Road, making it clear that access controls were fully in place and the question of public access formally addressed.

Rancho Entrance Road

The 1874 John Parrott Map shows a number of Rancho access options, but with closure of the ad hoc Jacinto and Butte City road the principal access was on the "Ranch Road" or "Home Place Road" leading to Rancho Headquarters from the north. The latter is the same road depicted as the main access in the foreground of the Smith & Elliott (1877) "Llano Seco Rancho, Property of John Parrott, San Francisco" illustration shown in Figure 19. The Ranch Road corresponds roughly to the route of present-day River Road, and in the 1860s-1910s provided a connector to Sacramento Avenue at John Bidwell's Chico Landing. John and Abby Parrott generally arrived and departed via steamship at Chico Landing, and took River Road south to the Ranch Road to reach the Rancho Headquarters offices and residences (Jostes 1972, 157-162). As noted, the 1907 Abby M. Parrott Map depicts the "Ranch Road" as the Rancho's gated sole access.

This access was little changed through the first two decades of the twentieth century. However, the *Minutes of the Parrott Investment Company Stockholder's Meeting of March 8, 1923*, contained a note instructing Rancho

Figure 15. 1874 John Parrott Map showing the ad hoc public roads
routed through Rancho Llano Seco in the first two decades
of Parrott ownership.

Jacinto-Dayton Road

Butte City-Dayton Road

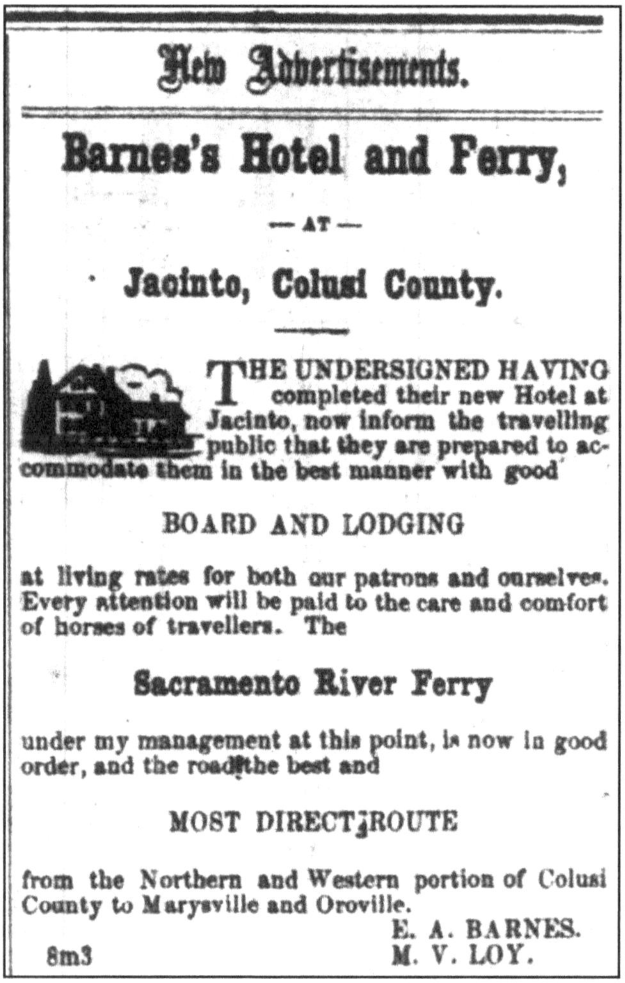

Figure 16. Jacinto Ferry and hotel advertisement from the *Weekly Colusa Sun*, March 8, 1862.

Manager Hugh Baber to oversee the installation of electrical power at Rancho Headquarters and concurrently to construct a new entrance road:

> The Board confirmed the authority given previously to install Electric Power on the ranch together with the installation of a pump in the tower with necessary pipes for connecting the water supply to the various buildings. The electric power is to be brought in along a new road to be opened from the county road to the tank tower in a straight line, which will avoid all water ways and will have only one gate. (PIC Minutes 3:142)

This new road provided a more efficient, direct connector to Ord Ferry Road and avoided the two ravine crossings necessary along the original "Ranch Road," no doubt a

hindrance to efficient ranch management due to frequent winter flooding. The re-build was completed in 1923; the new access route (present-day Hugh Baber Lane) was then planted with a parallel border of black walnut trees.

Access Spurs

The 1874 John Parrott Map shows that the southwest Rancho was accessed via three north-south spurs splitting off the Jacinto-Dayton Road (Figure 15). Access from Rancho headquarters to the Vermette Ranch was by way of a Jackson-Little Grant road crossing through present-day Stump Camp South and Oil Well Island fields. Access from Rancho headquarters to Newhart Landing was by way of a Miller-Newhart spur crossing through present-day Camp 2 West field. These two roads were also connected by east-west spurs, one connecting the Vermette Ranch to Newhart Landing through present-day Gangplank and Oil Well West fields, and the other connecting Jackson to Newhart through present-day Stump Camp South and Camp 2 West fields.

The 1907 Abbey M. Parrott Map and 1913 Polk Map (Figure 18) show that these connectors and the portion of the Jacinto-Dayton Road linking to these connectors stayed in use after the Jacinto-Dayton Road was closed to public use in 1880. Historic maps and aerial mosaics consulted for this study show little change in this basic access road configuration until the comprehensive clear-cuts and agricultural intensification of 1932-1939.

River Commerce and Landings

Travel and freight transport were slow on unimproved early Northern California roads, especially after wet weather. River transport along the axial Sacramento River and Delta waterways was soon established as a speedy and economical alternative (Johnson 2001; Mansfield 1918). Steam-powered river boats were the principal means of transporting the Sacramento Valley's wheat crops between 1849 and the mid-1870s when new rail lines were constructed. A revival of river traffic took place in the 1890s through 1910s (Hardwick and Holtgrieve 1996, 121; Stevens 1981, 15).

Historically, the Sacramento River above Colusa was shallow, turbid, and crooked, making it difficult to navigate (Dyke 1932, 17-22). Prior to 1849, John Sutter successfully navigated the river in his small boat, the *White Princess*, and Perry McCoon made occasional trips up the Sacramento and Feather rivers in his launch the

ROAD ABANDONED.—The Board of Supervisors of Butte county have abandoned the road located through the Llano Seco, or Parrott grant, while the same was in Colusa county. This leaves no road from Jacinto to Chico, and if Parrott closes the present traveled road up, it will put a stop to travel from the neighborhood of Jacinto, Germantown and Willows, to Chico. The Chico *Record* says that there was quite an excitement in that town on learning that the road had been abandoned. It was one of the most important roads that town had. The writer of this "local" surveyed and located the roads through the grant. One ran up parallel with the river from Colusa to a point about two miles north of Jacinto—the then line between Colusa and Butte, and the other ran from the ferry at Jacinto out to this road, a distance of some two miles. Neither of these roads gave an outlet entirely through the grant, in the direction of Chico, but the public have been permitted to pass over the grant. It seems, according to the *Record's* story, that Parrott, some two years ago, deeded to Butte county a road on the east and north of his grant, conditioned on the abandonment of the

oads through his land, and the Board then accepted the deed. There has been a contest as to whether the road should cross at Jacinto, where the road on the west side touches the river, and run through Parrott's land on the east, or cross at Parrott's north line and run out through Dr. Glenn's land. The Board of Supervisors of Colusa county recently refused the petition for the latter road, and now action has been taken for the closing of the one on the other side. We might say that if the merchants of Chico can stand it, the farmers of Colusa county can, but we believe in roads, and call the attention of our representatives in the Legislature to the fact that there should be some provision for the location of important thoroughfares, when the Supervisors of different counties cannot agree upon a common point of intersection. Sometimes, also, it is necessary to locate roads on county lines, as between Colusa and Yolo, and there should be some provision of law for such cases. Senator Glascock is personally interested in the latter case, and we hope he will get up a general law, covering both points.

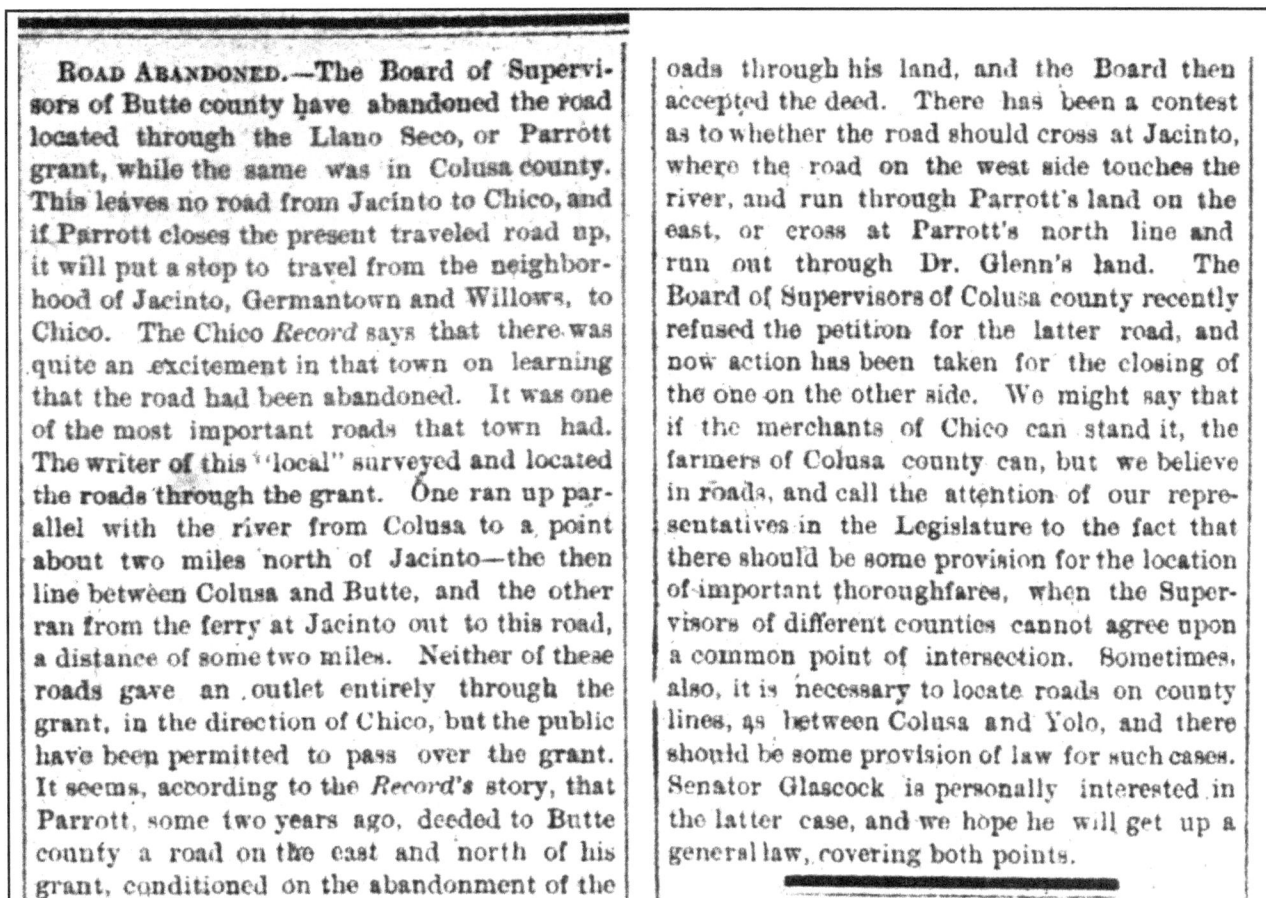

Figure 17. Article from the *Weekly Colusa Sun*, February 14, 1880, page 3, reporting the imminent closure of the Jacinto-Dayton Road.

Indian Queen (Dyke 1932, 1-4). However, once gold was discovered every available craft was used to negotiate the river: whale boats, ships, launches, barges using oars and sails, and row boats. Fares ranged from $50 to $200, and if the need arose the passengers were required to assist in propelling the vessel.

By 1849 a steady line of schooners ran the Bay and Delta between San Francisco and Sacramento (Dyke 1932, 4-7). Navigation of the upper Sacramento River was attempted as early as 1850 by Charles D. Semple and his steamer the *Martha Jane* (La Bourdette 1974, 13-15) and by Captain P. Le Fevre of the steamer the *Butte,* which began a regular run between Butte City and landings south along the Sacramento River (Dyke 1932, 21). Transportation companies ultimately had success piloting steamships north of Colusa once they made coordinated annual efforts to clear snags and grub out sand and gravel obstructions. Three steamboats, the *Orient*, the *Daniel Moore*, and the *Express*, made successful runs to Red Bluff

beginning in early 1852 (Dyke 1932, 25). Steamship companies profited from upstream and downstream postal contracts and passenger traffic but relied on contracts for mercantile goods and heavy equipment shipped to upriver suppliers, as well as agricultural commodities, cordwood, lumber, and cattle, meat, and hide products bound for downriver urban markets (Hardwick and Holtgrieve 1996, 122). By the late 1850s so many boats were on the river that competition was extremely keen (Dyke 1932, 10). In the 1860s, many owner-captains and small companies merged only to ultimately lose business when the California and Oregon Railroad, a subsidiary of Central Pacific, laid track to Chico in July 1870 (Hardwick and Holtgrieve 1996, 123; Stevens 1981, 22) and the Northern Railroad, also a subsidiary of Central Pacific, laid track to Willows in September 1878. Tremendous change would come to the regional economy with the rails, but not immediately. The new rail lines were developed at a distance from the river to avoid flood and erosion damage. Because

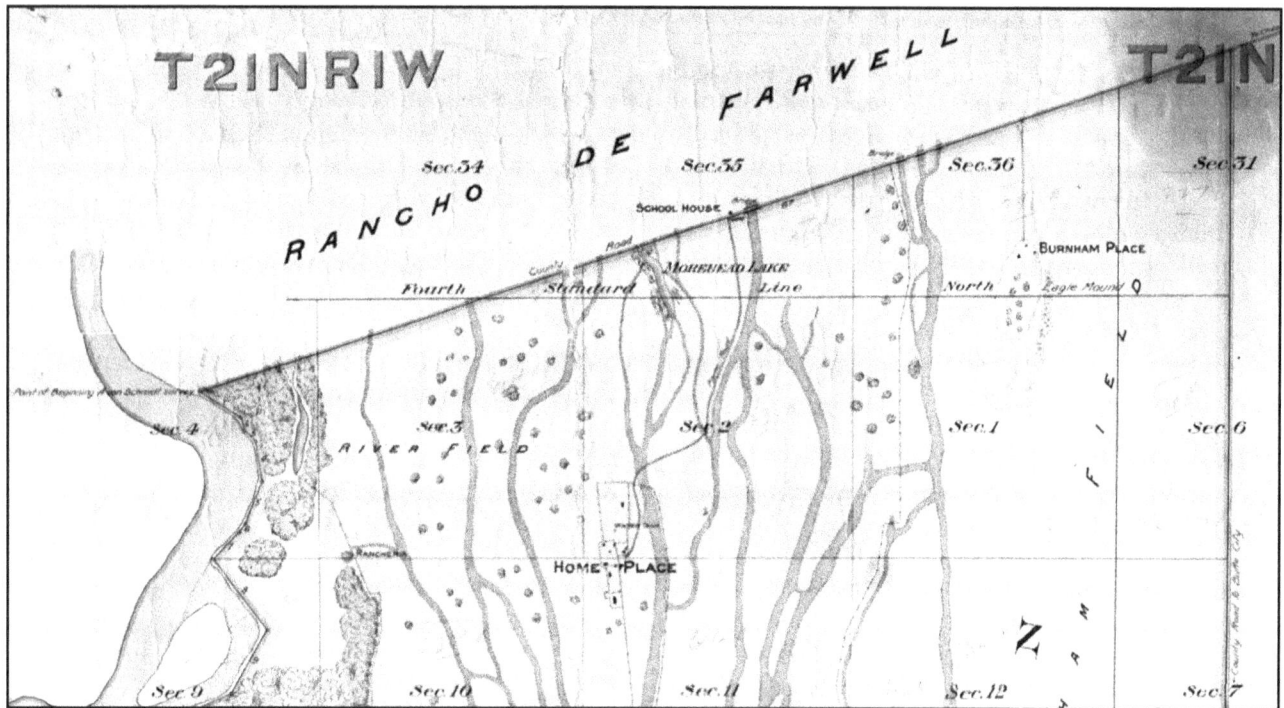

Figure 18. Northern portion of the 1907 Abby M. Parrott Map, showing the elimination of the original ad hoc county roads through the Burnham Field, the new Butte City-Dayton Road, and the bridges, schoolhouse and new gated Rancho entrance along the Ord Bend-Dayton Road.

roads from the river ranches were generally poor and conditions unreliable, and because freight wagons were too small to efficiently transport the tonnage typically produced by the Butte and Glenn County ranches, the grain and cordwood markets sustained steamboat transport along the Sacramento River for another three decades. Steamboats began towing barges to handle the heavy freight and transferred cargo to larger, deep-draft steamboats, each capable of towing up to four fully loaded barges in Delta and Bay waters (Hardwick and Holtgrieve 1996, 122). Magliari estimates that half of the state's 1890 wheat crop was transported by water (Magliari 1989, 453). The 1890s steamboat revival on the upper Sacramento River was also enabled by the introduction of light-draft stern wheel vessels and by the U.S. Army Corps of Engineers' success clearing river obstructions. Steamboats resumed weekly service to Red Bluff, and in this era new, large-scale grain elevators were constructed on the river banks at several locations (Hardwick and Holtgrieve 1996, 122).

Between the early 1850s and late 1860s local river transport needs were served at Newhart Landing, located off a gravel bar in the southwest corner of the

Rancho (Figure 20). The landing was named for two Rancho squatters who established a cabin and cordwood operation in what is now the southwest margin of the USFWS Riparian Sanctuary Unit around 1855. In letters to John Bidwell, John Parrott bemoaned conditions at Newhart Landing, which required grounding on a gravel bar. In the early years Parrott himself, when visiting the Rancho, frequently shipped to Bidwell's Chico Landing located at the western terminus of Sacramento Avenue west of the City of Chico (Jostes 1972, 153-162).

Among the most active local steamship operators at the turn of the century, the Sacramento Transportation Company prospered with seven steamers and 23 barges running oak cordwood and wheat between Chico Landing, Sacramento, and San Francisco Bay until 1913 (McGowan 1961, 305; Hardwick and Holtgrieve 1996, 121-122). Research in Rancho archives produced receipts for cordwood and grain sacks loaded on Sacramento Transportation Company steamers.

Sometime between 1874 and 1877 John Parrott ordered construction of a new landing for Rancho Llano Seco. Like Chico Landing, Parrott Landing was located at

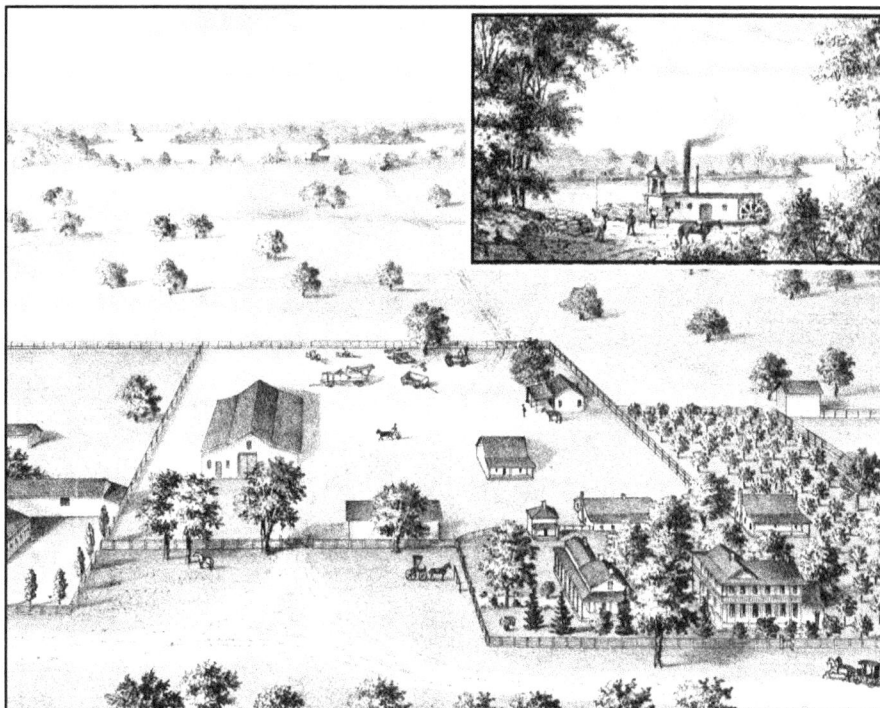

Figure 19. Detail of "Llano Seco Rancho, Property of John Parrott, San Francisco" (Smith & Elliott, 1877).

the end of a long east-west access road routed from Rancho Headquarters (Figure 19). Detail from an 1877 illustration "Llano Seco Rancho, Property of John Parrott, San Francisco" appearing in the portfolio volume *Butte County Illustrations, Descriptive of its Scenery, Residences, Public Buildings, Manufactories, Fine Blocks, Mines, and Mills* (Smith & Elliott 1877) depicts the landing and queued steamships (Figure 19). Parrott Landing was put out of operation sometime before the turn of the century. The 1907 Abby M. Parrott Map shows the former location of Parrott Landing isolated by a meander cutoff, the landing location and riverbed by then completely congested with gravel and partially overgrown. The 1907 map also depicts an active Newhart Landing. Invoices, receipts, and the minutes of Parrott Investment Company Board from the 1909-1913 time frame describe significant tonnage of grain sacks loaded at a landing, and presumably this was Newhart Landing.

Western Timber Belt

The Rancho archives produced a raft of new historical maps and aerial photo montages and extensive documentary and photographic evidence related to the purpose, management, and sequence of clear-cuts on the Rancho Llano Seco between the late nineteenth and mid-

twentieth centuries. Significant documentation related to clear-cuts along the Sacramento River was also found in regional newspaper archives. These sources made it possible to definitively locate and measure the historical clear-cut locations and understand their larger economic relationships.

In addition to the primary historical research previously described, in order to more precisely quantify the location and acreage of the historical clear-cuts, five key maps/aerials were digitized and georeferenced using a modern mapping application: 1) the 1874 John Parrott Map, 2) the 1907 Abby M. Parrott Map, 3) the 1922 Chambers Aerial Photo Montage, 4) the 1938 USGS Aerial Photo Montage, and 5) the 1958 USGS Aerial Photo Montage. For each, clear-cuts were digitized, acreage was determined, and the cut per field, per calendar interval, and cumulative totals were calculated. These calculations were limited to the Martin Complex, Camp 2 Complex, and Little Grant Complex fields situated in deep floodplain loams. Consistent with the assumption, the quantity of open space in both fields cumulatively fluctuated no more than 65 acres high and low in the same 1874-1958 period when the other fields experienced a significant net and cumulative loss of arboreal habitats in each calendar interval.

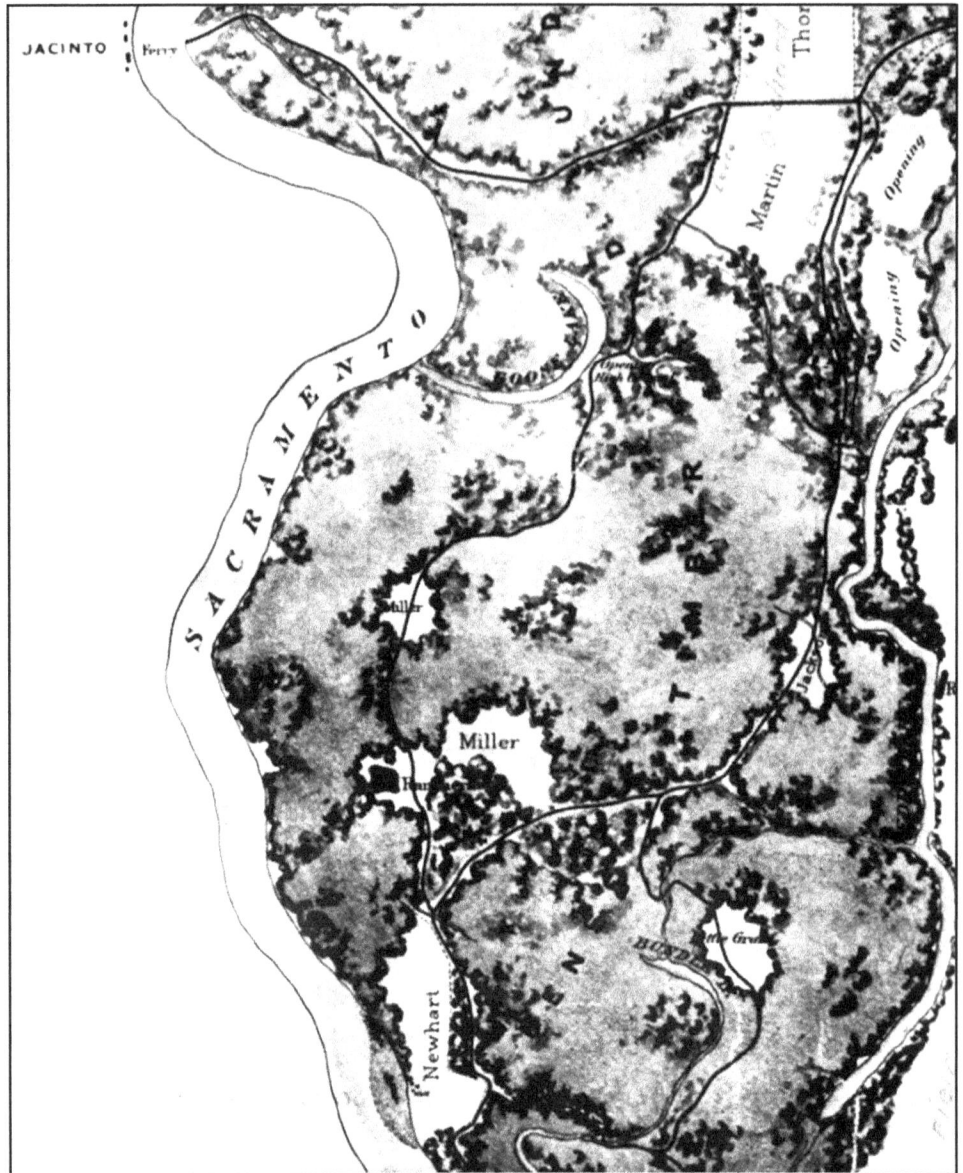

Figure 20. 1874 John Parrott Map showing road spurs linking Newhart Landing to the Jacinto-Dayton Road.

Pre-1844: Timber Density in the Prehistoric Period

Based on the archaeological survey findings described in the next section we can reasonably assume that at no point during the Holocene Epoch did the Llano Seco Project Area's native vegetation reach a "natural state" in the way that term is usually construed, that is, a state absent human agency. Archaeological findings indicate intensive human settlement and extensive harvest of surrounding landscapes for at least the last 7,000 years. As many as 500-1,500 people lived here in any one-time period, and these people depended on local natural resource extraction. In the prehistoric period, the Rancho bioscape was actively harvested and systematically modified by human occupants who conducted mass harvest of viable seed, nut, and sprouted plant crops, and probably most importantly, they likely altered plant communities systematically by setting fires. They also persistently depressed the density and diversity of large-bodied ruminant animals that would have otherwise produced additional checks on seed- and nut-bearing plant recruitment (Broughton 1994; Broughton and Bayham 2003; Winterhalder et al. 1988). These activities would have generated and maintained diversity, produced grassy openings, and constrained the tendency for understory overgrowth evident in today's unmanaged stands.

68

When the region was first depopulated in 1833-1837 due to introduced diseases, these checks probably ceased and it is likely that plant and animal populations responded. Immature tree recruitment probably increased in prairies and patches previously maintained by fire. Native American burning practices still occurred during this period, but the non-Indian population suppressed burning activity. For example, in March, 1850, as a member of the newly formed California legislature, State Senator John Bidwell advanced Senate Bill No. 54, "An Act Relative to the Protection, Punishment and Government of Indians" setting punishments and fines to be levied against California Indians apprehended in the act of setting fire to the woods or prairie, or for any Indian found not to "exert full force of effort to extinguish said fires at pain of $50.00 fine or corporal punishment not to exceed 100 lashes." As a result of the systematic curtailment and eventual elimination of traditional land management practices, we can assume that the first detailed depiction of Rancho habitat, the 1874 John Parrott Map, reflected the state of native vegetation 30 years after cessation of Native American fire management. Therefore, the uninterrupted, high-density western timber belt shown dominating the area in the 1874 map probably reflects several decades of invasive arboreal re-vegetation of tracts that were probably much more diverse and patchy in the prehistoric past.

1844-1861: Squatter Occupation and Cordwood Harvest

Between 1844 and 1860 the Rancho Llano Seco had absentee owners and there existed considerable and widely known uncertainty regarding the validity of the land grant title. In fact, the State Land Commission initially rejected the 1852 application, making validation appear more remote. In the interim, portions of the Rancho were occupied by squatters who viewed it as unclaimed land. For example, a travelogue newspaper article from 1859, "A Trip on the Sacramento River," mentions a visit to a cabin and landing run by partners Newhart & Fox, who "a few years ago, with only an axe in their hand, not a cent of money (earned their first meal with the axe)—settled on their present ranch and were last year assessed at $30,000" (*Daily Alta California* May 25, 1859). Regardless of the optimistic assessment, Newhart and Fox were squatting in the southwest portion of the Rancho. In fact, it is likely that all three of the named clearings depicted in the western timber tracts

in the 1874 John Parrott Map—Miller, Johnson, and Newhart—identify pre-1860 squatters and their clear-cuts. Individuals named "Miller" and "Johnson" appear in Parrott payroll records from 1874-1875, but Newhart and Fox may have moved on when John Parrott took possession; neither name appears in the early Rancho ledgers consulted to date.

These early squatters were equally interested in clear-cutting for profit and for agricultural development. Absent significant coal deposits in Northern California, in the era before electrical power and acetylene gas all domestic and commercial heating, lighting, processing, and industrial and mechanical steam power was produced by cordwood. A number of reports published during this period indicate that the river steamboats supplemented the wheat, passenger and mercantile trade by cordwood harvest and delivery to urban and industrial markets. For example, even in the earliest days of river travel there were "43 steamboats running upon our rivers and coast, where one year ago not eight or ten were engaged . . . wild forests of the Sacramento, San Joaquin, and their tributaries are fast yielding to the woodsman's axe" (*Daily Alta California* February 1, 1851). In a summary report of the status of cordwood supply and demand in Northern California, Will S. Green, publisher of the *Colusa Sun*, reported:

> Men generally attach too little value to the timber growing upon their lands. It will not be long before wood anywhere along the Sacramento River will be worth five dollars per cord in the tree. The supply in accessible localities in this State is very limited, and it is an article that must be had. (*Weekly Colusa Sun* December 26, 1868)

Green reports that live oak and white (valley) oak were the preferred species, commanding $7.50-$9.00 per cord in San Francisco. Cottonwood and sycamore were dropped and left in the clear-cuts in favor of oak owing to the "punky" and poor-burning nature of these soft woods. Elsewhere, Green encouraged "men of small means" to attempt homesteading via the wood-cutting formula exercised by Newhart and Fox:

> [I]t is easy to so locate farms that while they have a sufficient frontage on the river, they may extend back to the plains. This is the best wooded portion of the Sacramento Valley, and the lands near the river are covered with a fine growth of oak timber. In many places the trees are of great

size and age, in other places there is a younger growth. Owing to the great scarcity of timber in all the valley portions of California, this wood is very valuable, and sells readily on the banks of the river at about $3.50 per cord. We know one land owner in this neighborhood, who, after making a fair estimate, asserts that an average-sized oak is worth as much standing on his land as a two-year old steer. We knew one instance where the owner of a piece of land below Colusa cut and sold from it 100 cords per acre, the wood netting him $2 per cord. Land located as we have described can be bought at from $6 to $10 per acre, and a good title obtained, now that the land grants in this section of country are pretty well determined. Any enterprising man can pay for his land in one year, in either one of two ways: by cutting a portion of the wood and selling it for cash on the bank of the river, or by raising grain. (Weekly Colusa Sun December 13, 1862)

An article on river boat tonnage statistics for deliveries to the port of Sacramento in the year 1863 demonstrates the stunning quantities of cordwood harvested from the upper Sacramento River floodplain (Figure 21). This activity produced a heavy cut and the effects were immediate and progressive, reaching farther upriver and deeper into the floodplains each year:

> Fire-wood is brought to market from various inland sources. The Sacramento River in the vicinity of Colusa, and considerably above that point, and the upper San Joaquin supply a large amount. Formerly the "Slough," a portion of the Sacramento, yielded largely, but continual cutting has quite denuded the lands there. On both of these streams large wood barges, carrying from eighty to two hundred cords, drop down with the current to where steamers take them in tow for San Francisco. The wood is seen along the river banks, piled up where it has been hauled by teams and placed convenient for shipment; the woodman's solitary, smoke-begrimed cabin forming a curious looking foreground to the silent forest beyond. (*Weekly Colusa Sun* December 26, 1868)

Quantification and analysis of the historical map data suggests that the squatters and riverboat teams clear-cut 79.6 acres of oak forest in the Camp 2 Complex and Little

FIREWOOD.—The quantity of firewood brought to the city during the past year on barges, according to statistics furnished us by Harbormaster Whitney, amounts to 14,588 cords. This amount is much smaller than that brought to the city during 1861, as the demand this year for wood was not so great as it was last year. Our brickyards consume large quantities of wood when engaged in manufacturing, and they were prevented from being actively employed during the early part of the season, owing to the floods. The number of steamers on the river being smaller than last year is another reason for the smaller consumption of fuel. The bulk of the wood used is brought from between one hundred and one hundred and thirty miles above this city, on the Sacramento, in flatboats. The following are the names of the barges in use, the names of their owners, and the number of cords brought during the year by each:

Names.	Owners.	Cords.
Widow	Wm. Raught & Co.	1,435
Sacramento	Morse	1,000
Maid of Orleans	Manuel Castro	1,000
Star of the West	N. McNair	1,305
Two Brothers	Fred. Miller & Co.	1,190
Pioneer	E. D. Wheatley	1,563
St. Louis	— —	350
Mary Leng	Klotz & Co.	1,000
Caroline	H. Cook	900
Eliza	San Jun	700
Dayton	E. Rogers & Co.	800
Isabel	The Arcega estate	1,000
Taylor	The Arcega estate	1,000
Clinton	The Arcega estate	1,340
Total cords		14,588

Figure 21. "Tonnage Statistics" article appearing in the *Sacramento Daily Union*, January 1, 1863.

Grant Complex fields near the Sacramento River in the 1851-1860 time frame.

1861-1922: Wood-Cutting and Pasture Expansion

The percentage of clear-cuts evident in the 1874 John Parrott Map consisted of 122.4 acres opened in the Martin Complex fields representing cordwood production and clearing for wheat and pasture; I will assume that these were made under John Parrott's direction and carried out by Rancho foreman William Martin between the years 1861 and 1874. Between 1874 and 1907, the historical map data shows a slow pace of clear-cuts primarily focused on further expansion of the existing Martin Complex and Camp 2 Complex openings. Just 75 acres were added to the clear-cut inventory in this span. The archives show that, in the mid to late 1880s Rancho development was under the oversight of John Parrott II. For example, a handwritten receipt dated October 15, 1885 and endorsed by Parrott promises to pay Hong Gen (No. 7) for clearing 40 acres and bucking cordwood (Figure 22). Turn-of-the-century ledgers on file in the Rancho archives also list wages paid to members of the Mechoopda Tribe of Chico Rancheria for woodcutting work. Notes stored in the archives order the distribution of cordwood to perimeter camps and to headquarters households and cook houses. Another receipt found in the Rancho archives records the sale of 294 cords of oak cordwood (498 cords to date) sold by John Parrott II to the Sacramento Transportation Company on April 24, 1888, and loaded at Parrott Landing on steamship San Joaquin No. 3 (Figure 23).

Quantification of the historical map data indicates that there was a reduction in the pace of clear-cuts in years between 1874 and 1907 (Figure 24). This probably reflects on the one hand the relaxation of dedicated farm and pasture expansion practices after the death of John Parrott, and on the other a shift to centralized operations closer to Rancho Headquarters. The western timber belt was no longer used for grain production and instead was focused primarily or exclusively on range cattle operations. Based on research in the Rancho archives, John Parrott II took an active, on-site role at the Rancho through the 1880s, but less so in the 1890s. His Rancho

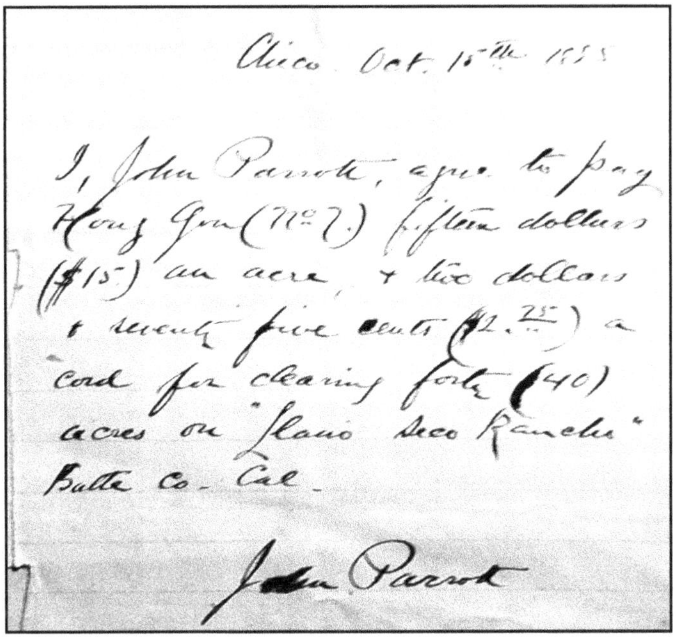
Chico Oct. 15th 1885

I, John Parrott, agree to pay Hong Gen (No. 7) fifteen dollars ($15) an acre, & two dollars & seventy five cents ($2.75) a cord for clearing forty (40) acres on "Llano Seco Rancho" Butte Co. Cal.

John Parrott

Figure 22. Handwritten receipt dated October 15, 1885, John Parrott II to Hong Gen (No. 7) agreeing to payment for clearing 40 acres and bucking cordwood.

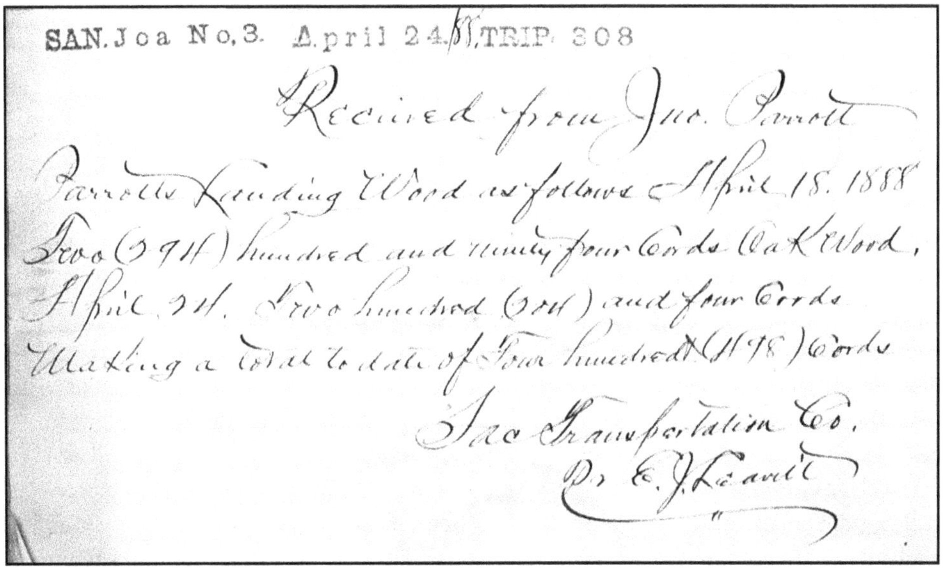
SAN. Joa No. 3. April 24/88 TRIP 308

Received from Jno. Parrott
Parrotts Landing Wood as follows April 18. 1888
Two (294) hundred and ninety four Cords Oak Wood,
April 24. Two hundred (204) and four Cords
Making a total to date of Four hundred (498) Cords

Sac Transportation Co.
Pr E. J. Leavitt

Figure 23. Receipt for 294 cords of oak cordwood sold to the Sacramento Transportation Company and loaded on the steamship *San Joaquin No. 3*, April 24, 1888, Parrott Landing.

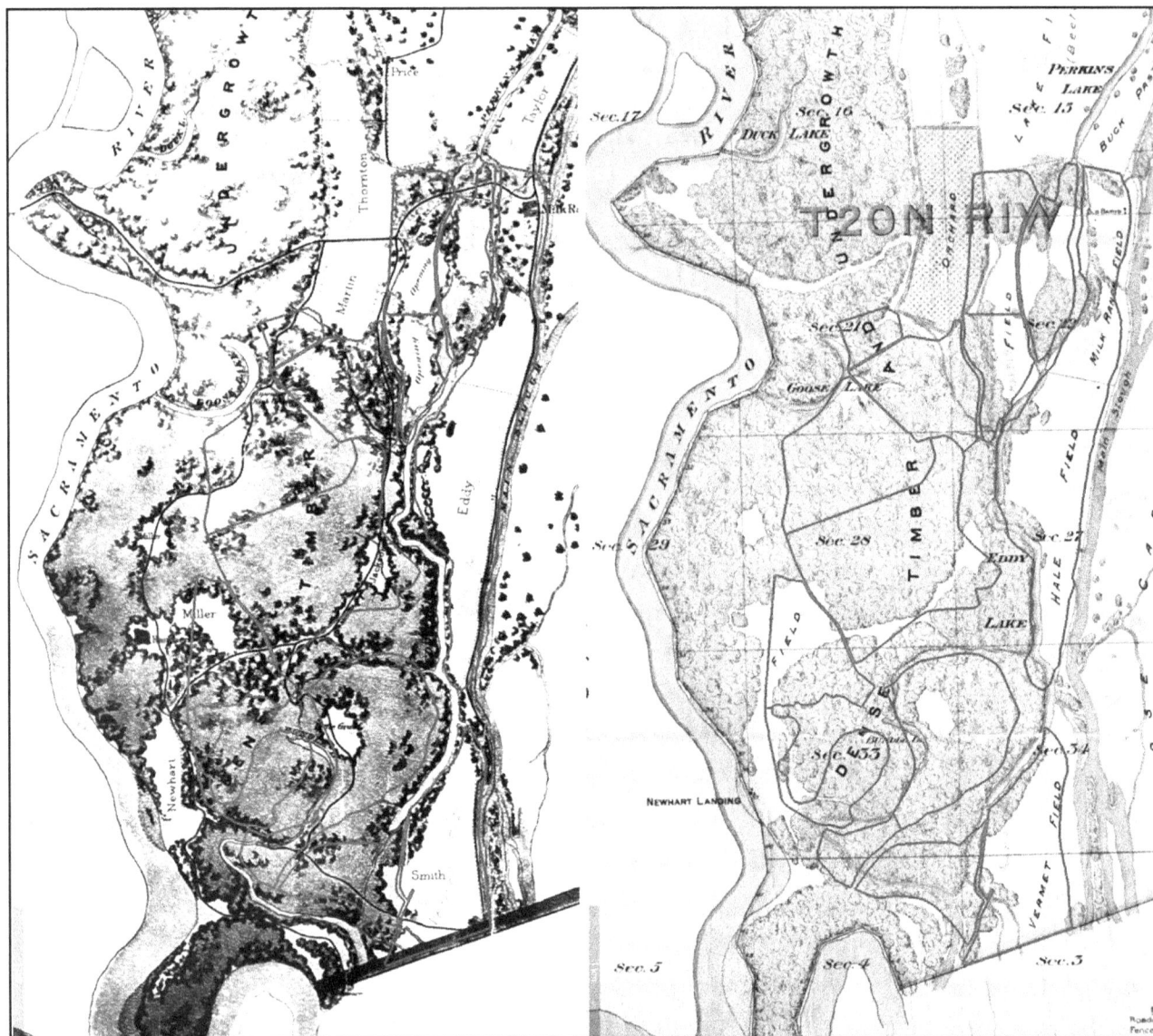

Figure 24. The extent of timber tracts in 1874 (left) and 1907 (right) in relation to Project Area field boundaries.

authority was terminated in 1907 when his mother, Abby M. Parrott, purchased his interests in a debt settlement precipitated by transfer of Rancho management to the PIC Board of Directors.

The period between the years 1907 and 1922 was characterized by an increase in the pace and scale of clear-cutting and an expansion into previously undeveloped fields. Quantification of the historical map data indicates that clear-cuts during this span totaled 230 acres, matching the clear-cuts made in the peak era of steamship-enabled harvest. The new clear-cuts doubled the size of the Martin Complex tilled grain and pasture lands, including two new rectangular patches contained

within the boundaries of the Project Area's DWR 2 field, and expansion of pasture lands in four of the Project Area's Camp 2 Complex and Little Grant Complex fields (Figure 24).

This period also saw an increasingly aggressive effort on the part of the PIC Board to install a Rancho manager willing to implement the Board's instructions and capable of producing solid bookkeeping and regular communications. For example, PIC minutes reflect an increasing dissatisfaction with G. A. Waugh, hired as Rancho Manager in 1912. Even at the beginning of his term, the PIC Board found it necessary to supply Waugh with instructions related to reporting and bookkeeping

(PIC Minutes 1:87, June 13, 1912). Waugh reported difficulty carrying out Board instructions because he could not keep men on staff, many leaving for duty in the Great War (PIC Minutes 2:95, April 12, 1917). Waugh was forced out in 1919, and for a time the Board operated the Rancho with a more diffuse management structure. In December 1919, the Board identified F. Julian as the new Rancho Manager.

1922-1939: Wood Cutting and Agricultural Intensification

A marked shift in the scope and scale of Rancho development and agricultural and animal production hinged on an appearance before the PIC Board by stockholder William G. Parrott on June 23, 1921. The PIC Minutes recorded Parrott's presentation calling for an expansion of operations in the "western timber belt." He noted that the lands could be developed to run an additional 1,800 to 2,400 head of cattle. This was a sound strategy because PIC financial records made it plain that beef cattle operations were the Rancho's most profitable undertaking, and Parrott argued that the expansion was both manageable and beneficial to the financial health of the company.

The Board viewed the proposal favorably, and at the meeting of July 14, 1921, invited Rancho Manager Julian to appear before the Board and discuss the proposal and how such an expansion might be handled on the ground. At this meeting the Board also formed a committee to investigate the proposal's various implications and profit potential.

It is unclear just what happened in the ensuing five years, but it is clear that the PIC Board was increasingly impatient, and by 1922 Julian's brief term at the helm was done. In December 1922, bringing an end to a string of short-term managers, the Board appointed W. Hugh Baber to the position. In Baber—who came to work on the Rancho as a laborer in 1919 and quickly moved up in the company— the Board found an individual who could act on instructions and add efficiency, quality, energy, and additional, unanticipated benefits.

The western development plan must have been put on hold for want of additional resources, although in this span Baber oversaw expansion and construction of hog and dairy facilities as well as field levelling for installation of new orchards in the northwestern quadrant of the

Rancho. In 1927, the first measures toward western Rancho development were taken when the Board instructed Baber to conduct a pilot program to clear a section of the western timber tract to ascertain total costs and potential yields on a per-acre basis (PIC Minutes 5:57, December 15, 1927). Archival research to date has not discovered Baber's report of findings; however, a positive outcome is indicated by the Board's move six weeks later to investigate the additional income potential of making charcoal (coke) from burned oak wood (PIC Minutes 5:70, February 9, 1928). Around this time, the Board must have given Baber the go-ahead, but the record is unclear, and it is likely that Baber planned the work to begin in the winter of 1928-1929 based on his prior decisions to put timber crews to work in winter in order not to conflict with agricultural production. It is likely that the clear-cut proceeded, but it is also evident from Rancho financial records that the stock market crash of October 1929 severely depressed the dairy, beef, and pork belly markets, hitting the Rancho where it had invested most heavily in the previous seven years, and also undercutting the purpose of western Rancho expansion. Rancho archives revealed a number of stiff measures implemented by the PIC. Baber cut back on staff size, and imposed first a 50-cent and then a one-dollar reduction in daily wages.

After two years Rancho finances stabilized, and the PIC and Baber were clearly inclined to bet on a coming prosperity. Baber's weekly report to the PIC Board of Friday, December 11, 1931 discussed an 11-man team of "timber slashers" kept at work through the winter at $2.00 per day, the crew foreman at a rate of $3.00 per day. According to employment ledgers on file in the Rancho archives, development of the Rancho's western timbered lands became Baber's primary focus, and by 1935 the Rancho annually employed large crews dedicated to clearing the western timber belt. Receipts and shipping manifests on file in Rancho archives indicate that cordwood sales also burgeoned during this period (Figure 25). By 1938 the primary clear-cut work was done. In 1939, Baber committed heavy equipment to the final step necessary to convert the former timberland to productive fields—pulling stumps and burning slash piles (Figure 26). A comparison of aerial photo mosaics (Figures 27 and 28) shows the scale of this effort. In 1922 the Camp 2 Complex was densely overgrown but the same area was sheared to bare earth in 1938, the ground littered with logs and slash piles.

Figure 25. W. Hugh Baber, Llano Seco Ranch manager (from *Condensed History of Butte County, California* by Charles H. Deuel, 1940).

Bottom: Section from Hugh Baber's Friday, November 18, 1932 weekly memorandum to the Parrott Investment Company reporting the sale of cordwood.

```
                                           Llano Seco Rancho,
                                           Friday, November 18 1932.
    WOOD.

        Out of the 397 cords of 4-foot wood cut last summer at a cost of
    {2.00 per cord there remained unsold on the 12th of November 173 cords,
    and this was disposed of to T. J. Dodds of Sacramento at {2.75 per cord
    f.o.b. the ranch, or {475.75 for the lot.

        Mr. Fite, who had charge of the timber slashing operations last
    winter, has been engaged to cut cord wood from this slashing and haul
    it to the headquarters wood yard for a contracted price of {2.50 per
    cord delivered.  He is being given the use of the Fageol truck to
    haul this wood from time to time as he accumulates enough to make
    several loads.  He can haul 4 cords to the load and can make four or
    five trips a day.
```

Ranch Operations

The history of the Project Area built environment is important here because cultural resources related to structures (framed, roofed, fixed human domiciles) and buildings (framed, roofed, fixed storage, work, or animal housing) built in the late-eighteenth through mid-twentieth centuries were identified in Project Area fields making this an important historical context.

None of these features were still standing. Some were marked by well-defined evidence and others by traces that might have been missed except for supporting documentary information found in Rancho archives. Research in the Rancho archives yielded a number of useful sources including: 1) historical maps; 2) historical aerial photo montages; 3) insurance appraisal asset inventories dated 1913 and 1944, the former featuring numerous maps and the later a photographic inventory of structures and buildings; and 4) work orders and reports related to building materials and construction progress. These sources made it possible to define the age, purpose, and composition of four Rancho structure and building complexes described in this section.

Figure 26. Bulldozer clearing stumps from Camp 2, 1939.

Organization and Management
of the Early Rancho

In the first decade of his ownership, John Parrott leased Rancho Llano Seco land for ranches and farms, in some cases to neighboring major land-owners whose Rancho leases allowed them to expanded their operations (for example, the Crouch and Burnham ranches in the eastern Rancho), and in other cases smaller-scale ranches and farms run by capable individuals, many of whom appear to have settled with their families and built homes on the Rancho. Dr. George Griffith, a former medical doctor who surrendered his practice in order to live a quiet life on the Rancho, was the first manager, serving a dual function as general manager and accountant. Around 1871, Parrott modified the organizing principal and retained A. B. Collins at a rate of $100.00 per month to serve as the Rancho's first manager for farm and ranch operations, to work alongside Griffith who then focused on financial records and fiscal management. An 1877 summary of major Butte County ranches described the Parrott operation:

> "Llano Seco Rancho" the property of John Parrott, Esq., is situated on the Sacramento river, with a frontage of six miles on the river, with landings for steamboats by which the immense grain crop of the ranch is easily transported to market. The ranch runs back from the river about four miles. There is now in cultivation about 14,000 acres, principally in wheat. On the ranch are about 6,000 sheep, 400 head of cattle, 200 horses and mules, and about 800 head of hogs. There is a large and commodious farmhouse and a large number of out-buildings for storage of farming tools and products. On the place is a blacksmith shop and carpenter shop where all ordinary repairs are made. A steam mill for grinding feed is also in operation. Water is pumped by horse-power and distributed about the buildings and grounds. There are several hundred fruit trees and all necessary requisites for a pleasant home. The ranch is in charge of A. B. Collins as superintendent, who has taken care of the place for six years past. Dr. Griffith has acted as book-keeper on the place for sixteen years past, and has been largely identified with its successful management. (Smith & Elliott 1877, 14)

Griffith's accounting ledgers from 1875-1877 show continued income from the major leaseholders, but also the presence of five foremen, each overseeing a different farm or ranch operation consisting of a specific field or set of fields engaged in specific economic activities. The five, Hercules Vermette, C.P. Hale, William Smith, Andrew Jackson, and William D. Martin probably all began living and working on the Rancho around 1862, after Parrott first acquired control of the Rancho. Each lent their names to and probably cleared timber from specific field complexes in the current Project Area where they appear on the 1874 John Parrott Map. Eventually, the ranch and

75

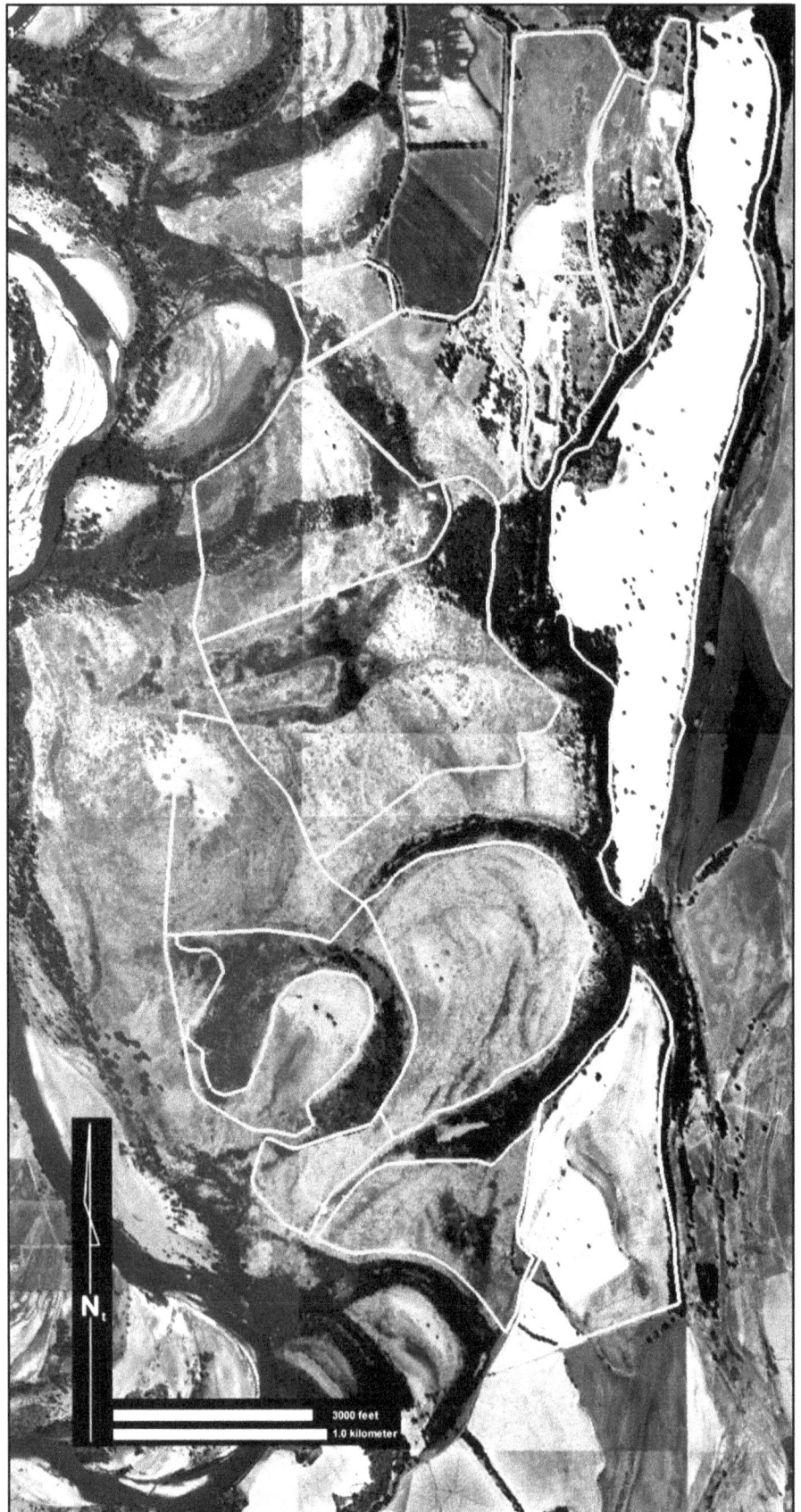

Figure 27. 1922 Chambers aerial photo montage of the Llano Seco Project Area showing the dense western timber stands little changed from their 19th century status.

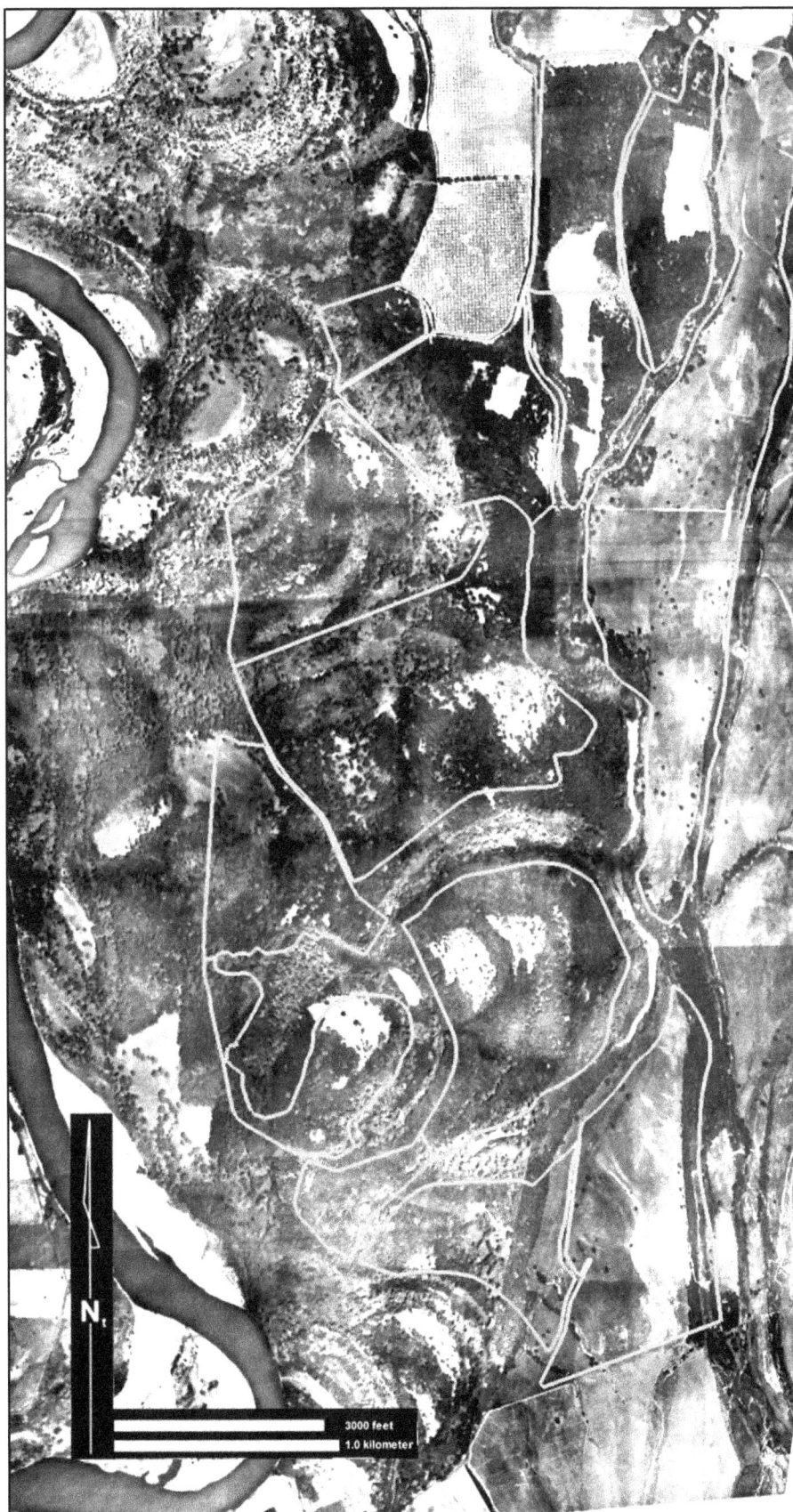

Figure 28. 1938 USGS aerial photo montage of the Llano Seco Project Area showing the western timber clear-cut and reduced to stumps and slash piles (adapted from sacramentoriver.org).

farm operations faded but the field names lived on. Built environment features associated with each are described below

The Milk Ranch

William D. Martin, listed with his wife and five children in the 1860 U.S. Census for Butte County, appears to have been among the first ranch foremen retained by John Parrott in 1862, and his name is commemorated in Martin 1–3 fields immediately adjoining the north end of Hale Field. Owing to a lack of documentary evidence from this time frame, the exact nature and duration of Martin's early role on the Rancho is uncertain. No payroll or financial ledgers predating 1875 are known to exist. However, The Martin family cemetery is located in Graveyard Field 0.8 miles (1.3 kilometers) northeast of the north end of Hale Field in a small valley oak grove. Grave markers associated with the cemetery commemorate the loss of Martin's wife Minerva and three Martin children in the period 1866–1870 (Cross 2001). The presence of his family on the Rancho clearly indicates Martin was a resident. Based on proximity of the cemetery and named fields it is likely that the Milk Ranch, situated in-between the Martin Fields and Martin Cemetery, was originally managed by William D. Martin. It is likely that the Milk Ranch began in the 1860s as the original Martin headquarters and was later expanded to accommodate the Rancho's principal dairy. However, this expansion took place at a time when Martin's role

diminished after the loss of his wife and children. Ledger entries dated 1875-1877 show that William Martin was by then working for the Rancho as a laborer at a rate of $1.16 per hour. The entries also show that his hours were uneven and irregular, indicating he had a steadily declining role on the Rancho in the 1870s, and his role on the Rancho probably terminated completely sometime between 1877 and 1880; he is not listed as an employee of the Rancho in the U.S. Census of 1880, and instead he is listed in the 1880 census for the Chico Precinct as a single, white laborer aged 53.

The Milk Ranch was located along the Jacinto-Dayton Road near its junction with a spur connecting to the Butte City Road, which may have accommodated sales and deliveries to Chico and other markets. The 1875-1877 ledgers list David Wiseman as Milk Ranch foreman, and in this capacity he managed sales and purchases. Dairy products were the Milk Ranch's principal focus, although the ledgers also tally earnings from egg, chicken, and hog sales and expenses related to feed and building materials (Figure 29). The Milk Ranch served as the Rancho's principal dairy through at least the early 1880s, but was probably swept away by fire and replaced by a new Main Dairy operation located in the west Rancho sometime in the late 1880s or 1890s. The 1907 Abbey M. Parrott Map shows the original complex reduced to two "Old Barns" (Figure 30) and the 1922 Chambers aerial mosaic shows a single barn and corral (Figure 31).

Llano Seco thresher, c. 1900. Written on the back of the photograph: "12 mules pulled the thresher, 10 mules saved up sacks of grain, and 4 more mules." (Larry V. Richardson collection, CSU, Chico, Special Collections 18273)

Vermette Ranch

Hercules Vermette was among the first foremen engaged by John Parrott after his acquisition of the Rancho in 1862 and he held this position until 1901. Guinn provides the following biographical summary:

Hercules Vermette. Third in order of birth and the eldest son in a French-Canadian family of thirteen children, Mr. Vermette early learned the lesson of self-reliance. His father, Augustine Vermette, and his mother, formerly Clarice Marchand, were both natives of Canada, in which country they spent their entire lives, the father being a farmer at St. Justin, near Quebec, where Hercules Vermette was born, October 20, 1837, receiving a limited education in the common schools, and at the age of fourteen helping his father to clear his farm. In 1852 he came to California, making the trip by way of the Isthmus of Panama and for several years after his arrival worked in the gold mines at Downieville, Laporte and other places, coming in 1862 to the Parrott grant, in the Sacramento Valley, to take charge of nine thousand sheep, seven hundred cattle and five hundred head of horses and mules. He remained in this responsible position for thirty-nine years, when, deciding to engage in independent farming, he rented two hundred and fifteen acres which he cultivated until 1900,

when he came to his present home, having purchased the property in 1898. Here he has a nice home ranch of one hundred and sixty acres, lying eight miles south of Chico and one miles south of Dayton, where he is engaged in general farming, the cultivation of wheat and barley and the raising of stock.

In Oroville, CA, Mr. Vermette married Amy Casey, a native of Rock Island, Ill. having been born there August 16, 1852. Her father, John Casey, was a native of Ireland, who immigrated to Illinois and engaged in railroad work with the Chicago Rock Island and Illinois Railway Company. His death occurred in early life and his daughter came to California with friends in 1877, locating at Chico. Mr. Casey's, family were Catholics. To Mr. and Mrs. Vermette have been born four children, as follows: Mary Louise, Marie Clarice, Albert Charles and Margaret Emma. With the exception of Marie Clarice, who died at the age of eleven years, all of the children are at home. Vermette is a Democrat in politics and fraternally is a member of long standing in the Independent Order of Odd Fellows. (1902, 1149-1150)

Like Martin, Vermette and his wife raised a family on the Rancho and given the presence of his family and possession of significant ranching responsibilities,

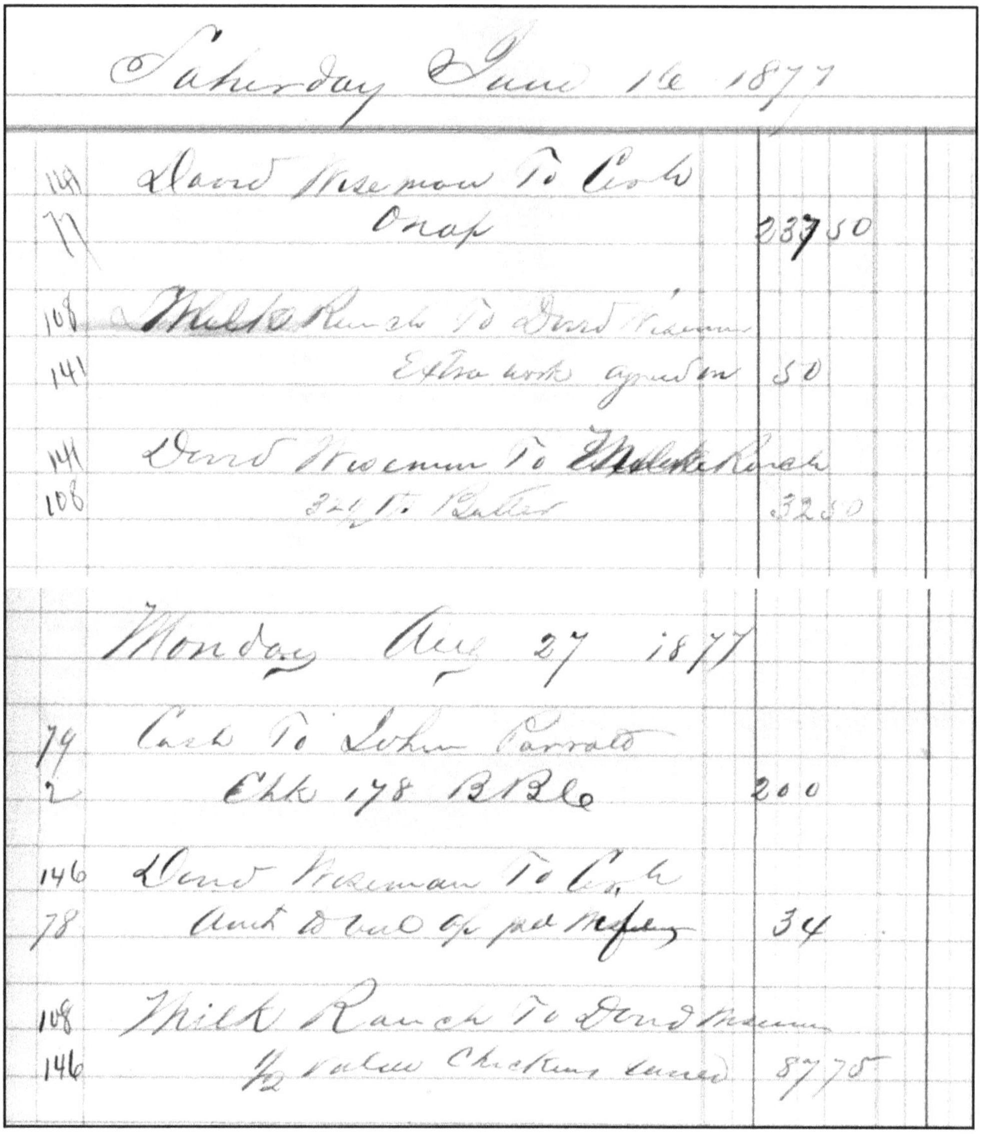
Saturday June 16 1877

Milk Ranch To David Wiseman
Extra work agreed on 50

Monday Aug 27 1877

Cash To John Parrott
Chk 178 B.R.Co 200

Milk Ranch To David Wiseman
1/2 value Chickens 87 75

Figure 29. 1877 Milk Ranch ledger entries.

he clearly would have required a domicile and ranch headquarters. Vermette's ranch was identified in two sources on file with the Rancho archives, the 1913 Polk Map where it is plotted as a filled square situated near the southwest border of Vermet Field, and captured in the 1922 Chambers Aerial mosaic where it is plainly visible in this location as a four-building ranch complex with two large corrals (Figure 32).

The 1875-1877 Rancho ledger tallies Vermette's wage of $50.00 per month, and he is frequently listed in the ledger immediately second to Ranch Manager A. B. Collins (e.g., Figure 33). By comparing the Guinn (1902) and Smith & Elliott (1877) quotes appearing above, it is evident that Vermette oversaw most of the Rancho's sheep, cattle, and working horse and mule pasture operations during his tenure, apparently having no role in hog and dairy production. Vermette's ledger entries also tally cash advances and recompense for tobacco, whiskey, and other sundries indicating he was responsible for Vaqueros and a bunkhouse; a Chinese cook and his food and related expenses are also frequently listed in the ledger alongside Vermette, suggesting the bunkhouse merited a mess and cook.

The location of the Vermette bunkhouse is uncertain. The 1922 Chambers Aerial image depicts a ranch house, a barn, and smaller outbuildings likely to represent a pump house and tack rooms, and does not depict a structure large enough to house a crew.

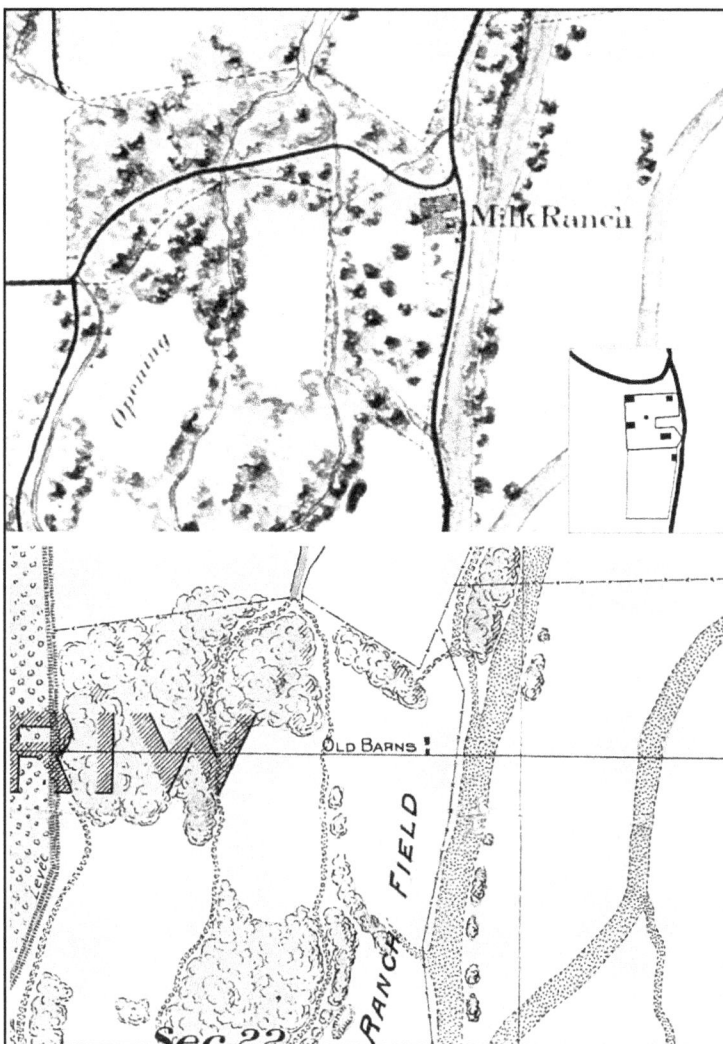

Figure 30. The Milk Ranch, 1874–1907.

Top: As depicted in the 1874 John Parrott Map showing the Milk Ranch in full operation, marked by one structure, five buildings, and a feed lot corral.

Bottom: The 1907 Abby M. Parrott Map showing the original six-building dairy and corral complex reduced to two "Old Barns."

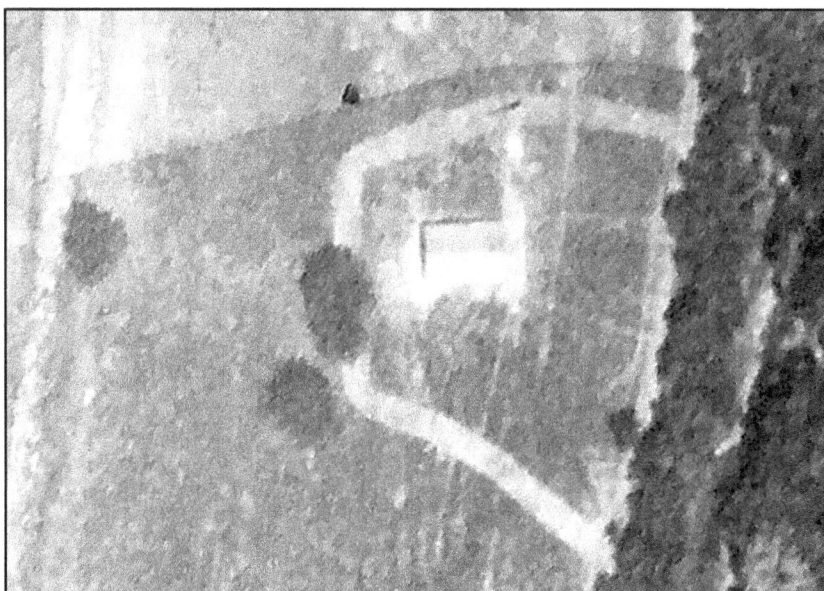

Figure 31. The 1922 Chambers Aerial mosaic showing a single standing barn and a portion of the corral still intact. The oak tree immediately west of the barn is standing today.

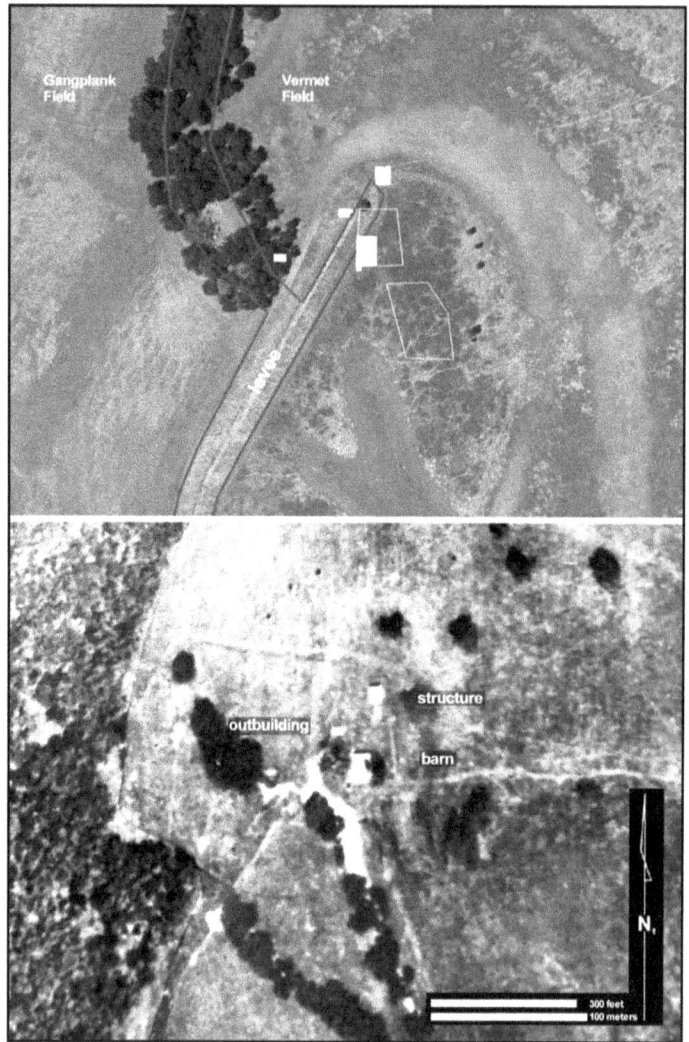

Figure 32. Vermette Ranch.

Top–Modern aerial showing georeferenced locations of Vermette Ranch features

Bottom–Vermette Ranch complex as depicted in the 1922 Chambers Aerial montage.

Figure 33. Rancho ledger payroll entry for September 29, 1877, showing Ranch Manager A. B. Collins at $100.00 per month and H. Vermette at $50.00 per month.

Reports, ledger entries, and other documents and notes contained in the Rancho archives show a shift in the field name over time. The 1875-1877 ledger entries list his name as "Vermette" or "Vermett." After he left the Rancho in 1901 during John Parrott II's management, Rancho crop maps and production tallies at first listed the field name as Vermette, but by 1919 the "Vermett" spelling predominated, and after 1939, as the administrative memory of Hercules Vermette's contribution to the early Rancho faded from memory, the field was listed as "Vermet."

The 1910 U.S. census for Butte County, California listed farmer Hercules Vermette aged 73, wife Amy Vermette aged 57, daughter Mary L. aged 28, son Albert J. aged 22, and daughter Margaret M., aged 19, all living at home. Hercules Vermette died in 1926 and Amy Vermette died in 1928. Son Albert J. Vermette died in Chico in 1959.

Jackson and Miller Fields

The 1874 John Parrott Map shows three named openings, one "Jackson" field and two "Miller" fields, situated in the Camp 2 Complex fields.

The Jackson field was 16 acres in extent and was traversed by one of two Jacinto Ferry-Newhart Landing spurs. The Miller fields were 50 acres in extent and were connected by the second Jacinto-Newhart spur. An earlier section speculated that these three named fields—Newhart, Miller, and Jackson—might represent the names of squatters dating to the era of absentee owners and uncertain legal claims between 1852 and 1861, and supporting evidence related to Newhart and Fox was presented indicating these individuals were engaged in production and sale of cordwood. The roads to Newhart Landing and proximity of the landing just 1.6 miles (2.7 kilometers) west must have facilitated transport of oak cordwood to the landing for sale to the steamship companies.

Four individuals named Jackson, all related, appear in the 1860 U.S. Census for the Chico Township, Alex Jackson, aged 24, a laborer from Tennessee, Joseph Jackson, aged 20, a laborer from Tennessee, and Alex's wife Sarah Jackson, aged 22, and Alex's and Sarah's daughter Elizabeth Jackson, aged 3. Only one Jackson appears in the 1875-1877 ledger, Andrew Jackson, who appeared once on April 16, 1876 for a 50-cent claim on account. It cannot be determined if Alex, Joseph, or Andrew Jackson bear any relationship to the Project Area's Jackson Field.

Only one Miller is listed in the 1860 U.S. Census for the Chico Township, a man aged 24 engaged as a laborer on another ranch. Similarly, no Newhart or Newhard was listed in the census, suggesting the pattern may have been deliberate and related to uncertainties of occupancy, that is, if they were squatters they may have avoided the census-takers.

No structures or buildings associated with the Miller or Jackson fields appear in the 1874 John Parrott Map or 1907 Abbey M. Parrott Map, and no building or structure traces are visible in the 1922 Chambers Aerial.

All considered, if we are correct that the Miller and Jackson openings were produced by squatters between 1844 and 1860, and if the squatters established camps or residences in these areas, then the archaeological evidence could be among the Rancho's oldest non-Indian historical traces. Positive evidence of early historical occupation has already been identified by a recent archaeological investigation of the Rancho's Newhart Landing area for the US Fish and Wildlife Service (White 2014B). In addition to the potential early historical features, it should be noted here that late eighteenth- and early to mid-twentieth century historical resources could be found in the Miller and Jackson field areas. For example, the road spurs depicted on the 1874 John Parrott Map served wagon, horseback, and stock-drive traffic to and from Rancho Headquarters and to the steamship landing and remote farms and pastures through 1913. The east spur crossing through Project Area field Stump Camp South also served as the Rancho access road to Vermette Ranch.

In the 1938 CADWR Aerial, the first aerials photographed after the comprehensive Camp 2 clear-cuts, several historical features are evident that have potential archaeological associations. Notably, a grassy patch is evident representing the location of the original Jackson field, and the 1874 Jacinto-Newhart spur passing through the Jackson field was also clearly visible. One interesting feature was a small cluster of four or five large trees deliberately left standing, presumably per instructions from Ranch Manager Hugh Baber, in the otherwise clear-cut landscape. These trees are visible in aerial photos dating through the 1958 CADWR Aerial, suggesting the trees were preserved because they served to shade a camp or cattle post still in use through the mid-twentieth century. Rancho senior staffer Shannon Samuelson reported that the tree cluster was identified as "Stump Camp" or "East Camp" and was still used as a work camp and cattle shade prior to full-scale tilling of Stump Camp South Field in the late 1970s.

Camp 2 Cattle Operation: Structures and Buildings

Project Area Camp 2 West Field encloses the clearing labelled "Miller" on the 1847 John Parrott Map. No historical record was found of a Miller occupation; however, the Rancho archives did produce evidence of built resources associated with Miller Field, the earliest depicted on the 1922 Chambers Aerial. Several lines of evidence identify this as "Camp 2," a cattle operation which apparently originated in the late nineteenth-century and developed and augmented after the 1932-1939 clear-cuts. Sharing a crop plan with most of the newly opened western fields, after 1939 the Camp 2 Complex fields—Stump Camp North, Stump Camp South, and Camp 2 West—were managed as one major beef cattle operation headquartered at Camp 2.

Sometime between 1939 and 1942, concurrent with agricultural intensification of the western fields, Ranch manager Hugh Baber constructed a new Camp 2 headquarters complex). Plainly visible as fully developed and operational on the 1942 USBR/USACE Aerial and the 1947 USGS Aerial, the layout and function of the Camp 2 buildings was detailed in an amended insurance coverage map filed by the PIC with the A. R. Johnson Insurance Company of San Francisco in February 1953. The map, confirmed by detailed aerials from the 1942-1970 time frame, consisted of the original large, polygon-shaped feed lot measuring 220 feet north-south by 255 feet east-west, a large "L"-shaped, single-story wood framed "boarding house" or bunkhouse measuring 55 x 20, a large single-story tack shed, and a well and tank house. By 1955, the entire southwest quadrant of the Rancho, inclusive to the current Oil Well Complex fields, was identified as "Camp 2" and the fields were used for a mix of grain (mostly, wheat and barley), hay, and pasture. The Camp 2 beef cattle headquarters, including the bunkhouse, buildings, and corral, as well as the former main road route was demolished and the site plowed-under shortly after Baber's death in 1968, and the entire field was turned over to grain production (Figure 34).

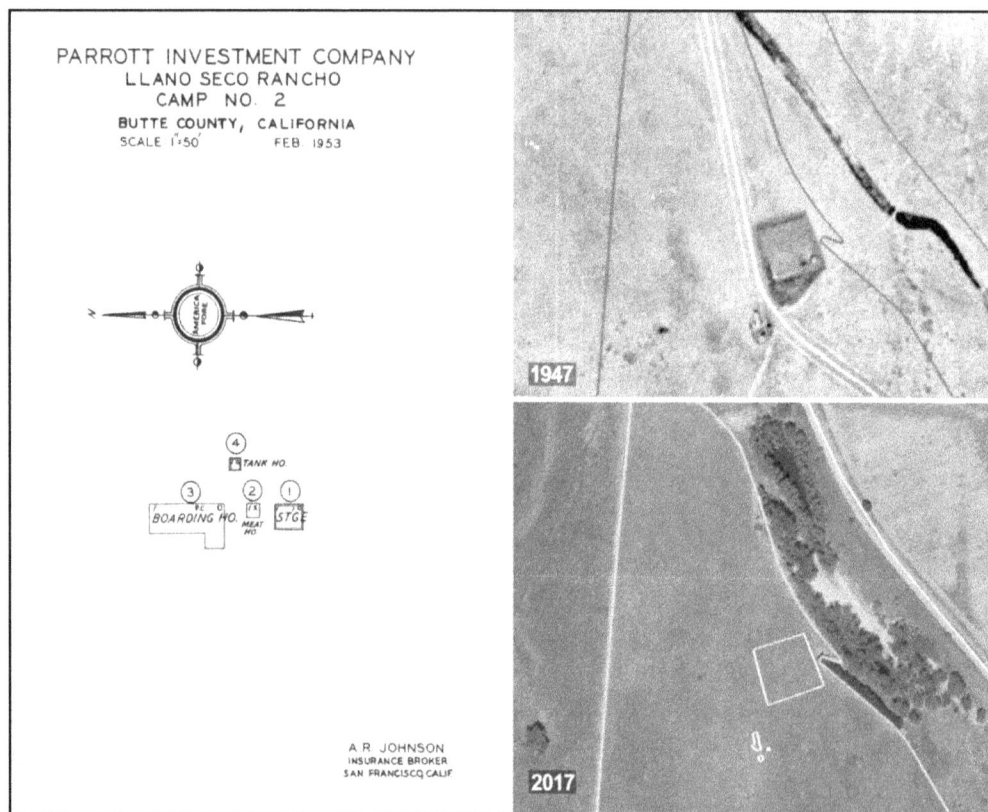

Figure 34. Location and composition of the 1939–1972 Camp 2 beef cattle operation, current Camp 2 West field.

Natural Gas Production

Geological Context

Layers of sediment extend thousands of feet below the surface of the Sacramento Valley, and these layers record a shift from marine to terrestrial rocks. About 170 million years ago the edge of the North American continent was in the area now occupied by the Sierra Nevada mountain range. The Sacramento Valley's deepest rocks are marine continental shelf debris including marine turbidites and deltaic sedimentary deposits washed down from the ancient mountain range. Around 130 million years ago, continental plates crashing together resulted in the folding and uplift of older seafloor deposits which were added to the continent and produced the Coast Ranges. This created a seaway depression behind the Coast Ranges which collected alluvium derived from the erosion of surrounding uplands, eventually filling the depression to form the Sacramento Valley. The valley has been a land-bound freshwater basin for about 40 million years (Almgren 1978; Harwood and Helley 1987; Olmstead and Davis 1961). Natural gas fields have been identified and developed in the Sacramento Valley since the 1920s. These deposits are buried between 0.5 and 1.25 miles (0.8–2.0 kilometers) deep, and they are associated with Upper Cretaceous sands dating approximately 80 million years old and partially contained in layers of shale produced at the end of the seaway phase, when the valley was a shallow, productive inland sea and marsh.

Early Leases

In the late 1930s, one of the State's largest natural gas fields—the Willows-Beehive Bend Gas Field— was discovered and developed just 5.0 miles (8.0 kilometers) west of the Llano Seco Project area in the Jacinto area of Glenn County. The Jacinto wells tapped gas in Upper Cretaceous "Forbes Formation" marine shale, siltstone, and interbedded sandstone deposits at a depth of 6,000 feet (Alkire 1968; Barrett 1967; Bowen 1962, 105–109). Standard works on the petroleum geology of Northern California state that the Llano Seco Rancho natural gas deposits were discovered and developed in 1954–1955 (Bowen 1962; Harding in Bowen 1962). However, documentary evidence on file in the Rancho archives demonstrates that drilling and geophysical exploration actually began 20 years earlier, concurrent with the first wells drilled in the Willows-Beehive Bend Gas Field.

Probably based on a growing body of geological evidence for widespread Forbes Formation deposits, concurrent with the Jacinto discovery, in March, 1936, San Francisco investment banker Charles R. Blythe approached the PIC Board with an application for a lease of 5,243 acres for natural gas prospecting on Rancho Llano Seco (PIC Minutes 6:138–139). After review and further negotiations, the lease was approved in October 1936 (PIC Minutes 6:145). Research in the Rancho archives failed to turn up a map, contract, or physical description related to this lease, but it can be assumed that the drilling took place in the western part of the Rancho where the geology was comparable to that found in the Jacinto-Beehive Bend gas field. Since Blythe was a money-man, not an oil-man, he must have engaged a petroleum company to do the drilling. The PIC received a first-year lease check from Blythe in December, 1936 (PIC Minutes 6:147). After expiration of the Blythe lease, in May 1942, the PIC received a request from W. B. McLeod of McLeod Oil asking for a lease of 1,161 acres for the purpose of drilling for oil and gas (PIC Minutes 8:4), and in October 1942 the PIC Board approved an oil and gas lease of 5,200 acres to William Myron Keck's Superior Oil Company (PIC Minutes 8:28). No records were found pertaining to the outcome of the Blythe, McLeod, and Superior leases, but there is also no evidence of a second-year renewal for any of the leases and no record of gas production in the petroleum industry literature, suggesting either that these leases were not fulfilled by drilling or the first prospects were unsuccessful.

General Petroleum

The straight-to-drill approach and lack of prospection was typical of early oil and gas exploration and resulted in low rates of success. In January 1943, General Petroleum Corporation (GPC, a subsidiary of Socony, later absorbed by Mobil Oil Company, and in turn by Exxon) addressed this concern by approaching the PIC Board with a proposal to conduct a geophysical operation on the Rancho employing newly-developed reflection seismography technology (PIC Minutes 6:138). The PIC Board approved this lease, but also based on prior experience spelled out a number of terms: strict limits on the times and locations of use of explosive shot, coordination with Ranch Manager Baber on dates and locations in order not to conflict with animal and agricultural operations, strict observance of fire prevention practices, and strict observance of limits on damage to fields and roads (PIC Minutes 6:146). Research in the Rancho archives failed to turn up a map, contract, or physical descriptions related to this lease; however, word of potential finds must have leaked out to the petroleum industry. In September 1943, R. P. Hopper applied for an oil and gas lease (PIC Minutes 8:66), in November of that year H. H. Magee of Amalgamated Oil also applied (PIC Minutes 8:68), and in February 1944, Standard Oil Company of California applied for a lease to perform new geophysical work (PIC Minutes 8:81). The PIC Board denied the Hopper and Magee requests but approved Standard Oil's, contingent on terms similar to those written into the General Petroleum agreement.

Llano Seco Well No. 1 and No. 2

Based on analysis of their geophysical results, GPC approached the PIC with a specific proposal for drilling within a lease area of approximately 1,000 acres, situated in cattle range on the south end of Camp 2, in current Oil Well Island and Oil Well West Fields (PIC Minutes 8:123). The first well, named "Llano Seco No. 1," was dug in November-December 1946. According to a PIC report, GPC successfully:

> drilled a well to a depth of 5,000 feet, but had been compelled to cease drilling operations because its rig was not heavy enough and that to move a heavier rig to the well during the rainy season would be difficult and costly. (PIC Minutes 8:150)

Consequently, GPC abandoned Llano Seco No. 1. Llano Seco No. 2 was dug in early summer 1947. The No. 2 well pad and rig are visible in USGS aerial photographs taken on June 13, 1947, accessed from the Sacramento River Forum's online Geospatial Library (sacramentoriver. org 2018), situated on the west edge of Oil Well Island Field adjacent to Bundle Lake. Notably, the 1947 aerial is sufficiently detailed to identify the rig, holding pond, lab, and material storage tanks, and an improved access road routed around Camp 2 (Figure 35). Probably based on geological mapping of the Willows-Beehive Bend finds where gas was up to 6,000 feet deep, by July, 1947 Llano Seco No. 2 reached a depth of 8,306 feet, still the deepest well ever drilled in the Rancho. This well did not produce but did serve to map stratigraphy. Later mapping (Harding in Bowen 1962) determined that Llano Seco No. 2 had penetrated more than 3,500 feet beyond the gas-bearing sand, ultimately tapping Upper Cretaceous

Sites Formation marine turbidites and continental debris. The GPC effort appears to have ended in uncertainty. The Minutes of the Meeting of the Board of Directors of Parrott Investment Company, August 28, 1947 noted that:

> The President advised the Board that the General Petroleum Co. was arranging to with draw [*sic*] all its machinery from the Ranch and that, under the circumstances, did not want their lease extended. (PIC Minutes 9:20)

In a reversal, an entry dated November 26, 1947 documents the PIC Board's approval of GPC's request for an additional 60 days for the drilling of a new well (PIC Minutes 9:32). General Petroleum later asked for a three-year extension, and this was also granted, securing rights through fall 1950 (PIC Minutes 9:48). No evidence was found for a third well, and there is no record of gas production any time between 1947 and 1950.

In anticipation of GPC's lease expiration, in October 1950 the Texas Oil Company (parent company of Texaco, Inc.) applied for a gas well lease (PIC Minutes 9:140); discussion and investigation by the PIC Board continued through the following month (PIC Minutes 9:141) leading to rejection of the application based on disagreement over acreage lease fees and the royalty rates. With no productive wells in place, natural gas development was on hold for two years until April 1952, when Honolulu Oil Company requested a five-year lease agreement for geophysical exploration (PIC Minutes 10:37). In the same meeting, Ranch Manager Hugh Baber reported a recent communication from GPC also requesting a new lease for geophysical exploration. Based on GPC's excellent compliance with prior lease provisions, on April 24, 1952 the PIC Board voted to deny the Honolulu Oil Company request and—pending negotiations regarding royalty provisions of the agreement—approve the GPC lease (PIC Minutes 10:39).

Mapping and Development

In May 1953, immediately after conclusion of the GPC lease, Humble Oil & Refining Company (HOC) approached the PIC Board with a gas well lease proposal (PIC Minutes 10:94). Negotiations for a one-year lease at one-sixth royalties continued through the summer, and an agreement was executed in September (PIC Minutes

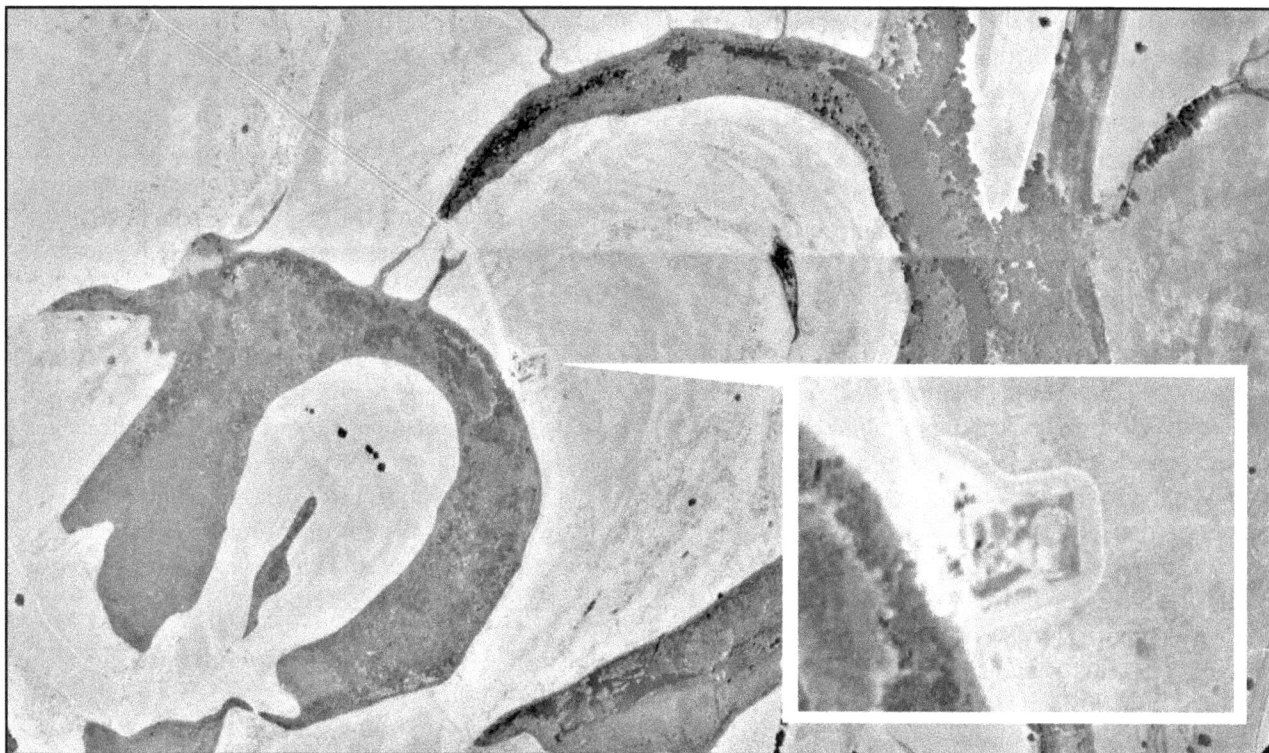

Figure 35. GPC's Llano Seco No. 2, visible in USGS aerial photo dated June 13, 1947.

10:106). HOC focused drilling in the same area drilled by GPC, and used the combined well log and geophysical data to complete a more accurate geological model and pinpoint the gas-bearing deposits. This effort defined two gas fields, the "Llano Seco Gas Field" centered near the current Project Area's Oil Well Complex fields, and the "Perkins Lake Gas Field" centered near the current Project Area's Martin Complex fields. Definition and stratigraphic mapping of the two gas fields was accomplished by petroleum geologist Tod P. Harding:

> Production is from the Upper Cretaceous Estes and Sannar sands at a depth of approximately 3,300 feet. Structurally, the field is on a broad, symmetrical north-trending anticline. The larger Perkins Lake field, discovered in September, 1955, produces from the lower Eocene "Perkins Lake" sand at depths ranging from 3,365 to 3,505 feet. The structure is an elongate, northeast-trending anticline. Stratigraphically, the two fields are quite dissimilar. The Llano Seco field has an almost normal sequence of lower Eocene and Upper Cretaceous beds, whereas the Perkins Lake field, being in an Eocene erosional gorge, has a lower Eocene section

which is greatly thickened at the expense of the Upper Cretaceous section. The pronounced unconformity at the base of the Eocene is found 1,300-1,800 feet lower at Perkins Lake than at Llano Seco, whereas within the Cretaceous the two fields are nearly flat structurally. (Bowen 1962, 216)

HOC's second well produced gas, and as a result focused more resources on the area. In response, the PIC Board ordered a new civil survey of the southwest corner of the Rancho in order to generate a better definition of Rancho boundaries in the area, cast into doubt by recent Sacramento River migration (PIC Minutes 10:153). HOC dug at least nine wells on Rancho lands between 1954 and 1958, and four produced gas. Commercial gas deliveries began in July 1957 (Bowen 1962, 105–109). In November 1959, the HOC lease was reassigned based on HOC's merger with Standard Oil of New Jersey (PIC Minutes 12:88). Notably, around this same time GPC assets were acquired by SOCONY-Mobil Oil Company.

HOC-Standard filed a quitclaim on the Rancho lease in January 1961, and at this point the PIC Board took a new tack, generating separate leases for the Perkins Lake Gas

Field, the Llano Seco Gas Field, and exploration of other parts of the Rancho. That same month the Board was approached by Franco-Western Oil Company (FWOC) regarding lease rights in the Bedrock and Goose Camp fields west of the current Project Area (PIC Minutes 12:189). FWOC filed a quitclaim in August 1963 (PIC Minutes 13:169), and Westrep Oil Company and Jade Oil Company sought this lease in 1963 (PIC Minutes 13:170 and 14:65, 70, 72, 78, 143).

The PIC Board also soon accepted new proposals for leases on the Llano Seco Gas Field, and in April 1961 favorably reviewed a lease proposal submitted by A. A. Hopkins, President of the Sacramento Oil and Gas Company (SOGC), described in the Board report as an "outstanding oil and gas geologist" and his company a "small and recently incorporated firm" (PIC Minutes 12:207). A three-year term was discussed with the acreage fees waived for the first year contingent on one-fifth royalties (PIC Minutes 12:207, 232). SOGC's first two wells, completed in December 1961, produced gas and further defined the Llano Seco Gas Field reserves. SOGC subsequently sublet the lease, first to Neaves Petroleum (1962–1964), then to Gant Oil (1965), and California-Time Petroleum (1965–1968). In this period the PIC minutes reflect increasing impatience with SOGC's sublet practices, and in two instances denied SOGC's lease renewal pending reimbursement for crop and road damage, sludge pit backfilling, and fulfillment of other cleanup provisions of the existing lease agreement (PIC Minutes 14:131). In June 1967, the Board sought counsel's advice on the matter and inserted a new clause in the SOGC lease specifying that no sublet could take place without written permission from the PIC Board (PIC Minutes 15:45). In July 1967, the Board added additional provisions requiring a minimum 5,000-foot drill depth and a $20,000.00 deposit, to be returned if the well was dry (PIC Minutes 15:51).

A 1962 California Division of Mines and Geology publication on the gas and oil fields of California reported that 10 wells had been drilled in the Llano Seco Gas Field. Five of the wells were completed, and all five were producing gas from the center of the field, centered over the southwest corner of the Rancho in the vicinities of the current Project Area's Oil Well North, Oil Well South, Oil Well West, Little Grant, and Fish Camp Fields. As of 1962, the five wells produced 2,241,763,000 cubic feet of gas, at an average of 1,119,000 cubic feet per day, with peak production of 1,207,119,000 cubic feet in 1957 (Bowen 1962, 105–109).

By the late 1960s the Llano Seco Gas Field was 10 years past its peak and production tailed off annually. In September 1968 California-Time Petroleum quitclaimed its sublet back to SOGC. This prompted the Board to again inform SOGC of its responsibility for damaged roads, to be repaired as a condition of any new well agreements. (PIC Minutes 15:185). In 1972, SOCONY-Mobil Oil was acquired by Exxon, and in 1973, Exxon acquired the Humble-Standard assets and proceeded to clear up legal issues potentially attached to the Rancho wells, filing quitclaims when the field was closed in 1980, on file in the Rancho archives. The quitclaims filed at this time specified that all remaining equipment including tanks, compressor gear, and pipelines were the property of the PIC for salvage or repurpose.

In June, 1975, Western Geophysical Company of America filed a lease request with the Board and received permission to complete an extensive reflection seismology grid spanning the western reach of the Rancho in an effort to define previously undiscovered reserves. No records were found of the outcome but it was apparently unsuccessful since no new wells were dug and no new leases were secured.

Summary

- Wells. In preparation for the field investigation, a thorough assessment was made of all documents, physical descriptions, and maps associated with gas exploration and production in the Rancho archives. This effort benefited from the identification of maps filed by Humble Oil in 1954, GPC in 1974, and two undated, hand-plotted 1:150,000 maps, one compiling the locations of all SOGC wells probably filed with PIC in 1968, and another plotting all wells combined probably filed with PIC by Exxon in 1980. Both of the latter maps were wildly inaccurate and served better as a general guide and inventory. Following up, to the extent possible all physical locations were confirmed by aerial photo analysis, and in several cases well locations and conveyance alignments were confirmed. There were 32 confirmed wells, 15 of which produced gas and 17 dry. Gas wells were dug in nine of the Project Area's 15 fields, the majority dug in a block formed by the Stump Camp South, Oil Well Island, and Oil Well West

Fields. These fields also yielded the majority of the productive wells and contained most of the gas pipelines.

- Pipelines and Compressor Facilities. Owing to poor documentation it was frequently difficult to identify the original locations of conveyance pipelines and compressor/holding tank facilities. In November, 1958, PG&E filed and was granted an easement for a gathering line connecting well lines to a central pump and compressor, probably situated in west-central Oil Well Island Field. In May, 1962, PG&E approached the PIC Board seeking an easement for a gas main to connect the two productive SOGC wells to this same compressor facility (PIC Minutes 13:58). Aerial photo analysis indicates that gas lines originating from all productive Little Grant Complex gas wells were routed to the compressor/holding tank facility located in the west-central Oil Well Island Field, the facility still today marked by an elevated fill pad square in plain view measuring 195 feet north-south by 180 feet east-west and still marked by thick concrete pads and scrap pipe. Aerial photographs indicate this facility was built after 1958 and before 1970, and the timing here indicates it was built by SOGC.

A 1974 Exxon map shows an additional PG&E gathering line routed along the Rancho's main access road from Martin 3 Field to a Mobil/Exxon compressor/heater facility located on the northwest margin of Martin 2 Field. As the fields developed, gas from the Oil Well Island and Martin 2 compressors was pumped via the large PG&E gathering line routed along the main access road and north through Lake field, outside the present Project Area. Diagonal orange-white striped gas line warning signs are still in place marking the route of a gathering line from a well situated near the west-central river bank in the USFWS Llano Seco Riparian Sanctuary to the east where it crosses the main access road and holding the same bearing through the northwest corner of Stump Camp South Field, through the southwest corner of Stump Camp North Field, bisecting Martin 3 Field diagonally and joining the gathering line buried along the main access road shoulder as described. This pipeline is clearly still in-place but its status is unknown.

The original concrete pads, some steel mounts, and some rigging for the Martin 2 plant are still in-place readily visible immediately adjacent to the main Project Area access road. The 1974 map also shows that gas from two wells in the Martin Complex fields was routed in 2.5-inch flow lines buried 3.0 feet deep to this compressor facility. Long-time Rancho employees tell me that these pipelines were dug out in the 1980s in anticipation of deep tilling for irrigated row crops in the Martin Complex, Camp 2 Complex, and Little Grant Complex fields. Some of the pipes were found during the current survey, two located in the timbered east margin of Martin 1 Field and 10 piled on the concrete pad in west-central Oil Well Island Field.

REFERENCES CITED

Adam, D.P., and G.J. West. 1983. "Temperature and Precipitation Estimates Through the Last Glacial Cycle from Clear Lake, California, Pollen Data." *Science* 219 (4581): 168-170.

Alkire, J. 1968. "Natural Gases of North America, Volume One, Chapter F. Willows-Beehive Bend Gas Field: Occurrence of Natural Gas in Mesozoic Rocks of Northern California (Abstract)." *American Association of Petroleum Geologists Memoirs*:639–642.

Almgren, A. 1978. Timing of Tertiary Submarine Canyons and Marine Cycles of Deposition in the Southern Sacramento Valley, California. In *Sedimentation in Submarine Canyons, Fans, and Trenches*, edited by D.J. Stanley and G. Kelling. Dowden, Hutchinson, and Roth.

Bates, Craig. n.d. "Personal Research Notes." Manuscript on-file, tribal offices of the Mechoopda Tribe of Chico Rancheria.

Barrett, D. E. 1957. "History of Exploration and Development of Willows-Beehive Bend Gas Field" (Abstract). *American Association of Petroleum Geologists* 41 (2): 350–352.

Bauer Jr., William J. 2009. *We Were All Like Migrant Workers Here*. University of North Carolina Press.

Bayham, F.E. and K.L. Johnson. 1990. *Archaeological Investigations at CA-GLE-105: A Multicomponent Site Along the Sacramento River, Glenn County, California. Prepared for the US Army Corps of Engineers, Sacramento District.* Northeast Information Center of the California Historical Resources Information System, California State University, Chico.

Beals, R. L. 1933. "Ethnology of the Nisenan." *University of California Publications in American Archaeology and Ethnology* 31(6): 335-414.

Bean, L.J. and S.B. Vane. 1978. "Cults and Their Transformation." In *Handbook of North American Indians Vol. 8*, edited by Robert F. Heizer. Smithsonian Institution.

Beardsley, R.K. 1954. *Temporal and Areal Relationships in Central California Archaeology: Part Two*. Reports of the University of California Archaeological Survey, No. 25.

Bennyhoff, J.A. 1994. "The Napa District and Wappo Prehistory." In *Toward a New Taxonomic Framework for Central California Archaeology*, edited by R.E. Hughes. Contributions to the University of California Archaeological Research Facility, Berkeley.

Benson, L., M. Kashgarian, R.Rye, S. Lund, F. Paillete, J. Smoot, C. Kester, S. Mensing, D. Mekoh, S. Lindstrom. 2002. "Holocene Multidecadal and Multicentennial Droughts Affecting Northern California and Nevada." *Quaternary Science Reviews* 21:659–682.

Bibby, Brian. 2002. *Historical Use and Occupancy Report for the Mechoopda Tribe of Chico Rancheria, Report 59-2002*. Submitted to National Indian Gaming Commission. Washington, DC.

Bidwell, Annie K. 2002. "Diaries of 1864, 1866, 1868-1900." Bidwell Mansion Association, Chico, California. [CD-ROM]. California State University, Chico, Meriam Library.

Bidwell, John. 1904. "Early California Reminiscences." *Out West, A Magazine of the Old Pacific and the New* XX (3): 285-287.

Bidwell, John. "Mapa del Valle del Sacramento" (pen-and-ink and watercolor. U.S. District Court. California, Northern District. Land case 301 ND, page 310; land case map E-610. Online Archive of California. cdlib.oac.org.

Bidwell, John. 2002. "The John Bidwell Diaries: A Transcription of John Bidwell's Diaries from 1864-1900." Transcribed and edited by Shirley Connolly and Lois McDonald. Bidwell Mansion Association, Chico, California. [CD-ROM]. California State University, Chico, Meriam Library.

Blackburn, T.C. 2006. *An Artist's Portfolio: The California Sketches of Henry B. Brown, 1851-1852*. Malki Press.

Bowen, O.E., ed. 1962. *Geologic Guide to Oil and Gas Fields of Northern California*. Bulletin 181. California Division of Mines and Geology.

Brice, J. 1977. *Lateral Migration of the Middle Sacramento River, California*. United States Department of the Interior Geological Survey Water Resource Investigations.

References Cited

Broughton, J.M. 1994. "Late Holocene Resource Intensification in the Sacramento Valley, California: The Vertebrate Evidence." *Journal of Archaeological Science* 21:501-515.

Broughton, J.M. and F.E. Bayham. 2003. "Showing Off, Foraging Models, and the Ascendance of Large-Game Hunting in the California Middle Archaic." *American Antiquity* 68 (4): 783-789.

Bureau of Reclamation. 2008. *Finding of No Significant Impact: Llano Seco Ranch Bedrock & 80-90 Fields -Habitat Restoration for Special Status Species; Vernal Pool Restoration at Sacramento River National Wildlife Refuge and Colusa National Wildlife Refuge.* Northeast Information Center of the California Historical Resources Inventory System, California State University, Chico.

Chant, C. and J. Batchelor. 2002. *A Century of Triumph: The History of Aviation.* The Free Press.

Cook, S.F. 1955. "The Epidemic of 1830-1833 in California and Oregon." *University of California Publications in American Archaeology and Ethnology* 43 (3): 303-326.

Cook, S.F. 1964. "The Aboriginal Population of Upper California." Proceedings of the 35th International Conference of Americanists, Mexico.

Cook, S.F. 1976. *The Conflict Between the California Indians and White Civilization.* University of California Press.

Cross, M. 2001. *Restoration Plan for the Martin Family Cemetery Project.* Northeast Information Center of the California Historical Resources Inventory System, California State University, Chico.

Currie, A. H. 1957. "Bidwell Rancheria." *California Historical Society Quarterly* 36 (4):313-325.

Deal, K. 1987. "The Archaeology of the Cana Highway Site, CA-BUT-288, Butte County, California." Master's thesis. Department of Anthropology, California State University, Chico.

DeTristan, M. 1960. *Historical Notice and Resume of Transactions Involving the Llano Seco Rancho from 1844 to This Date.* Rancho Llano Seco Archives, Chico., CA

Dixon, R.B. 1905. "The Northern Maidu." *American Museum of Natural History Bulletins* 17 (3): 119-346.

Dreyer, W.R. 1984. "Prehistoric Settlement Strategies in a Portion of the Northern Sacramento Valley, California." Masters thesis. Department of Anthropology, California State University, Chico.

Driver, H.E. and W.C. Massey. 1957. "Comparative Studies of North American Indians." *Transactions of the American Philosophical Society* XLVII:165-456.

DuBois, C. 1939. "The 1870 Ghost Dance." *Anthropological Records* 3:1. University of California Press.

Dunne, T. and R. Aalto. 2013. "Large River Floodplains. In *Treatise on Geomorphology*, edited by J. Shroder and E. Wohl. Academic Press.

Dyke, D.J. 1932. "Transportation in Sacramento Valley 1849-1860." Masters thesis. Department of History, California State University, Chico.

Ellison, W. H. 1922. "The Federal Indian Policy in California, 1846-1860." *The Mississippi Valley Historical Review* 9 (1): 37–67.

Elsasser, A.B. 1978. "Development of Regional Prehistoric Cultures." In *Handbook of North American Indians Vol. 8*, edited by Robert F. Heizer. Smithsonian Institution.

Eugster, S.E. 1990. "Freshwater Mussel Utilization at a Late Prehistoric Period Archaeological Site (CA-BUT-12) in the Northern Sacramento Valley, California." Masters thesis. Department of Anthropology, California State University, Chico.

Fagan, J.L. 1988. "Clovis and Western Pluvial Lakes Tradition Lithic Technologies at the Dietz Site in South-Central Oregon." In *Early Human Occupation in Far Western North America: The Clovis-Archaic Interface*, edited J.A. Willig, C.M. Aikins, and J.L. Fagan. Nevada State Museum Anthropological Papers 21.

Fiedel, S.J. 1999. "Older than We Thought: Implications of Corrected Dates for Paleoindians." *American Antiquity* 64 (1): 95-116.

Fiedel, S.J. 2000. "The Peopling of the New World: Present Evidence, New Theories, and Future Directions." *Journal of Archaeological Research* 8 (1): 39-103.

Fischer, V., trans. 1992. *The Diary of Captain Luis Antonio Arguello: October 17-November 17, 1821: The Last Spanish Expedition in California.* Series of Keepsakes Issued by the Friends of the Bancroft Library by its Members, No. 40. University of California. Berkeley.

Fredrickson, D.A. 1974. "Social Change in Prehistory: A Central California Example." In *ANTAP: California Indian Political and Economic Organization*, edited by L.J. Bean and T.F. King. Anthropological Papers 2. Ballena Press.

Fredrickson, D.A. 1984. "The North Coastal Region." In *California Archaeology*, by M.J. Moratto. Academic Press.

Fredrickson, D.A. and G. White. 1988. "The Clear Lake Basin and Early Complexes in California's North Coast Ranges." In *Early Human Occupation in Far Western North America: The Clovis-Archaic Interface*, edited by J. A. Willig, C.M. Aikens, and J.L. Fagan. Nevada State Museum Anthropological Papers No. 21.

Gifford, E.W. 1927. "Southern Maidu Religious Ceremonies." *American Anthropologist* 29 (3): 214-257.

Gillis, M. and M. Magliari. 2003. *John Bidwell and California: The Life and Writings of a Pioneer, 1841-1900*. Arthur H. Clark Company.

Guinn, James Miller. 1906. *History of the State of California and Biographical Record of the Sacramento Valley, California: An Historical Story of the State's Marvelous Growth from Its Earliest Settlements to the Present Time; Also Containing Biographies of Well-known Citizens of the Past and Present.* Chapman.

Haines, F.D., ed. 1971. *The Snake Country Expedition of 1830-1831, John Work's Field Journal*. University of Oklahoma Press.

Hardwick, S.W. and D.G. Holtgrieve. 1996. *Valley for Dreams*. Rowman & Littlefield.

Harwood, D.S. and E.J. Helley. 1987. *Late Cenozoic Tectonism of the Sacramento Valley, California*. U.S. Geological Survey Professional Paper 1359. U.S. Government Printing Office.

Heizer, R.F. 1949. "The Archaeology of Central California, I: The Early Horizon." *University of California Anthropological Records* 12 (1): 1-84.

Heizer, R.F. 1972. *The Eighteen Unratified Treaties of 1851-1852 Between the California Indians and the United States Government*. Archaeological Research Facility, Department of Anthropology University of California, Berkeley.

Heizer, R.F., ed. 1979. *Federal Concern About Conditions of California Indians 1853 to 1913: Eight Documents*. Publications in Archaeology, Ethnology, and History No. 13. Ballena Press.

Heizer, R.F., ed. 1993. *The Destruction of California Indians*. University of Nebraska Press, Bison Books.

Heizer, R.F. and A.J. Almquist. 1971. *The Other Californians*. University of California Press.

Heizer, R.F. and T.R. Hester. 1970. "Names and Locations of Some Ethnographic Patwin and Maidu Indian Villages." In *Papers on California Ethnography*, 79-116. Contributions of the University of California Archaeological Research Facility, No. 9. University of California Archaeological Research Facility. Berkeley.

Helley, Edward J. and David S. Harwood. 1985. *Geologic Map of Late Cenozoic Deposits of the Sacramento Valley and Northern Sierran Foothills, California*. U.S. Geological Survey Miscellaneous Field Studies Map MF-1790.

Hildebrandt, W.R. and J.F. Hayes. 1983. *Archaeological Investigations on Pilot Ridge, Six Rivers National Forest*. Northwest Information Center of the California Historical Resources Inventory System, California State University, Sonoma.

Hill, D. 1978. *The Indians of Chico Rancheria*. California Department of Parks and Recreation.

Hill, D. , ed. 1980. *Rancho Chico Indians by Annie E. K. Bidwell*. Bidwell Mansion Association.

Ide, Simeon 1880. *Biographical Sketch of William B. Ide*. Published by subscription.

Johnson, R.L. 2001. A Short History of Transportation in Colusa, Glenn and Tehama Counties. *Wagon Wheels* 51 (2): 1, 4-28.

Jones, T.L., G.M. Brown, L.M. Raab, J.L. McVickar, W.G. Spaulding, D.J. Kennett, A. York, and P.L. Walker. 1999. "Environmental Imperatives Reconsidered: Demographic Crises in Western North America During the Medieval Climatic Anomaly." *Current Anthropology* 40 (2): 137-170.

Jones, T.L., R.T. Fitzgerald, D.J. Kennett, C.H. Miksicek, J.L. Fagan, and J. Sharp. 2002. "The Cross Creek Site (CA-SLO-1797) and Its Implications for New World Colonization." *American Antiquity* 67 (2): 213-230.

Jostes, B. D. 1972. *John Parrott, Consul 1811-1884: Selected Papers of a Western Pioneer*. Lawton and Alfred Kennedy.

Katibah, E.F. 1984. "A Brief History of Riparian Forests in the Central Valley of California." In *California Riparian Systems: Ecology, Conservation, and Productive Management*, edited by R.E. Warner and K.M. Hendrix. University of California Press.

Kowta, M. 1988. *The Archaeology and Prehistory of Plumas and Butte Counties, California: An Introduction and Interpretive Model*. Northeast California Information Center, California Historical Resources Information System, California State University, Chico.

References Cited

Kroeber, A.L. 1922. "Elements of Culture in Native California." *University of California Publications in American Archaeology and Ethnology* 13 (8): 259-328.

Kroeber, A.L. 1925. *Handbook of Indians of California: The Wintun.* Smithsonian Institution, Bureau of American Ethnology, Bulletin 78.

Kroeber, A.L. 1932. *The Patwin and Their Neighbors.* University of California Publications in American Archaeology and Ethnology, 29 (4).

Kroeber, A.L. 1954. "The Nature of Land-Holding Groups in Aboriginal California." *University of California Archaeological Reports* 56:19-58.

La Bourdette, L. 1974. "Charles Donald Semple, Co-Founder of Colusa." *Wagon Wheels* 24 (1): 13-15.

Lillard, J.B., R.F. Heizer, and F. Fenenga. 1939. "An Introduction to the Archaeology of Central California." Sacramento Junior College, Department of Anthropology Bulletin 2. Board of Education of the Sacramento Unified School District.

Lindsey, Bill. 2015. "Bottle Glass Colors." Society for Historical Archaeology's Historic Glass Bottle Identification & Information. http://www.sha.org/bottle/colors.htm.

"Llano Seco, Diseños 289, GLO No. 12, Butte County, and Associated Historical Documents." (2018). Butte County. 7. https://digitalcommons.csumb.edu/hornbeck_usa_4_a_bc/7

Magliari, M. F. 1989. "Populism, Steamboats, and the Octopus: Transportation Rates and Monopoly in California's Wheat Regions, 1890-1896." *Pacific Historical Review* 58:449-469.

Magliari, M. F. 2012. "Free State Slavery: Bound Indian Labor and Slave Trafficking in California's Sacramento Valley, 1850–1864." *Pacific Historical Review* 81 (2): 155–192.

Maloney, A.B., ed. 1945. *Fur Brigade to the Bonaventure: John Work's California Expedition, 1832-1833, for the Hudson's Bay Company.* California Historical Society.

Mansfield, G. C. 1918. *History of Butte County, California with Biographical Sketches of the Leading Men and Women of the County Who have been Identified with its Growth and Development from the Early Days to the Present.* Historic Record Company.

Mathes, V. S. 1983. "Indian Philanthropy in California: Annie Bidwell and the Mechoopda Indians." *Arizona and the West* 25 (2): 153-166.

McCullough, D.R. 1969. *The Tule Elk: Its History, Behavior, and Ecology.* University of California Publications in Zoology No. 88.

McDonald, L. H. 2004. *Annie Kennedy Bidwell: An Intimate History.* Stansbury Press.

McGowan, J. A. 1961. *A History of the Sacramento Valley, Vol. 1.* Lewis Historical Publishing.

McKearin, H. and K.M. Wilson. 1978. *American Bottles and Flasks and Their Ancestry.* Crown Publishers.

McKern, W.C. 1923. "Patwin Houses." *University of California Publications in American Archaeology and Ethnology.* 20 (10): 159-171.

McKinstry, D. G. 1872. *Documents for the History of California, 1846-9.* University of California, Berkeley.

Memorial and Biographical History of Northern California, Illustrated. 1891. Chicago: Lewis Publishing.

Merriam, C. H. 1977. *Ethnogeographic and Ethnosynonymic Data from Northern California Tribes.* Assembled and edited by R. F. Heizer. Archaeological Research Facility, Department of Anthropology, University of California, Berkeley.

Meyer, J. and J. S. Rosenthal. 2008. *A Geoarchaeological Overview and Assessment of Caltrans District 3 Cultural Resources Inventory of Caltrans District 3 Rural Conventional Highways.* Northeast Information Center of the California Historical Resources Inventory System, California State University, Chico.

Moratto, M.J. 1984. *California Archaeology.* Academic Press.

National Register History, and Education. 1995. *How to Apply the National Register Criteria for Evaluation.* U.S. Department of the Interior: National Park Service Cultural Resources.

Nunis, D.B. 1968. *The Hudson's Bay Company's First Fur Brigade to the Sacramento Valley: Alexander McLeod's 1829 Hunt.* Sacramento Book Collectors Club.

Olmsted, F. H. and G. H. Davis. 1961. *Geologic Features and Ground-Water Storage Capacity of the Sacramento Valley, California.* Geological Survey Water-Supply Paper 1497. U.S. Government Printing Office.

Ornduff, Robert. 1974. *Introduction to California Plant Life.* University of California Press.

Phillips, G. H. 1976. *The Conservation of the California Tule Elk.* University of Alberta Press.

Phillips, G. H. 1981. *The Enduring Struggle: Indians in California History*. Boyd & Frazer Publishing.

Powers, S. (1874) 1975. *The Northern California Indians: A Reprinting of 19 Articles on California Indians Originally Published 1872-1877*. Contributions to the University of California Archaeological Research Facility, No. 25. University of California Berkeley Archaeological Research Facility.

Preston, R.N. 1983. *Early California Atlas, Northern Edition*. Binford & Mort Publishers.

Rawls, J.J. 1984. *Indians of California: The Changing Image*. University of Oklahoma Press.

Riddell, F.A. 1978. "Maidu and Konkow." In *Handbook of North American Indians Vol. 8*, edited by Robert F. Heizer. Smithsonian Institution.

Roberts, W.G., J.G. Howe, and J. Major. 1980. "A Survey of Riparian Forest Flora and Fauna in California." In *Riparian Forests in California: Their Ecology and Conservation*, edited by Anne Sands. The Regents of the University of California, Davis.

Robertson, K. G. 1987. "Paleochannels and Recent Evolution of the Sacramento River, California." Master's thesis. Earth Science and Resources, University of California, Davis.

Rosenthal, J.S. 1996. "A Cultural Chronology for Solano County, California." Masters thesis. Department of Anthropology, Sonoma State University, Rohnert Park, CA.

Rosenthal, J. D., G. White, and M. Q. Sutton. 2007. "The Central Valley: A View from the Catbird's Seat." In *Colonization, Culture, and Complexity: California's Chaotic Prehistory*, edited by T. L. Jones and K. Klarr. Alta Mira Press.

Sampson, C. G. 1985. "Nightfire Island: Later Holocene Lakemarsh Adaptation on the Western Edge of the Great Basin." *University of Oregon Anthropological Papers* 33.

Schulz, P.D. 1981. "Osteoarchaeology and Subsistence Change in Prehistoric Central California." PhD diss. Department of Anthropology, University of California, Davis.

Shover, M. 1998. "John Bidwell, Reluctant Indian Fighter, 1852-1856." *Dogtown Territorial Quarterly* 36:32–56.

Shover, M. 1999. "The Politics of the 1859 Bidwell-Kibbe Campaign Northern California Indian-Settler Conflicts of the 1850s." *Dogtown Territorial Quarterly* 38:4–39.

Shover, M. 2000. "John Bidwell and the Rancho Chico Indian Treaty of 1852: Seduction, Betrayal, and Redemption." *Dogtown Territorial Quarterly* 42:4–39.

Smith, E.S. 1973. *Effects of Three Possible Reservoir Development Projects on the Cache Creek Tule Elk Herd* (Cervus elaphus nannodes). California Department of Fish and Game, Environmental Services Branch Administrative Report No. 73-2.

Smith, S. L. 2013. *Freedom's Frontier: California and the Struggle over Free Labor, Emancipation, and Reconstruction*. University of North Carolina Press.

Smith & Elliott. 1877. *Butte County Illustrations, Descriptive of its Scenery, Residences, Public Buildings, Manufactories, Fine Blocks, Mines, and Mills*. Smith & Elliott.

Stevens, K.J. 1981. "Iron Horse North – Railroads in the Sacramento Valley." *Northern California Review*.

Sullivan, M. 1934. *The Travels of Jedediah Smith: A Documentary Outline Including the Journal of the Great American Pathfinder*. Fine Arts Press.

Taber, R.D. 1956. "Deer Nutrition and Population Dynamics in the North Coast Range of California." In *Proceedings of the Twenty-First North American Wildlife Conference*.

Tod, J. H. 1988. *Porcelain Insulators: Guide Book for Collectors*. Privately Printed.

Trafzer, C. E. and J. R. Hyer, eds. 1999. *Exterminate Them: Written Accounts of the Murder, Rape, and Enslavement of Native Americans During the California Gold Rush*. Michigan State University Press.

USDA. 2018A. "Soils Series Description for Llano Seco Series soils." https://soilseries.sc.egov.usda.gov/OSD_Docs/L/LLANOSECO.html.

USDA. 2018B. "Soils Series Description for Vermet Series soils." https://soilseries.sc.egov.usda.gov/OSD_Docs/V/VERMET.html.

USDA. 2018C. "Soils Series Description for Parrott Series soils." https://soilseries.sc.egov.usda.gov/OSD_Docs/P/PARROTT.html.

USDA. 2018D. "Soils Series Description for Whitecabin Series soils." https://soilseries.sc.egov.usda.gov/OSD_Docs/W/WHITECABIN.html.

USDA. 2018E. "Soils Series Description for Dodgeland Series soils." https://soilseries.sc.egov.usda.gov/OSD_Docs/D/DODGELAND.html.

References Cited

USDA. 2018F. "Soils Series Description for Farwell Series soils." https://soilseries.sc.egov.usda.gov/OSD_Docs/F/FARWELL.html.

USDA. 2018G. "Soils Series Description for Gianella Series soils." (https://soilseries.sc.egov.usda.gov/OSD_Docs/G/GIANELLA.html) accessed February 2018.

USDA. 2018H. "Soils Series Description for Columbia Series soils." https://soilseries.sc.egov.usda.gov/OSD_Docs/C/COLUMBIA.html.

U.S. Court of Claims. 1861. *Reports from the Court of Claims submitted to the House of Representatives During the Second Session of the Thirty-Sixth Congress, 1860–1861.* Government Printing Office.

Valentine, N. 1996A. *Cultural Resource Report for the Llano Seco Unit Fields 2 & 3 Project, Butte County, California.* Northeast Information Center of the California Historical Resources Inventory System, California State University, Chico.

Valentine, N. 1996B. *Cultural Resource Report for the Rancho Rio Chico Project, Butte County, California.* Northeast Information Center of the California Historical Resources Inventory System, California State University, Chico.

Valente, N. 1998. "Resource Intensification and Foraging Efficiency at The Patrick Site (CA-BUT-1)." Master's thesis. Department of Anthropology, California State University, Chico.

Waterman, J.S. 1934-1940. Looseleaf file of photocopied and transcribed newspaper articles clipped from the *Chico Record* pertaining to the history of Butte County and the City of Chico. Northeast California Special Collections, Meriam Library California State University, Chico.

Weber, D.J. 1990. *The Californios Versus Jedediah Smith, 1826-1827: A New Cache of Documents.* Arthur H. Clark.

Welden, B. 1990. "The Physical Being and Lifeways of the Indians of the Llano Seco Site, CA-BUT-233, Butte County, California." Master's thesis. Department of Anthropology, California State University, Chico.

Wells, Harry L., Frank T. Gilbert, and W. L. Chambers. 1882. *History of Butte County in Two Volumes.* Harry L. Wells.

White, G., ed. 2002. *Bidwell Mansion Grounds Historical and Archaeological Research: Summary of Findings and Results of Geophysical Studies. Completed for Northern Service Center, Park Design and Construction Division, California State Department of Parks and Recreation.* Northeast Information Center of the California Historical Resources Inventory System, California State University, Chico.

White, G. 2003A. *Cultural Resource Overview and Management Plan Sacramento River Conservation Area, Tehama, Butte, Glenn, and Colusa Counties, California. Prepared for the Nature Conservancy.* Northeast Information Center of the California Historical Resources Inventory System, California State University, Chico.

White, G. 2003B. *Testing and Mitigation at Four Sites Along the Level(3) Long Haul Fiber Optic Alignment, Colusa County, California.* Northeast Information Center of the California Historical Resources Information System, California State University, Chico.

White, G. 2003C. "Population Ecology of the Colusa Reach." PhD diss. Department of Anthropology, University of California, Davis.

White, G. 2014A. *Archaeological Site Boundary Determination for Ca-But-2658, the Sanctuary Mound, U.S. Fish and Wildlife Service, Llano Seco Riparian Sanctuary, Sacramento River National Wildlife Refuge, Butte County, California. Prepared for Kelly Moroney, Wildlife Refuge Manager, U.S. Fish & Wildlife Service Sacramento River NWR.* Northeast Information Center of the California Historical Resources Information System, California State University, Chico.

White, G. 2014B. *Archaeological Reconnaissance and Site Boundary Determination for a Proposed Habitat Restoration Project, U.S. Fish and Wildlife Service, Llano Seco Riparian Sanctuary, Sacramento River National Wildlife Refuge, Butte County, California. Prepared for Kelly Moroney, Wildlife Refuge Manager, U.S. Fish & Wildlife Service Sacramento River NWR.* Northeast Information Center of the California Historical Resources Information System, California State University, Chico.

White, G. 2016. *The Loveliest of Place: A study of the Pre-Mansion Historical Resources of Bidwell Mansion State Historic Park.* California Department of Parks and Recreation, Cultural Resource Division, Publications in Cultural Heritage, No. 32. Sacramento.

White, G. 2017A. *Results of U.S. Fish and Wildlife Service, Llano Seco Riparian Sanctuary, Ca-But-2658/H Site Review Seed Drill Preparation, Sacramento River National Wildlife Refuge, Butte County, California. Prepared for Joe Silveira, Wildlife Refuge Manager, U.S. Fish & Wildlife Service Sacramento River NWR.* Northeast Information Center of the California Historical Resources Information System, California State University, Chico.

White, G. 2017B. *Results of U.S. Fish and Wildlife Service, Llano Seco Riparian Sanctuary, Ca-But-2658/H Site Review for Seed Drill Preparation, Sacramento River National Wildlife Refuge, Butte County, California. Prepared for Joe Silveira, Wildlife Refuge Manager, U.S. Fish & Wildlife Service Sacramento River NWR.* Northeast Information Center of the California Historical Resources Information System, California State University, Chico.

White G., D.A. Fredrickson, L. Hager, J. Meyer, J. Rosenthal, M. Waters, J. West, and E. Wohlgemuth. 2002. *Culture History and Culture Change in Prehistoric Clear Lake Basin: Final Report of the Anderson Flat Project.* Center for Archaeological Research at University of California, Davis,

Wilkes, C. (1845) 1958. *Columbia River to the Sacramento.* Bio-Books.

Will, M. 2015. "The Evolution Sacramento River During the late Quaternary and the Influence of an "Inherited" Topography on Modern Floodplain Sedimentation Rates." PhD diss. College of Life and Environmental Science, University of Exeter, Exeter, United Kingdom.

Will, M., R. E. Aalto, and M. Fuchs. 2011. "Evolution and Floodplain History of the Middle Sacramento River from the late Quaternary to Modern Times (Abstract)." American Geophysical Union, Fall Meeting 2011.

Willig, J.A. and C.M. Aikens. 1988. "The Clovis-Archaic Interface in Far Western North America." In *Early Human Occupation in Far Western North America: The Clovis-Archaic Interface*, edited by J.A. Willig, C.M. Aikens, and J.L. Fagen, pp. 1-40. Nevada State Museum Anthropological Papers No. 21.

Winterhalder, B., W. Baillargeon, F. Cappelletto, I.R. Daniel, Jr., and C. Prescott. 1988. The Population Ecology of Hunter-Gatherers and Their Prey. *Journal of Anthropological Archaeology* 7:289-328.

Zancanella, J.K. 1987. "A Study of Projectile Points From the East Central Sacramento Valley, California." Masters thesis. Department of Anthropology, California State University, Chico.

Zorn, Frank J., ed. 1922. "A New Departure in Map Making." *Buildings and Building Management* XXII (1): 17–18.

Mapa del Valle del Sacramento (facsimile), John Bidwell, 1851

APPENDIX

Sebastian Keyser

Sebastian Keyser

Rancho Llano Seco was identified and claimed by Sebastian Keyser in 1843, late in the history of Mexican California. After decades of financial insolvency, the provincial government was left unable to defend an enormous territory increasingly hemmed in between the intensifying competitive interests of the United States and Great Britain. As early as 1828, Mexican legislators pushed efforts to solve the problem of frontier defense by liberalization of the naturalization process and by introducing new land grant rules codified in the Mexican Reglamento, permitting the issuance of frontier land grants to "foreigners"—mostly Americans who promised to become naturalized Mexican citizens.[1]

Even though the province of California "went through twelve governors and experienced four major revolts,"[2] each regime maintained policies favoring land grants and liberalized naturalization; consequently, interior lands continued to be colonized progressively deeper into the frontier by a mix of foreign expatriates and Californios with Mexican service. These first Alta California colonizers targeted Coast Range foothill lands, which were suitable for wheat and hide-and-tallow operations that had long formed the backbone of Alta California's agrarian economy—an economy reliant on Native labor conditioned to servitude by the mission experience. At the same time, many rancheros initially resisted colonization of remote, interior land grants because they feared the "wild tribes" living in the unclaimed and rarely penetrated Sacramento Valley lands.[3]

Sebastian Keyser and John Sutter

John Augustus Sutter was among the first of the "foreign" settlers in Alta California, and, in 1839, became the first to shoulder the challenge of settling among the "wild tribes" in traditional Maidu-Nisenan territory. A native of Switzerland who served as an underlieutenant in the Swiss Reserve under Charles X, Sutter immigrated to the United States in 1833 to escape imprisonment for debts incurred by his dry goods enterprise, thus abandoning his wife and four children in the process.[4] Of Sutter's career in the U.S., Bancroft concluded that:

He was great only in his wonderful personal magnetism and power of making friends for a time of all who could be useful to him . . . .. Of principle, of honor, of respect for the rights of others, we find but slight trace in him. There was no side of any controversy that he would not readily adopt at the call of [self] interest.[5]

John Sutter initially led a mobile existence in the U.S., creating and using elaborate fictitious origin stories to talk his way through an existence filled with grift and adventure. Sutter fled debt several times through his first five years in the States, ultimately latching on in 1838 with a cross-country trapping party heading to Oregon, whose members included Nicholaus Allgeier and Sebastian Keyser. Along the way, Sutter learned the lay of California from the trappers and became determined to make the Great Central Valley his new home.

After shipping from Oregon to Hawaii on a Sandwich Island trader, Sutter secured supplies on credit and negotiated with King Kamehameha III for the services of nine *Kanaka maoli*[6] for three years, including seven men, two of whom also brought their Hawaiian wives. After arriving in Yerba Buena, Sutter immediately traveled to Monterey, where he informed Governor Juan Bautista Alvarado of his intention to settle in the Sacramento Valley, establish Mexican citizenship, and petition for a land grant.

Alvarado was pleased to support the plan, with the condition that Sutter enlist in the Mexican government's efforts to suppress the still-active eastern Delta Plains Miwok rebellions and to curtail the incursion of American and British trapping parties into the Alta California interior.[7] Thus granted the right to colonize, in August 1839, he set out to explore the lower Sacramento and Feather River,[8] establishing a rough camp near the confluence of the American and Sacramento Rivers.

After convincing San Joaquin Valley rancheros to provide him with cattle on credit, Sutter initiated a small hide-and-tallow operation in 1840 and subsisted on wild game.

---

1 Cleland; Rives.

2 Warren, 93.

3 Hittell, 2:275–281.

4 Hurtado.

---

5 Bancroft, 1886B, 739.

6 The indigenous peoples of the Island of Hawaii.

7 McGowan, VI:25.

8 Ibid., VI:104.

The little colony grew quickly,[9] and "[I]n August, 1840, Sutter was joined by five men who had crossed the Rocky Mountains with him, and whom he had left in Oregon."[10]

Missionized Plains Miwok formed the core of Sutter's 1839–1841 Native work force, but in these first years, Sutter's herds and rancho crops were frequently raided and threatened by Valley Nisenan and Plains Miwok tribes living outside his sphere of influence. Sutter's cattle were killed for food, and his horses stolen—a possibility presaged by Governor Alvarado in his first meeting with Sutter in Monterey when he described the tribes as "very hostile" and unlikely to permit any white settlement.[11] Sutter's response was to commence expeditions of reprisal to suppress the tribes, an effort made possible by the 1840 arrival of Nicholaus Allgeier and Sebastian Keyser.[12]

Allgeier was born in Freiberg, Germany, in 1807, and Keyser was born 400 miles to the south in the Austrian Tyrol in 1811. It is not known if they interacted before both migrated to North America circa 1830, but both took up work as trappers in British-held territories for the Hudson's Bay Company.[13] Both were members of the Missouri-to-Oregon cross-country party that Sutter joined in 1838, and both stayed on at Fort Vancouver when Sutter went south in 1839.[14] Sutter appears to have written Allgeier and Keyser soon after establishing the New Helvetia operation, inviting them to join him in California. After their arrival in spring 1840, the hard-scrabble pair became the core of Sutter's "praetorian guard":

> Their [Allgeier's and Keyser's] presence at New Helvetia made it unlikely that a force of disgruntled [Nisenan] Indian workers or

independent [Plains] Miwoks would eject him from the valley. Too many hard men with weapons stood in the way.[15]

Sutter also maintained an elite contingent of Native fighters decked out in articles derived from Russian military uniforms.[16] Bidwell reports the contingent was trained in Western military practices:

> [T]he soldiers were Indians, and every evening after coming from work they were drilled under a white officer, generally a German [probably Allgeier or Keyser], marching to the music of a fife and drum. A sentry was always at the gate, and regular bells called men to and from work.[17]

In spring 1840, Sutter began a series of punitive attacks on Plains Miwok and Northern Yokuts communities south of New Helvetia, the most substantial conducted by Allgeier, Keyser, and the Native contingent in retribution against an unidentified village, probably the Plains Miwok resistance center of *Junizumne*, located at the mouth of the Mokelumne River.[18] Similar attacks were made against independent Valley Nisenan settlements on the Sacramento River twenty-five river miles north of New Helvetia, where members of the 1841 United States Exploring Expedition found evidence of severe actions resulting in the abandonment of two villages above the confluence of the Feather and Sacramento Rivers.[19]

In June, 1841, Sutter was granted Mexican citizenship and received title to 48,827 acres in two grants: the New Helvetia land grant (named in honor of the traditional Swiss Confederacy), centered in the present-day City of Sacramento, and the Rancho Terreno de Sutter land grant, the site of the future Hock Farm located on the Feather River stretching from its confluence with the Sacramento River north to the latitude of the Sutter Buttes, near present-day Live Oak.[20] Governor Juan

---

9 Angel, 42. Angel solved the debate regarding the number of Sutter's Hawaiian workers by securing Sutter's testimony that, after adding another Kanaka maoli then residing in the port of Yerba Buena to his team, he sailed up the Sacramento with five Anglos and "8 Kanacas (two of them married) [for a total of 10 Hawaiian natives]."

10 Angel, 40.

11 Ibid., 39.

12 Bancroft 1886A, 700. Keyser's early arrival at New Helvetia is confirmed by Bancroft, who references a letter of introduction written by Sutter to South Coast Range rancho tycoon Antonio Sunol in 1841.

13 Bancroft, 1886A, 700; Delay, 46.

14 Ibid., 120.

15 Hurtado, 79.

16 Elements acquired in Sutter's purchase from the Russians of the Fort Ross/Bodega facilities (see McGowan, VI:30).

17 Bidwell, 1890, 169.

18 *Sacramento Daily Union*, February 23, 1858; see also Angel, 40.

19 See Wilkes, 73, and Pickering, 104.

20 The Rancho Terreno de Sutter land grant was grossly under-calculated as originally proposed by Sutter; its original mapped extent occupied approximately 350,000 acres.

Bautista Alvarado also conveyed to Sutter the title of "Representende del Govierno en las Fronteras del Norte Encargado de la Justicia" (Governor's Representative at the Northern Borders in Charge of Justice). Alvarado later amended the title to include "Commandante Militare."[21] These new roles enabled Sutter to identify and coordinate new land grant applications, which was important because Sutter's headquarters at the confluence of the American and Sacramento Rivers soon became a storied destination for travelers and emigrants arriving in California from the U.S. and its territories. In its first years of operation a number of the new American arrivals stayed on to serve on Sutter's staff, including individuals who would go on to play outsized roles in Sacramento Valley history—John Bidwell (arrived 1841), Peter Lassen (arrived 1840, joined Sutter's staff 1842), Charles Flugge, Theodor Cordua and Theodore Sicard (arrived 1842), Thomas Hensley and Pierson Reading (arrived 1843), Samuel Neal (arrived 1844), and James Marshall (arrived 1845).

At some point before 1843, Sebastian Keyser transitioned out of the militia and took up work for Sutter as a saddle-tree maker, a fine woodcraft entailing the production of the hardwood core of traditional Spanish riding and pack saddles.[22] Keyser continued in this role at New Helvetia through 1844, and his reported skill as a saddle-maker makes it likely that Keyser worked at times with Peter Lassen, who arrived in California the same year as Keyser and, after two years as an itinerant blacksmith specializing in fine fittings for Mexican saddles, in 1842 took employment with Sutter at New Helvetia where he "obtained great local distinction as a manufacturer of bridle bits and Spanish spurs."[23]

Between 1841 and 1843, John Bidwell assumed several tasks in Sutter's operation, including exploration and mapping of the Sacramento Valley, as well as Spanish language skills, which combined to enable him to take on a burgeoning role in land grant survey and conveyance. Five grant applications he prepared for legislative and executive review were located in the lower watersheds of Butte and Chico Creeks: Rancho Llano Seco (Sebastian Keyser), Rancho de Farwell (Edward Farwell), Rancho Esquon (Samuel Neal), Rancho Willy

(Michael Nye), and Rancho del Arroyo Chico (William Dickey). Four of these ranchos experienced few or no improvements through 1848, and they largely served as investment properties with little to no owner-occupancy. Only Samuel Neal's Rancho Esquon saw significant development in the pre-Gold Rush period.

Sebastian Keyser was among the first to apply for a land grant via Bidwell's recommendation and agency. After qualifying for Mexican citizenship in 1842, Keyser applied for the 17,767-acre Rancho del Llano Seco, concurrent with William Dickey' naturalization and application for Rancho del Arroyo Chico. Keyser made one visit to Rancho del Llano Seco, an event documented by a unique coincidence.

In spring 1843, Sebastian Keyser and William Dickey forged a plan to visit their newly proposed Rancho del Llano Seco and Rancho de Arroyo Chico land grants. While staging their expedition at Sutter's Hock Farm, located on the west bank of Feather River near Shanghai Bend, the pair met and invited Swedish naturalist, illustrator, and journalist G. M. Waseurtz af Sandels,[24] who at the time was visiting Sutter's operations. The adventurous Sandels joined them, chronicling the expedition in his journal.[25] Concurrent with the trio's departure from Hock Farm, the 1842–1843 Lansford Hastings emigrant party, which arrived in Oregon in 1842 and entered California in spring 1843, was in transit along the Sacramento River south to New Helvetia.

Two self-styled "Indian killers" travelling with the Hastings company had adopted the practice of firing at Natives from a distance as the company moved south through the Sacramento Valley. Near Red Bluff, one of the men even stabbed an unsuspecting Wintu to death and mortally shot another from a sniper's position. Reaching the area of present-day Hamilton City, the two men continued to fire at the curious Nomlaki following the train. News of the murders reached tribes to the south, and when the company neared the River Patwin village of *Coru*, located on the Sacramento River 20 miles

---

21 Angel, 39–40.

22 Royce, 129–130.

23 *Memorial and Biographical History of Northern California, Illustrated*, 267.

24 Hereafter referred to as "Sandels," in keeping with his own practice.

25 G.M. Waseurtz af Sandels's journal was later translated and published by the Book Club of California and The Society of California Pioneers (1945): *A Sojourn in California by The King's Orphan: The Travels and Sketches of G. M. Waseurtz af Sandels, a Swedish Gentleman Who Visited California in 1842–1843.*

(33 kilometers) west of Hock at the present-day site of Colusa, a large number of River Patwin warriors formed up and fired arrows toward the emigrants. Emigrant casualties were minor due to the distances involved, but return rifle fire was heard by Keyser, Dickey, and Sandels as they travelled around the western skirt of the Marysville Buttes on their way north to the grant lands.[26] The conflagration resulted in injuries to members of the emigrant party and the deaths of several *Coru* Patwin. When the emigrant company reached Sutter's Fort, Sandels also returned and was available to render medical aid to the wounded settlers.[27]

Having been informed of the incident and despite the cautions expressed by cooler minds that the emigrants were at fault, "Sutter came to the conclusion that the Indians where the arrows had been shot . . . were hostile and should be punished," and therefore, in a conclusion reported by a still-shocked John Bidwell, Sutter:

> went with fifty men and attacked the Indians at daylight. His forces were divided, part having gone above and crossed on the Indian bridge, so that they would be ready simultaneously at daybreak to begin the attack. The Indians fled and mostly jumped into the river, where they were fired on and great numbers of them killed. After that time the Indians in that part of the valley were never known to be hostile to the whites. I do not believe that there was sufficient reason for considering them hostile before. At any rate I remember of no hostile act on their part, having gone among them almost alone a year after, twice at least, and once, with only five men with me, camped all night near a village without molestation.[28]

No records exist of the militia composition, but it is highly likely that Keyser and Algeier joined the fray, probably Keyser's last punitive expedition. The following year, in 1844, Keyser received title to Rancho del Llano Seco, a 17,767-acre grant issued on July 26, 1844, by Governor Pio Pico. Keyser never took formal possession by occupation or improvement of Rancho del Llano Seco, and he sold the grant to William Dickey on November 10, 1844, even before it was fully finalized.

26 Sandels, 69.

27 Ibid.

28 Bidwell, 1904, 286.

Rancho de Gutierrez & Rancho de Johnson

In 1843, Sutter instructed a Mexican vaquero named Don Pablo Gutierrez, a native of Sinaloa, Mexico, to join Bidwell at Hock Farm.[29] Taking up residence at Hock Farm, Gutierrez purchased a Hill Nisenan wife in the mountains east of Hock Farm, and in early spring 1844, the woman ran away. When Gutierrez left Hock Farm "to find and bring her back," he ascended Bear River canyon and did not appear for work the next day.[30] On his return, Bidwell scolded Gutierrez, who replied that:

> he had seen signs of gold. After my lecture, he said, "Señor, I have made an important discovery; there surely is gold on Bear River in the mountains." This was in March, 1844. A few days afterward I arranged to go with him up on Bear River. We went five or six miles into the mountains, when he showed me the signs and the place where he thought the gold was. "Well," I said, "can you not find some?" No, he said, because he must have a "batea." He talked so much about the "batea" that I concluded it must be a complicated machine. "Can't Mr. [Sebastian] Keiser, our saddle-tree maker, make the batea?" I asked. "Oh, no." I did not then know that a batea is nothing more nor less than a wooden bowl which the Mexicans use for washing gold. I said, "Pablo, where can you get it?" He said, "Down in Mexico." I said, "I will help pay your expenses if you will go down and get one," which he promised to do. I said, "Pablo, say nothing to anybody else about this gold discovery, and we will get the batea and find the gold."[31]

No doubt hoping to capitalize on his find, in mid-1844, Gutierrez selected and applied for a 22,197-acre (five Mexican leagues) land grant on the north bank of the Bear River, 12.5 miles north-northeast of Rancho Olash and approximately the same distance east of Hock Farm. Honoring his preemption commitments, that same

29 Sandels, 70. Likely the same individual identified by G. M. Waesurtz af Sandels in an 1844 Hock Farm observation: "at Captain Sutter's newly established cattle range, then managed by a young North American by the name of Bidwell and Sutter's trusted old servant, Padde."

30 Royce, 129–130.

31 Ibid.

year Gutierrez built an adobe structure "at the place afterwards called Johnson's Crossing."[32] However, at Bidwell's urging, Gutierrez stayed at work on Hock Farm, and for a time Bidwell also delayed the planned foray to Mexico.[33] Ultimately, the delay meant that they were unable to capitalize on the opportunity, and both men were soon drawn into the Micheltorena War, which lasted from November 1844 to March 1845. John Bidwell—a naturalized citizen of Mexico—served as an officer on the side of the Governor, and Pablo Gutierrez, early in the conflict, served as Sutter's courier to the Mexican Governor, when he was captured by the insurgents and "hanged to a tree, somewhere near the present town of Gilroy. That, of course, put an end to our gold discovery; otherwise Pablo Gutierrez might have been the discoverer instead of [James] Marshall."[34]

In 1845, acting in his role as the Mexican Governor's representative on the northern frontier, John Sutter sold Rancho de Gutierrez and all associated stock and improvements at auction. The winning bid was offered by the partnership of William Johnson and Sebastian Keyser, who purchased the grant for $150 U.S. dollars. Johnson, who claimed Irish birth,[35] was a sailor out of Boston when he engaged as a mate on the *Alciop* and jumped ship in Yerba Buena in 1840. Johnson became a naturalized citizen of Mexico, acquired a schooner, and "for several years . . . had traded between the Sandwich Islands and Yerba Buena."[36]

In 1844, Johnson purchased a building lot in Yerba Buena and secured a lighter vessel used in bay shipping. During this period, Johnson engaged in trade with Sutter and plied the river routes to New Helvetia, becoming a member of Sutter's Micheltorena Battalion during the 1844–1845 insurrection.[37] With his purchase of Rancho de Gutierrez, Johnson also acquired Gutierrez's cattle, supplementing them in October 1845 with cattle likely purchased from San Joaquin Valley ranchers and driven through New Helvetia, where they were noted in Sutter's diary.[38]

The Johnson and Keyser partnership was short-lived. The rancho headquarters was situated in the foothills of the Sierra, on the principal California Emigrant Trail route, at a point where the trail diverged into several Sacramento Valley spurs. The rancho was identified in newspapers and circulars carried by emigrants who saw it as a destination to end their travails, confounding the troll-like Johnson. The rancho's fame grew exponentially after January 17, 1847, when seven Donner Party and Forlorn Hope survivors were guided by Bear River Nisenan to Johnson's domicile, where they reported that the rest of their emigrant party remained trapped in the high Sierra.[39] Johnson's Ranch then became the center for planning, outfitting, and expediting four Donner relief expeditions, the first joined by cross-river neighbor and Rancho de los Nemshas partner Joseph Verrot, and the fourth joined by Rancho de Johnson co-owner Sebastian Keyser.

William Johnson hosted and fed the survivors at his ranch, where he met 15-year-old Mary Murphy, whom he married just six months later. The marriage quickly failed. Johnson was intemperate, domineering, and probably shared his home with his very young wife while continuing to consort with his Native concubines.[40] Mary left Johnson in December 1847, accusing him of cruelty and violence, and obtained an annulment with the assistance of her family. Johnson, who may have regretted surrendering his privacy, stayed on at the ranch two more years, but in November 1849 sold his assets and roamed to parts unknown. Johnson re-appears in the record in 1852, when he filed an affidavit with the Land Commission (U.S. District Court. California, Northern District, Land case 397), but soon after "either died or went to the Sandwich Islands.[41]

Keyser Crosses the Rubicon

Sebastian Keyser apparently took part in the Bear Flag revolt of 1846, where he lost part of his left hand in a

---

32 Delay, 44.

33 Royce, 129–130.

34 Ibid.

35 Bancroft, 1886A, 694.

36 Delay, 44.

37 Ibid., 120.

38 Sutter, 4.

39 The reader may refer to the vast and devoted literature on the Donner Party event, discussed in relation to Johnson's Ranch by Steed and Steed (1988) and covered admirably in the annotated links posted by the Donner Relief Expedition (2022).

40 Following an approach to marriage pioneered locally by John Yates.

41 Bancroft, 1886A, 694.

munitions accident.[42] On October 24, 1846, he married the former Elizabeth Rhodes, late of Roy County, Missouri; the ceremony took place on the Bear River and officiated by the Reverend J. G. T. Dunleary.[43] Elizabeth joined Keyser for a time on the Bear River but soon left him for her family's home on the Cosumnes River. Sutter's *New Helvetia Diary* records Sutter's discovery of Keyser's divorce on July 25, 1847, and an attempt to carry a letter between the separated parties on July 31, 1847.[44] With the apparent failure of these efforts, in early September, Sebastian Keyser ran an ad in The California Star announcing: "My wife, having left my bed and board, the subscriber would inform the public that he will not be accountable for any debts of her contracting after this date. Bear Creek, August 20th, 1847."[45]

Perhaps providing a clue to the Keysers' destiny, Sutter's New Helvetia Diary also records six visits to New Helvetia between September 1847 and January 1848 made by Thomas Rhodes and his family, arriving from and departing to their residence on the Cosumnes. Bancroft reports that Elizabeth Rhodes returned to Sebastian Keyser in 1847, and Keyser sold his half-interest in the Johnson Ranch in 1849.[46] Sebastian and Elizabeth Keyser next sought a home near her parents, and Sebastian Keyser immediately took work with two men he knew from New Helvetia, William Daylor and William R. Grimshaw, who had left their employment with Sutter to open a store at a popular Cosumnes River crossing. In winter 1849-1850, Daylor and Grimshaw were engaged in building a ferry "with a large scow, capable of transporting a wagon and team" to be readied for use "as soon as the high water renders it necessary."[47] Sebastian Keyser went to work for Daylor and Grimshaw operating the ferry, and in 1850, he drowned when the craft was swamped; "he left one child and $15,000 in gold dust."[48]

---

42 Bancroft, 1886A, 700. Bancroft expresses skepticism toward the report of Keyser's Bear Flag action.

43 *The Californian*, December 12, 1846.

44 Sutter, 62, 64.

45 *The California Star*, September 4, 1847.

46 Bancroft, 1886A, 700.

47 *Daily Placer Times and Transcript*, December 22, 1849.

48 Bancroft, 1886A, 700.

References

Angel, M. 1882. *History of Placer County, California with Illustrations and Biographical Sketches of its Prominent Men and Pioneers.* Thompson & West.

Bancroft, H.H. 1886A. *The Works of Hubert Howe Bancroft, Volume XXI; History of California, Volume IV, 1840–1845.* Bancroft and Company.

Bancroft, H.H. 1886B. *The Works of Hubert Howe Bancroft, Volume XXII; History of California, Volume V, 1846–1848.* Bancroft and Company.

Bidwell, J. 1890. "Life in California Before the Gold Discovery." *The Century Magazine* XLI (2): 163–183.

Bidwell, J. 1904. "Early California Reminiscences." *Out West, A Magazine of the Old Pacific and the New* XX (3): 285-287.

Cleland, R.G. 1914. "The Early Sentiment for the Annexation of California: An Account of the Growth of American Interest in California, 1835-1846." *The Southwestern Historical Quarterly* 18 (2): 121–161.

Delay. P.J. 1924. *History of Yuba and Sutter Counties, California, with Biographical Sketches of the Leading Men and Women of the Counties Who Have Been Identified with Their Growth and Development from the Early Days to the Present.* Historic Record Company.

"Donner Relief Expedition." 2022. History Expeditions. https://historyexp.org/front-pagenew3-0-relief-parties/

Hittell, T.H. 1898. *The History of California, Volume 2.* San Francisco: Pacific Press Publishing House and Occidental Publishing Company.

Hurtado, A.L. 2006. *John Sutter: A Life on the American Frontier.* University of Oklahoma Press.

McGowan, J.A. 1961. *A History of the Sacramento Valley, Vols. 1, 2, 3.* Lewis Historical Publishing.

Memorial and Biographical History of Northern California, Illustrated. 1891. Chicago: Lewis Publishing.

Pickering, Dr. Charles. 1848. *United States Exploring Expedition During the Years 1838, 1839, 1840, 1841, 1842.* Philadelphia: C. Sherman Publishing.

Rives, G.L. 1918. *The United States and Mexico, 1821-1848; A History of the Relations Between the Two Countries from the Independence of Mexico to the Close of the War with the United States.* Two Volumes. Charles Scribner and Sons.

Royce, C.C. 1907. *Addresses, Reminiscences, &tc. of General John Bidwell, Pioneer, Statesman, Philanthropist.* Chico: Privately printed.

Sandels, G.M. Waseurtz af. 1945. *A Sojourn in California by The King's Orphan: The Travels and Sketches of G.M. Waseurtz af Sandels, a Swedish Gentleman Who Visited California in 1842–1843.* Translated and edited by H. P. Van Sicklen. The Book Club of California. San Francisco.

Steed, J. and R. Steed. 1988. *The Donner Party Rescue Site: Johnson's Ranch on Bear River.* Fresno: Pioneer Publishing Company.

Sutter, J.A. 1939. *New Helvetia Diary: A Record of Events Kept By John A. Sutter and his Clerks at New Helvetia, California, From Sept. 9, 1845 to May 25, 1848.* The Grabhorn Press for the Society of California Pioneers.

Warren, Major T.R. 2016. *Operations in California during the Mexican-American War: A Monograph.* United States Army School of Advanced Military Studies, United States Army Command and General Staff College, Fort Leavenworth, Kansas.

Wilkes, C. (1845) 1958. *Columbia River to the Sacramento.* Bio-Books.

www.ingramcontent.com/pod-product-compliance
Lightning Source LLC
Chambersburg PA
CBHW080519110426
42742CB00017B/3172